D0018799

ALSO BY ROBERT W. BLY

The Copywriter's Handbook
Selling Your Services
Business-to-Business Direct Marketing
The Elements of Business Writing
The Elements of Technical Writing
How to Promote Your Own Business
How to Get Your Book Published
Write More, Sell More
Direct Mail Profits
Ads That Sell
Careers for Writers
Creating the Perfect Sales Piece
Targeted Public Relations
Keeping Clients Satisfied

SECRETS OF A FREELANCE WRITER

SECRETS OF
A FREELANCE
WRITER

THIRD EDITION

How to Make
$100,000 a Year or More

Robert W. Bly

A Holt Paperback
Henry Holt and Company
New York

Holt Paperbacks
Henry Holt and Company, LLC
Publishers since 1866
175 Fifth Avenue
New York, New York 10010
www.henryholt.com

Library of Congress Cataloging-in-Publication Data
Bly, Robert W.
   Secrets of a freelance writer : how to make $100,000 a year or more /
Robert W. Bly.—3rd ed.
     p. cm.
   Includes index.
   ISBN-13: 978-0-8050-7803-9
   ISBN-10: 0-8050-7803-7
   1. Authorship.   I. Title.
PN151.B63 2006
808'.02—dc22   2005058458

Henry Holt books are available for special promotions and
premiums. For details contact: Director, Special Markets.

Originally published in hardcover in 1988
by Dodd, Mead & Company

First Owl Books Edition 1990

Second Owl Books Edition 1997

Third Owl Books Edition 2006

Designed by Kelly S. Too

Printed in the United States of America

D 10 9 8 7 6 5

To my assistants, advisors, and vendors—Ilise Benun,
Peter DeCaro, Fern Dickey, Jon Kauffmann,
Wayne Kolb, Paul and Carolyn Mazza, Nurit Mittlefehldt,
Stanley Dumanig, Edward Mueller, Brett Ridgeway,
and Jodi Van Valkenburg—for helping to run my office
so smoothly so I can sit here and do nothing but
read, think, and write for our clients

On writing—a matter of exercise. If you work out with weights for 15 minutes a day over the course of ten years, you're gonna get muscles. If you write for an hour and a half a day for ten years, you're gonna turn into a good writer.

—Stephen King,
Time, October 6, 1986

No one writes as well as he ought. He is fortunate if he has written as well as he could.

—Bliss Perry,
Bedside Book of Famous British Stories

CONTENTS

ACKNOWLEDGMENTS

I'd like to thank my writer friends and colleagues — freelancers who, over the years, have given me countless ideas on how to build my business, get new clients, expand my services, and increase my income. I won't name them all here, but they know who they are. Thanks, folks!

Special thanks to Don Hauptman, Richard Armstrong, Milt Pierce, Sig Rosenblum, Roger C. Parker, Joan Harris, David Yale, Dr. Andrew Linick, John Finn, and Bob Kalian — successful writers and marketers whose brains I greedily pick whenever the opportunity arises.

I would also like to thank my editors, Cynthia Vartan and Flora Esterly, for being the best editors an author could have . . . and the most patient. And Henry Holt, for allowing me to reprint portions of my book *Successful Telephone Selling* in chapters 14 and 16 of this new edition of *Secrets of a Freelance Writer*.

Some of the networking tips in chapter 6 are from Carolyn Campbell's article "Networking," which appeared in the April 2005 issue of *Freelance Writer's Report* (page 5) and are reprinted with permission.

And, of course, thanks to my assistant, Carolyn Mazza, and my project manager, Ilise Benun, for handling the details of running my office so I can just sit and write. And to my agent, Dominick Abel, for shepherding this book through its many editions and printings.

PREFACE

This book was written to help you make a lot of money as a freelance writer.

To my mind, too many writers spend too many hours laboring over work for which they are paid only a pittance. We live in a society that often forces writers literally to give away their writings, either for free or for wages that, when figured on an hourly basis, are barely competitive with what an unskilled laborer can earn pushing hamburgers in a fast-food restaurant or moving crates in a warehouse.

This book is dedicated to the proposition that writers should be paid a fair dollar for a fair day's work . . . and that writing is a professional service worth the fees that other professions command.

Think about the last few articles or stories you sold. Were you satisfied with the pay? If not—if you feel frustrated by editors and publishers who seem to begrudge you every penny when it comes time to negotiate your fee or advance—this book can change your life!

• If you're tired of being underpaid as a writer, of spending long hours on projects that barely provide a decent living wage, I'm going to show you a different side of freelancing—one that can put you in an income bracket that even a corporate executive, attorney, or physician might envy.

• If you're a new or established freelancer handling commercial projects for corporate clients, I'll tell how you can double or triple your writing income, how to get new clients, and how to get more business from current clients—and I'll give you new ways to market your services and expand your business as never before.

• If you're a staff writer employed by a corporation, advertising agency, newspaper, or other organization and you want to quit your job and become a freelancer, I'll show you how to do it. By following my techniques, you'll be able to match—or even double—your present salary in your first year of freelancing.

• If you dream of writing the Great American Novel, or short stories, poetry, plays, essays, articles, or other literary forms—great! This book will show you how to get lucrative commercial assignments that pay the rent and free you to pursue more artistic interests.

• If you're a moonlighter, a part-timer, or you want to expand your regular income, the type of writing described in this book is ideal for you, because you can work as much or as little as you choose. It's all up to you.

• If you've never written for money in your life but you have a hankering to write, or you're looking for a second career, or to make some money in your spare time working from home, you've come to the right place.

When I wrote the first edition of *Secrets of a Freelance Writer* for Dodd, Mead in 1987, I was thirty years old and had five years' experience as a freelance commercial writer.

Now it's nearly two decades later, I'm 48, and I've been a freelance corporate writer for twenty-three years. In the eighteen years between editions, I've written hundreds of freelance projects for dozens of clients—and I pass along the new tips, techniques, and methods I've learned in this new edition.

The question readers of the first and second editions most often ask me is "Can you still make $85,000 to $125,000 a year or more doing freelance writing for the business market?" The answer is yes, although market conditions have changed over the past two decades. Here are the key differences between then and now.

First, the bad news:

• The recession of the late 1980s and early 1990s—and the uncertain economy of the twenty-first century—put us into a "buyer's market" from which we will never recover. There is more competition, and, at the same time, budgets are more limited and clients are more cost-conscious. You can still make $100,000 a year or more as a freelance corporate writer, but it's more difficult than when I started in 1982—no doubt about it.

• We live in the Age of Now. Deadlines are shorter. Speed, convenience, efficiency, and client service are becoming ever more critical to many buyers of writing services. For some assignments, how fast you can get the copy to the client—and in what file format—seems at times to overshadow the quality of the writing itself.

• There have always been clients who do not care about writing and treat it as a commodity. Such clients have always been and are still a small minority, but their ranks have grown over recent years. You value your craft. Be aware that some buyers do not.

• Downsizing has motivated many downsized corporate workers to try freelancing, flooding the market with new writers. Some stay. Most seem to freelance only until they can find another corporate or ad agency job.

• Clients expect and demand freelance writers to have adequate office technology and be knowledgeable in a variety of programs and computer skills, including Internet access and e-mail. If you are low-tech or computer-phobic, you are far behind the times—and you need to enter the world of modern computing without further delay.

Now, the good news:

• Demand for freelance writing services among businesses, government agencies, and nonprofit organizations has never been higher. Many freelancers are struggling to keep up with the workload and fill orders. There are more than enough assignments to go around. Unlike the book and magazine publishing fields, demand for corporate writing greatly outweighs supply.

• There is still a lot of money to be made. For the first and second editions of *Secrets of a Freelance Writer*, I picked the subtitle "How to Make $85,000 a Year," because that seemed like a lot of money at the time. It's still a nice income for a freelance writer, but many of my readers report earnings of $100,000 to $175,000 a year—and several make more. One called me the other day to tell me he just hit the $200,000 mark!

• Instead of seeing the Internet and CD-ROM as competition for the printed word, see them for what they are: lucrative markets for writers. Do you prefer print? Writing for the World Wide Web has more in common with writing a brochure than it does with writing a movie. It's easy for print writers to adapt to and enjoy this medium.

• Downsizing has resulted in more outsourcing by corporations. They no longer have large staffs of writers and editors. Many documents once produced mainly in-house are now routinely outsourced to freelancers like us, often for big bucks.

• Technology lets you get more work done in less time and makes your life easier. With the PC, fax, and e-mail, I can get twice as much work done as I did in the days of the electric typewriter and no fax or e-mail. For the freelance writer, computers and related technology dramatically increase output, which translates directly into greater earnings.

For many writers, freelancing is where it's at! Freelance writers enjoy significantly greater freedom, flexibility, and—for the most part—more income than writers employed at full-time jobs. When copywriter Nick Usborne asked subscribers of his online newsletter "Excess Voice" in late 2004 their work preference, more than six out of ten said they would prefer to be self-employed.

"Before we can accumulate riches in great abundance, we must become money-conscious until the desire for money drives us to create definite plans for acquiring it," wrote Napoleon Hill in *Think and Grow Rich* (Fawcett Crest). *Secrets of a Freelance Writer* gives you those "definite plans" for acquiring wealth through freelance commercial writing, saving you the headache of creating those plans for yourself—and the costly trial and error of testing them out.

This new edition of *Secrets of a Freelance Writer* has been revised and expanded to address today's new marketplace. It has been reorganized to give you many more tips and strategies for running a successful freelance commercial writing business. It also provides more guidance on using technology, the Web, and e-mail, both as a source for writing assignments and for marketing and self-promotion.

Here's what you'll find in this third edition of *Secrets of a Freelance Writer:*

Chapter 1 defines "freelance commercial writing" and gives an overview of this lucrative but often overlooked writing opportunity.

Chapter 2 provides special guidance for novices. It was written in response to readers who have asked me, "Can you do this if you have no experience?" This chapter outlines strategies for those who want to be writers but have limited or no writing experience, as well as for writers who have done journalism, fiction, or poetry but have little or no experience doing corporate work.

Chapter 3 shows how to set up your freelance writing business, including computers, software, e-mail, Internet access, and other recommended equipment for your home office.

Chapter 4 answers the question "What will I be writing?" It discusses some of the commercial writing assignments you can handle for pay as a corporate freelance writer.

Chapter 5 shows you how to set your fees, present cost estimates, and get the client to agree to your price. You will see what other writers are charging and be given effective strategies for dealing with the objection "Your price is too high." You'll also reduce the number of times you hear this objection, by finding out what the client wants to spend before you give him or her your quotation.

Chapter 6 answers the question "Who will hire me?" You'll learn what types of organizations hire freelance commercial writers, who within these organizations does the hiring, and where to find affordable directories and mailing lists containing the names, companies, addresses, and phone numbers of these potential clients.

Chapter 7 shows how to use direct mail, advertising, the telephone, and other direct-marketing techniques to generate interest in your services among this target audience, resulting in direct inquiries for more information about who you are, what you do, and what you would charge to handle specific projects.

Chapter 8 covers public relations and self-promotion for the freelancer. Here you learn how to generate additional sales leads and build your reputation through giving speeches, writing articles, and other promotional methods.

Chapter 9 shows you how to create an effective Web site for your freelance writing business.

Chapter 10 explains how to get leads and assignments on the Internet by writing, publishing, and distributing a free online newsletter or "e-zine."

Chapter 11 explains how to follow up sales leads so that a significant percentage of those prospects hire you to do projects for them, thus becoming clients of your practice.

Chapter 12 provides helpful hints on running the day-to-day operations of your freelance writing business. It focuses on making the most efficient use of the primary asset you sell for money: your time.

Chapter 13 covers the basics of effective copywriting and business writing and focuses on how to complete assignments so your clients are satisfied.

Chapter 14 gives tips on client service. It's not just the quality of your writing that determines client satisfaction, it's also how you deal with and treat your clients. Here are easy ways to strengthen your relationships with clients.

Chapter 15 describes common problems in this business and provides effective strategies for coping with each one.

Chapter 16 shows you how to ride the ups and downs of your writing career and integrate freelance writing so it complements your total lifestyle.

Chapter 17 outlines a plan in which, by steadily increasing your income as a freelance writer, living conservatively, and saving, you can become a self-made millionaire well before retirement age (although I don't necessarily advocate retiring).

The appendices provide a wealth of resources, including organizations, publications, and model documents.

Whether you write for a living or just for the sheer pleasure of it, or both, wouldn't it be nice to be paid $130 an hour instead of $30 an hour? Or $4,500 for an assignment instead of $450?

After reading this book, you'll be in a position to earn big money from your writing whenever you need it.

Your attitude about writers and money will change for the better. You will have more money, more earning power, and the freedom, security, happiness, peace of mind, pride, contentment, and self-esteem that go with it.

Countless writers have already achieved these goals using the techniques in this book. You can, too. Good luck!

SECRETS OF A FREELANCE WRITER

1

AN INTRODUCTION TO HIGH-PROFIT WRITING

When asked by *Esquire* magazine what he would have done if it hadn't been for writing, novelist Richard Ford replied: "Make more money." And that, I think, sums up the plight of the freelance writer in America today.

When I speak to groups of writers and would-be writers, I ask, "How many of you think it's possible to earn $40,000 this year from your writing?" A few hesitant hands make their way into the air, but most of the audience members sit silently, staring down at their laps . . . because they don't think they'll ever make a living at the computer keyboard, and $40,000 seems a fantastic sum.

They are shocked when I tell them that it's ridiculously easy to earn $40,000 a year writing.

That an annual income of $40,000 can be theirs without much sweat.

That, if they're willing to reexamine their attitude toward the writing life — and commercial, moneymaking writing in particular—they can earn $100,000 or $150,000, or even $200,000 or more.

It's true.

I've done it. And so can you.

IS A SIX-FIGURE INCOME IN YOUR FUTURE?

What does it take to make $100,000 or more a year, every year, writing?

First, it doesn't take genius. You have to be reasonably intelligent to be a writer, I suppose. But not brilliant. Intellectual curiosity and enthusiasm are far more important than sheer brainpower when it comes to being a good and successful writer. "From what I can tell, copywriting isn't rocket science," says copywriter John Forde. "True, it does take a certain knack, but patience and dedication will get you far."

Second, it doesn't take greatness. To succeed as a commercial writer, you have to be good at what you do. But you don't need to be great. Clients look to freelance writers for solid, reliable work, not creative genius. If you rate yourself good, excellent, or even just competent as a writer, you can make $100,000 a year writing. "Being the very best at what you do is not essential," says Cam Foote, a successful freelance corporate writer. "Good is all that's required; excellent isn't."

Now if you don't need genius or greatness, what does it take? Three things:

1. *A new attitude.* If you've always looked down your nose at the type of commercial writing I'm going to describe in this book, take another look. There can be great joy, dignity, and pride in being a successful commercial writer—not to mention more opportunities and better pay. Although 90 percent of my time is devoted to handling projects for corporate clients, I love my work, and I am proud of consistently earning a six-figure income year after year in a profession where most full-time writers are scrambling to make the rent payment each month.

2. *Dedication.* Whether you handle commercial projects full-time or part-time, you have to dedicate yourself to the

task. You must treat the work you do for your clients with respect, not contempt. If you can really muster no enthusiasm for writing an annual report, corporate brochure, Web site, or sales letter, your lack of enthusiasm will show in your writing.

3. *A businesslike approach.* Stockbroker Jim Hansberger says, "We are all salespeople . . . at least part of the time." This applies to stockbrokers, doctors, accountants, dentists, teachers, college presidents—and writers, too.

"There are dozens, perhaps even hundreds, of competitors doing what you do, going after the same business you go after," writes Cameron Foote in "Creative Business." "Marketing allows you to direct the course of your business, rather than being dependent on whatever happens to come your way."

Whether you're writing copy for an ad agency, or the Great American Novel for the Great American Publisher, you have to sell your work in order to live. Fortunately, selling is an easily acquired skill and it can be great fun, too. I know some writers who say they enjoy the selling part of this business almost as much as the writing.

THE AWFUL TRUTH ABOUT "TRADITIONAL" FREELANCE WRITING

When I ask beginning writers how they plan to earn money, they almost always reply, "By writing books and magazine articles." This is the conventional approach to freelance writing. Writers, would-be writers, and people outside writing think of a "real" writer as someone who writes magazine articles and, if fortunate, books, too.

But the sad fact is, writing magazine articles and books doesn't pay very well. A recent survey from the American Society of Journalists and Authors revealed that nearly 7 out of 10 freelance journalists earn less than $50,000 a year. And according to literary agent Michael Larsen, author of *Literary Agents:*

What They Do, How They Do It, advances for a full-length adult nonfiction book today are in the $5,000 to $25,000 range, but the advance for a genre novel or literary first novel may be less than that.

Says novelist and *Advertising Age* columnist James Brady, "Writing novels is not a career. Or an amusement. Or, God knows, a business. It is an addiction those of us afflicted by it are powerless to resist."

The first step to making a lot of money as a freelance writer is to avoid the "poverty mentality" so many writers have. This is the belief that (a) freelance writers earn very little money; (b) freelance writers deserve to earn very little money; (c) it's impossible to make a lot of money as a freelance writer unless you hit with a bestseller or big movie script; and (d) therefore you will never make or have a lot of money as a freelance writer.

Set your sights higher. Don't aim for an income of $40,000 a year. Aim for $100,000 a year, or even $250,000 a year. You may not make your goal. But even if you come only halfway to achieving those high goals, you'll be a lot better off than writers who deliberately aim low.

Believe that you deserve and can earn a good living as a writer because you do and, more important, you can.

Put the $25,000 to $50,000 a year you read about writers making out of your head. You will earn much more than that. When you think about it, $25,000 a year is easy. After all, the average poverty threshold for a family of four is an annual income of around $15,000 a year. Surely you don't expect to live in poverty.

The average New York City doorman makes about $37,300 a year. Doesn't it seem likely that corporations will pay you more to write their Web sites than landlords will pay you to open a door? An article in the New York *Daily News* told of a "squeegee guy" (a person who walks up to your car in Manhattan at a red

light, cleans the windshield, and asks for money) who, when booked for disorderly conduct by the police, was found to have $4,918 in cash in his pockets. If the squeegee guy can make this kind of money, you can, too.

A NEW TYPE OF FREELANCING: HIGH-PROFIT WRITING

Fortunately, there is another way to make money at writing. Some call it "corporate writing" or "business writing." My term is "high-profit writing."

It isn't hard to break into. And it gives you an opportunity to build a regular client base, a steady, solid career, and a business that grows and prospers year after year.

The odds of success are in your favor. In fact, if you are a competent writer, and follow the advice presented in this book, I can almost assure you of a steady, decent income for life.

It's fun. It's rewarding. It's a challenge. And it pays extremely well.

I know of no other area of writing that is so lucrative yet so easy to get started in. In High-Profit Writing, your client is a corporation, small business, or other commercial enterprise— not a magazine or book publisher.

My dictionary defines *commercial* as an activity "1: having profit, success, or immediate results as its chief aim," and "2: sponsored by an advertiser."

High-Profit Writing is work performed for a client who intends to use your copy for commercial purposes. The writing may be used to motivate, educate, inform, or persuade. Most commercial writing is designed to sell or help sell some product or service.

Usually, your client is a corporation that sells goods or services for profit, and your writing is aimed at helping the client achieve this sales goal. Some High-Profit Writers serve other types of clients, such as nonprofit organizations, colleges,

politicians, hospitals, trade associations, community centers, churches, fund-raisers, museums, and government agencies. Most, however, find their best client is corporate America—companies that manufacture products, distribute merchandise, publish information, or render services.

High-Profit Writing encompasses just about any type of printed, electronic, and online presentation clients may need to promote their products, services, organizations, or ideas. These assignments include, but are not limited to, advertisements, annual reports, articles, booklets, brochures, case histories, catalogs, CD-ROMs, circulars, data sheets, direct-mail packages, e-mail marketing campaigns, employee communications, film scripts, fliers, instruction manuals, invoice stuffers, newsletters, press releases, product labels and packaging, proposals, radio commercials, reports, sales letters, sales promotion materials, seminars, slide- and computer-based presentations, speeches, technical papers, trade show exhibits, training materials, TV commercials, videotapes, and Web pages.

In this book, I'll tell you everything you need to know to get started in this exciting business—including how the business works, who the clients are, where to find clients, how to get people to hire you, how to set and negotiate fees, how to complete assignments successfully, how to handle revisions, how to make sure you get paid, how to collect past-due bills, how to resolve difficulties and problems, how to market your writing services, plus how to get more assignments from current clients.

After reading this book, you will be able to start and run your own successful freelance writing business, specializing in commercial High-Profit Writing assignments. Of course, you are free to devote as much or as little time to this endeavor as you please.

If you work at it full-time, you can achieve an annual income in excess of $100,000. If you work at it part-time, you

can earn a nice sum and have many free hours to devote to writing novels, short stories, poems, or whatever else is your pleasure, without having to depend on these literary endeavors for your income.

I can't guarantee your success, of course. But I can point the way.

PROS AND CONS OF FREELANCE COMMERCIAL WRITING

Although it may not be what you dreamed of when you first got hooked on writing, being a commercial writer has its advantages. Among them:

1. You make much more money than in other types of writing. On average, freelance writers doing corporate work earn two to four times as much money as freelance writers doing magazine articles and books.
2. Commercial writing is a business that can build up nicely, with a regular client base and steady assignments. Freelancing for magazines and book publishers, on the other hand, is an uncertain occupation at best. In High-Profit Writing, the client is buying you as a writer, your writing services. If the service is good, she will come back to you again and again. In the publishing world, the publisher is buying your book or article idea; even if you did a good job the first time, they'll turn you down if your next idea doesn't turn them on.
3. There is tremendous variety in commercial assignments. Each client and each project is different. You will rarely be bored.
4. Corporations have a real and pressing need to get things written. There is a huge demand for commercial freelance writers. Assignments for competent freelancers are never in short supply. There is much less competition

than in books, magazine articles, television writing, or movies.

5. The relationship between writer and client is on a highly professional level. Writers are generally treated better by their corporate clients than by publishers.
6. There is little or no "on spec" work. With rare exception, commercial writers always get paid for services rendered.
7. There's no need for you to sit around and dream up ideas. Clients will come to you with projects and assignments. This eliminates the need to write query letters and proposals—a time-consuming activity for which writers do not get paid.
8. High-Profit Writers enjoy the sense of dignity, self-esteem, and peace of mind that comes from being well paid. They do not sit in cold garrets hunched over antiquated electric typewriters and outdated PCs bemoaning their poverty. Successful commercial writers earn enough to support a home, a family, and the other necessities and luxuries of life.
9. High-Profit Writers who know how to market themselves and are good at what they do can ensure a steady stream of new clients and new business all year long. The agony of sitting around with nothing to do, waiting for a letter or phone call from an editor, need not be a part of the commercial writer's life.

Of course, there are disadvantages as well:

1. You don't get a byline. Most of your copy, including ads, brochures, and catalogs, is sent out under the client company's logo. If you ghostwrite speeches or articles for a client, the client, not you, is credited as the author.
2. The work you are doing is, by its nature, commercial, not literary. This bothers some people. But most writers with

literary aspirations can enjoy both types of assignments, commercial and literary, for what they are.

"In the writer's youthful dreams, literature had been the freest of all countries and the thought of it the only possible way of escaping from the vileness and submissions of daily life to a proud equality, and no doubt many had pursued such dreams," writes Peter Handke in his book *The Afternoon of a Writer* (Minerva). As a freelance commercial writer, be prepared to deal with the real world of "crass commerce" and dispense with your literary illusions—at least while you're working on client projects. You can always create art on your own time.

3. The ideas are not your own. It is the client who dictates the nature of the assignment (the type of copy needed, the product to be promoted, the key sales points or themes to be stressed). Writers' creativity comes into play when they shape the raw material into an interesting, compelling, persuasive piece of copy. But the basic idea originates with the client. You usually do not work with material that is totally of your own choosing, as you would writing a novel, play, or poem.

4. The client dictates the final form. If the client wants revisions, you must make them, even if you disagree. The client, not the writer, is gambling his money on your TV commercial or sales letter or advertisement, so ultimately the client must be happy and comfortable with it. A smart client pays close attention to his writer's recommendations and opinions. But the client, not the writer, has the final say.

Most documents produced in organizations must be approved by multiple reviewers, which can make the revision process slow and sometimes tedious. No writer is immune to this. In her book *What I Saw at the Revolution* (Random House), White House speechwriter Peggy

Noonan says that every presidential speech was circulated for comments and reviewed by twenty to fifty people, depending on the importance of the occasion and the topic.

5. As with many other types of businesses, payments are sometimes slow in coming. This is not a deliberate attempt to cheat the writer. It is simply that many large corporations routinely take 60 or 90 days to authorize payment for a vendor's invoice. With 10 to 70 percent of your assets tied up in accounts receivable, slow payments can create serious cash-flow problems for the freelancer. This can be alleviated by building up a steady flow of business and a "rainy day" nest egg in the bank.

6. Disputes occasionally arise between client and writer. The client is displeased with the copy and refuses to pay. Or the writer thinks the client's suggested revisions are stupid. Few businesses operate without some complaints and dissatisfaction. But problems are amplified by the fact that commercial writing is a highly personal endeavor. Writers take criticisms of their writing as criticisms of themselves. In chapter 15, I'll show you how to handle and resolve the various types of client conflicts.

7. It can be difficult to achieve a balanced flow of work. "When it comes to both work and revenue, it's often feast or famine," writes Sally-Jo Bowman in an article in *Writer's Digest*. For instance, the day you accept three new assignments on a rush basis, three existing clients call with extensive revisions on jobs you thought were finished and done with. This creates a pressure situation that can result in stress. Also, some clients will try to force you to accept unrealistically tight deadlines, creating additional pressure. At other times, when things are

on a new ambulatory-care unit for a local hospital, asks you, "Can you send me any samples of eight-page brochures you've written for ambulatory-care units for local hospitals?" They are looking for a sample to clone—not a real writer—and may not be the type of prospect you want to work with anyway.

• One-third of the people who call are looking for a writer, have heard you are good (or believe you are when you tell them so), don't care about samples or credentials, and are ready to hire you today. This is the segment of the market easiest for you to sell to, if you are a novice with little or no experience.

The drawback is that these may be the smaller organizations with smaller budgets—and, quite frankly, are not paying a lot, or asking for a lot, either. They just want decent, clean copy; the quality of the work isn't life and death for them. Obviously, as you progress, you want to move away from this group to clients that need the best copy and are willing to pay for it. But for now, this "less fussy" group of buyers is a good place to start.

More good news: This is a sizable, substantial market that will always exist. There are approximately 10 million businesses in the United States. I estimate that one-third are in this category, which would give a total of 3.3 million potential clients for you to approach. That will keep you busy for quite some time.

YOU MAY NOT BE AS INEXPERIENCED AS YOU THINK

Many would-be writers complain to me that they lack experience. But do they? Most of us who want to be professional writers have done some writing. And, while you didn't think much of it at the time, that technical manual you edited at the selling of your professional writing services. In this chapter I will show you how a beginner with little or no experience can overcome this handicap and go on to land highly profitable assignments writing for corporations, ad agencies, and other clients.

WILL CLIENTS HIRE NOVICE FREELANCE COMMERCIAL WRITERS?

Although lack of experience prevents you from getting many assignments, it will not prevent you from getting assignments from certain clients.

Clients—their needs, perceptions, and concerns—vary amazingly. I have found in twenty-three years of freelancing that the following pattern holds true:

• One-third of the prospects who call me want me to send samples or show a portfolio, but the samples are not their key concern. They are primarily concerned with knowing that I am reliable, capable, and can do the job on time and within their budget.

But because we live in a society of credentials on paper, they ask for samples as a matter of routine; samples are the resumé of the freelance writer. Lack of good samples is a difficulty in selling to this group, but it can be overcome if you sparkle in person and are impressive in your preliminary conversations and sales meeting with the prospects.

• One-third of the prospects who call me give me the third degree concerning my samples, resumé, and other credentials. If the samples are not carbon copies of the new piece they want me to create, they ask for more samples. And more samples. Unless you or I have samples very close to the piece they want to commission, they'll pass on us and search around until they find a writer with such a sample in his or her portfolio.

This is the prospect who, if she needs an eight-page brochure

2

TIPS FOR BEGINNERS: GETTING STARTED

Can you really make $100,000 a year or more as a freelance writer serving local and national clients, even if you don't have a lot of writing experience?

This is what one of my readers wanted to know when she wrote me a letter after reading the first edition of *Secrets of a Freelance Writer*.

"I am very interested in your premise," her letter began. "However, most of your advice as to how to get started in commercial writing seems to be slanted to someone who has corporate experience or some sort of technical background. I have neither one of those things.

"How would you suggest that I, laboring under that handicap, go about marketing myself? I don't know if anyone would be receptive to an announcement like, 'Hi, I'm a good writer, hire me.' Do you have any suggestions? As I said, I'm very interested in this idea of commercial writing, and I would like to see how I could do. I'm a good writer and a fairly quick study, so I hope that would help offset my lack of any other type of experience. I'd really appreciate any ideas you might have."

I know from letters, e-mails, and phone calls that many of you are in a similar position and are wondering how it affects on the weekend or evenings. But when you do put in extra time, you get more money. This is an advantage not enjoyed by corporate employees, who put in long hours but are often not compensated for overtime.

I spent the rest of Tuesday writing a one-page sales letter for a client who sells electronic components. I completed the whole job that day. My fee: $700.

Another client, a school that trains computer programmers, needed a small ad and brochure describing a new course on micro-computer programming. I started that Tuesday and finished after lunch on Friday. I printed the copy on my computer, proofread it, and sent it by Federal Express for Monday delivery. My fee for the ad and brochure: $1,900.

I thought I was through for the week, but then, as a pleasant surprise, I received a package and check by messenger. Someone who had phoned earlier in the week had asked me what I would charge to read and critique an ad he had already written and prepared for publication. Apparently he thought my fee was reasonable. Reviewing the ad took about an hour. I printed out my report and sent it back by fax before five P.M. My fee: $200. My total income for those seven days: $4,800.

But this wasn't the only work I had on my desk during this period. I had several other high-paying commercial assignments I was able to put off because their deadlines weren't until later in the month. Plus ongoing publisher's contracts to write two magazine articles and three books, any of which could have kept me busy at the PC during the week.

Back then, I didn't make $4,800 every week. Some weeks, I made less. These days, the majority of weeks I make considerably more than that. But this diary of my week's activities shows that it is possible to make a lot of money in freelance writing.

Okay. Let's say you want to tap this lucrative market, either as your full-time business or as a part-time supplement to your other writing activities. Let's get started.

MY DAY: AN INTRODUCTION OF SORTS

What, exactly, is a typical day or week in the life of a commercial writer?

Actually, no day or week is typical. Each week brings something new. Today's assignment is different from yesterday's. That's what makes this business fun and exciting.

Some weeks will be hectic, crammed with projects and assignments. Others may be slow. But don't worry. You can use that slow time for many things. You can organize your office or update your files. You can buy that new piece of software you need and learn how to use it.

Or, you can work on your novel or play or short story. You can write query letters or turn out a magazine article or essay. You can generate more commercial business by phoning clients, writing sales letters, or going to meetings. You can spend the time polishing a current project. You can catch up on your Web surfing or e-mail. Or, you can take the day off to shop or drive in the country or do some household chores.

Years ago (when my fees were lower than they are today), I wrote this chapter for the first edition of this book. I wrote it on a Friday, at the end of a week that was fairly hectic. Let me describe that week for you.

The Friday before, I received a call from an ad agency account executive whom I had met with three months ago. They needed a brochure written over the weekend and ready the following Tuesday. Was I available?

I wanted to work with the agency, and the project, a brochure describing a new telecommunications system, was right up my alley. Although I normally don't like rush jobs, I knew I could meet the deadline. So I accepted.

They sent the background material over that morning, and I e-mailed the finished copy back to them on Tuesday. My fee: $2,000, all earned during the weekend. You don't have to work slow, you may worry about not being busy enough and not having enough money coming in.

8. The writer who runs a one-person commercial writing business is the proverbial one-man or one-woman band. You make the sales, service the clients, write the copy, keep the books, handle the paperwork, and take care of the numerous nagging details of running a small busi-ness. Sometimes you may tire of it. Burnout is always a possibility.

   In an article in the now-defunct "Self-Employment Survival Letter," one home-based entrepreneur commented: "The one thing no one ever gets across clearly about self-employment is the way it dogs you, waking and sleeping, especially when you know to the penny what every minute of your time is worth." A classic definition of entrepreneurs is people who gladly work 80 hours a week for themselves to avoid working 40 hours a week for someone else—although in today's downsized, reengineered corporate world, full-time employees seem to be putting in as many as or even more hours than we freelancers.

   Solutions? You might consider cutting back on your work, hiring an assistant, or subcontracting assignments to other freelancers.

9. Writing is sedentary work, so you must exercise to keep fit. According to the "UC Berkeley Wellness Letter" (March 1996), a 130-pound person burns only 48 calories during 30 minutes of typing—less than he or she would use drawing, walking, or playing the piano. I work out twice a week in one-hour sessions at a local gym with a personal trainer. And I keep in my office a Schwinn Airdyne stationary bicycle, purchased used for $400, which I ride not as often as I should.

work or the article you wrote for your church newsletter can often be enough to convince prospective clients to hire you to create similar material for their organization.

My own entry into the writing field is a good case study of this principle in action. After completing my undergraduate degree in chemical engineering, I decided I wanted to be a writer, not an engineer. But I had not done any professional writing. So who would hire me?

A wise guidance counselor asked whether I had done *any* writing. "Sure," I replied. "Some articles and columns for the college newspaper. But nothing professional—nothing that counts." The counselor disagreed. On the strength of some of those articles for the school newspaper, she got me an interview with Westinghouse, and in 1979 I was hired as a staff writer for $18,000 a year, a decent salary at the time. I was on my way!

Go through your education and career and take an inventory of all the writing you've done in your life. Also, comb your files for documents that can serve as your first samples.

I say this again, as strongly as I can: Everyone has done some writing. It's impossible to live in the twenty-first century and participate in business or get through the educational system and not write. Thanks to e-mail, now virtually everyone writes something, every day.

Here are some of the things you may have written that can serve as samples of your work when you speak to potential clients:

- *Business letters.* Did you ever write a business letter you thought was particularly persuasive? Clients pay $300 to $1,000 a page for good letter copy. Show them a sample or two and they just might hire you.
- *Other writing done on the job.* Reports, memos, e-mails, Web pages, proposals, instructional materials, press releases,

announcements, and articles can all serve as examples of
your writing ability.

- *Published or unpublished articles.* A book (especially if it
deals with communications or a subject related to the
client's business) also impresses.

The only things I would definitely not show a prospective
commercial client are unpublished short stories, novels, plays,
and poems.

IF YOU DON'T HAVE ANY WRITING EXPERIENCE,
GO OUT AND GET SOME

Not having any materials on file is no excuse not to pursue a
lucrative career or part-time income in commercial freelance
writing. With so many outlets for writing, if you don't already
have samples, it's easy enough to go out and create some. And
that's what you should do.

There are many low-pay/no-pay opportunities to get writing
assignments. Although you should work for low pay or no pay
as little as possible, and only until you get two or three good
samples out of it, this is one way to get experience if you really
have none. Here are some suggestions for getting experience
and samples:

1. Volunteer. Nonprofit organizations especially are always
on the lookout for volunteers to turn out newsletters, press releases, and fund-raising mail.

TIP: To find local nonprofit organizations, look at the news
items in your town newspaper. Most of the organizations featured in short news items — the library, parent/teacher associations, animal shelters, environmental groups — have active
publicity programs and can use your help. My son's preschool,
for example, asked one of the parents to volunteer to write

some press releases on school events for distribution to the local papers.

It goes without saying that you should always get copies of what you write to use as samples.

2. If you belong to a church or other organization, volunteer to write for, or even produce, their newsletter. There is a big demand among corporate clients for writers who do newsletters. Are you a member of a club, society, or association? Volunteer to do the newsletter for your local chapter. Also send contributions to the editor of the national newsletter, if there is one.

3. Write articles for trade journals that cover the industries or areas of specialty in which you'd like to get corporate clients. Once these clients see you can write a good article and get it published in their industry trade journal, they will hire you to ghostwrite and place such articles for them as promotional vehicles.

4. If you have friends or relatives who own small businesses, offer to create ads, brochures, or other marketing materials for them at a low fee in exchange for the experience and copies of the piece as a writing sample.

5. Take a course at a local college, university, community center, or online that requires you to do a weekly writing assignment as part of your homework. A course in advertising copywriting, public relations, or business communications would be a good bet.

Then, after the instructor grades your assignments, rewrite them to incorporate his comments and retype the copy neatly. Many of the students who took the copywriting class I used to teach at New York University told me they were able to secure a good full-time job or lucrative freelance assignments on the strength of samples created as homework assignments for the class.

Of course, when retyping homework, do not give any indication on the manuscript that the material was done for a class rather than a paying client. If the prospect asks, you can be truthful. But most will never ask.

In fact, you don't even need to take a course to create your own writing samples. Amil Gargano, the advertising genius who founded Ally & Gargano Advertising Agency and created those wonderful fast-talking commercials for Federal Express, suggests that you go through magazines and clip out half a dozen or so ads that interest you but that you think could be improved. Then, says Gargano, rewrite the ads to make them better. These become your first samples.

BUILDING YOUR SAMPLE PORTFOLIO

By taking inventory of your past experience, assembling materials you've written, and getting more experience as outlined above, you will soon have a file folder of samples.

You don't need many samples, and whether you have three samples or thirty really doesn't make all that much difference. It's getting the first few that matter.

If you're selling to prospects primarily by mailing out samples, you need only mail a handful. When someone calls and asks for information on my services, I usually send three or four samples. No more.

In the beginning, keep copies of your samples in a folder in your briefcase. (In chapter 3 we'll discuss using a portfolio to display your samples.) When you meet with clients, don't focus on your background, but instead ask questions about the clients' problems, the nature of the assignment, what the clients need, and how you can help them. Clients are not really interested in you per se, but rather in the writing they need done and how you can help them do it.

If clients then say, "Did you bring any samples?" you can hand over the folder. I prefer to bring photocopies I can leave behind. It is neither a bad nor a good sign that clients ask to see samples in a meeting. It may indicate genuine interest or be just a polite way of ending the meeting.

If clients do not want to see samples, this can be a positive sign, indicating that they like you and trust you to the point where looking at samples is unimportant. Of course, it could also indicate total disinterest in you and your services. You can usually tell which is the case from their attitude and body language.

Should your clients not ask to see samples, don't offer to show them or pull them out of your briefcase. The clients are probably already sold on you. Why slow down the sales process by forcing them to look at something in which they have indicated no interest? If they need to see samples before making a decision, they'll ask for them.

If you are truly a beginner at this, without reputation or experience, your focus—at least in the beginning—should be on gaining experience, establishing a track record of success, building a client list, and getting good samples for your portfolio.

Although I feel that too many writers are afraid to ask for the compensation they deserve, and that writers should not give away their services at low rates, this is one situation where an exception to the rule may be necessary.

When you're just starting out, no one knows you. You don't have a long list of clients, a lot of samples, or a proven track record, so demanding high fees may be hard to justify.

My advice is to take assignments from wherever they come, do them to the best of your ability, and thus build an experience base from which you can start climbing the ladder of success. Yes, of course, you want to get paid well, but if push comes to shove—if you feel that you need the assignment and the experience—then be willing to take a less-than-ordinary fee to get it.

This is the strategy I used in the beginning of my own freelance career to rapidly build a portfolio and list of prestige clients. Could I have charged higher fees and still landed all those assignments? Perhaps. More likely, I would have gotten a portion of them, while other clients would have gone to a less expensive or more experienced writer. And my goal then, as yours should be now, was to get as many client successes as possible into my portfolio as quickly as possible.

There is nothing wrong with being more aggressive and bolder about demanding higher fees. Just realize that if you quote a high fee, there is a possibility that you will not get the assignment. If you are psychologically able to allow that to happen at this stage in your career, fine. Stick to your guns and get top dollar. But if you feel you need to "hook" those first half-dozen clients right away, you can be a bit more flexible in the money department. It's your choice.

HOW TO FIND YOUR FIRST CLIENT

In her letter, my reader also asked, "Would simply an area of interest be a good place to start? Two categories that I would like to concentrate in, arising out of my own interests, are the pet-care industry and diabetes-related health care."

By all means, concentrate your initial marketing efforts in areas where you have a strong interest, aptitude, connections, or some prior experience. This is the best place for a novice freelance writer to start. After all, if you have a strong interest, you will be more enthusiastic, and when that enthusiasm shows through in your writing (as it invariably will), the client will spot it and appreciate it.

Also, your prior interest means you have probably done some reading or had some hands-on experience in the field, which makes you more knowledgeable and better able to provide clients with both copy and advice.

Be careful, though, that you don't make your field of choice so narrow that there are not enough clients to sustain your practice. For example, "diabetes-related health care" is too narrow; "health care," however, is a good specialty. It is narrow enough to give you an edge over other writers who don't specialize in it, yet broad enough for there to be enough prospective clients (hospitals, pharmaceutical companies, medical equipment manufacturers, doctors, HMOs, etc.) to keep you as busy as you want to be.

One of my students specializes in writing user manuals for software and computer systems. The field is so huge that it can easily support her and hundreds of other software documentation writers, yet it is specialized enough that good writers are constantly in demand. If she had told me she specialized in writing operating manuals for elevators, I would have advised her to expand and broaden her horizons, because there are only a handful of elevator companies—and if they already have writers, there is little or no market for her service.

HOW TO ANSWER THE PROSPECT WHO SAYS, "WHO ARE YOUR CLIENTS?"

An embarrassing question for the novice is "Who are your clients?" It's a classic catch-22 situation: You don't have clients because you're a beginner. Clients don't want to hire you because you don't have an impressive client list. But you can't get an impressive client list until some clients hire you.

Fortunately, there is a solution. The solution is to speak in terms of "clients and experience" rather than just clients.

The key to this principle is to lump together everyone you've ever written for in the past—full-time employers, book publishers, magazine editors, volunteer work, and freelance commercial clients—as your collective base of "clients and experience."

For example, the headline on my list of clients (which I send prospects who ask for further information on my services) doesn't say "Clients"; it reads "Clients/Experience." This legitimately allows me to put Westinghouse on my client list, even though I worked for Westinghouse as a full-time employee and not a freelancer. Prospects reading the list don't stop to question which names are clients and which are not; thus they get the impression that my client list is that much more impressive because Westinghouse is on it.

Most of us starting freelance careers have worked for one or two or three companies and may even have moonlighted for one or two clients. Clever language can make this limited base of experience seem like an impressive roster of clients.

When I started my career I had held, besides the position with Westinghouse, a full-time position with Koch Engineering. I had also written one freelance article for Dow Chemical, one ad for an ad agency, two press releases for a PR firm, and a short item for the employee magazine of ABC-TV (none of them were ongoing clients). In my first promotional mailing to potential clients I wrote: "My experience includes writing copy for such companies as Westinghouse Electric Corporation, Koch Engineering, Dow Chemical, ABC-TV, and many other organizations."

Sounds impressive, doesn't it? The statement is entirely truthful, yet gives the impression that my experience is much more than it actually is. This is not deception, it's skillful copywriting, and it's a technique that can work for you, too.

When your client roster is short—say, less than half a dozen actual firms—present it as a paragraph in your sales letter or brochure. When your client list grows to perhaps a dozen firms or more, you can print it on a separate sheet and distribute it to impress your prospects.

GET SOME BLUE-CHIP NAMES ON YOUR CLIENT LIST AS EARLY AS YOU CAN

It is useful in your sales letters, brochures, and conversations with prospects to rattle off the names of two or three well-known firms you have worked for. Even though you may have done great work for smaller or regional firms, prospects are still more impressed when you tell them that General Electric, Ford, Grumman, and AT&T are among the firms on your client roster.

If the opportunity to work for a Fortune 1000 company comes your way, grab it, even if the assignment isn't your dream project. You will have a far easier time convincing prospective clients to hire you when you can toss off two or three famous client names in your conversation.

You don't have to have a regular contract or even do a large assignment to legitimately include a company name on your client list. As mentioned earlier, ABC paid me $50 for a short article for their employee magazine; I used them on my client list for years.

SHOULD YOU WORK FOR A CLIENT ON SPEC?

Imagine this scene: You are in the offices of a prospective client. You feel the meeting has gone well. They have an assignment. And then the prospect says, "Well, why don't you take a crack at this and see what you can do? If we like what you've done, you'll get a real assignment." Or: "Why don't you take home this background material and write us a sample as a test?"

This is known as "spec work" (short for "speculative work"). On a spec assignment, you write the copy with no promise of pay. If the client likes it and wants to use it, you'll be paid. Or, if they like it but don't want to use it, they give you a real assignment. If they don't like it, they don't hire you, don't pay you, and don't owe you for your time.

Should you take on any assignment on spec? It really depends on the situation and your own needs. How badly do you want the work? How much potential does this client have in terms of prestige and income? Is the client seriously considering you for the assignment, or just jerking you around? (Some people in business delight at abusing outside vendors.)

There are basically two situations in which clients ask writers to work on spec. In the first situation, the client has an assignment. Unsure of how you will perform, she tells you to go ahead and do the job on spec. Although the idea is that you will be paid if the work is satisfactory, beware. Most legitimate clients do not engage in this practice.

Typically, people who call with a request for spec work never intend to pay and are just wasting your time while picking your brains for free. The best way to separate serious prospects from these time-wasters is to ask for a "kill fee"—a small partial payment—if the assignment is not accepted. The kill fee should be 10 to 50 percent of your normal fee for the project.

In the second situation, the client gives you a small "test" assignment to see how well you perform before engaging your services. Example: A client needs fifty photo captions written. He might ask you to write one or two on spec; if he likes them, you are paid for the two captions and get the contract to do the rest of the work. If he doesn't like them, you don't get paid.

Should you accept this type of spec assignment? In some cases, maybe. If your instincts tell you the client is on the level and you have a good chance of getting the assignment, you might agree to write one or two short samples on spec. Again, you might make the assignment more palatable, and raise your prestige in the client's eye, by insisting on a kill fee, however modest, explaining that you don't work for free.

If the client persists, go ahead with the test on spec, but

emphasize that this is an exception and that you are doing it as a special service for this client only. Don't make spec work a habit. Don't ever volunteer to do it unless the client insists.

CREATING YOUR FIRST MARKETING MATERIALS: SPECIAL CONSIDERATIONS FOR BEGINNERS

If you take a look at my marketing package (see appendix E), you will find an emphasis on credentials and past performance: client list, testimonials, samples of work completed. Writers ask me, "How can I put together a convincing package when I don't have this experience?"

The answer is simple. When you have a lot of experience, your marketing documents stress what you have done for others in the past and the results you have achieved—the inference being you can do the same thing for the prospect, too.

But when you are a beginner, without experience, your marketing documents stress who you are, the services you offer, the benefits of those services, and what you can and will do, rather than what you have done.

Your brochure or sales letter will stress:

- Who you are.
- Credentials (salaried positions held, results achieved for employers, academic degrees, awards won, memberships in professional associations).
- Abilities (e.g., "I write technical copy that is clear, crisp, and factually accurate").
- Services you provide (writing, Web site design, search engine optimization, editing, proofreading, consulting, etc.).
- Types of projects you handle (reports, articles, books, manuals, online copy, etc.).
- Types of clients or industries you will write for (e.g., nonprofits, colleges, hospitals, manufacturers, banks).

- Benefits of your services (your copy will produce more sales, recruit more employees, and cut down on customer service calls).
- Advantages of your copy over that of other writers who may be competing for the same clients you are (e.g., you write great auto copy because you are an amateur mechanic and race car driver).
- If your copy projects an image of competence and confidence, many clients will accept what you say without digging into your lack of experience, so your beginner status will not be a problem.

One of my readers, Roscoe Barnes III, sent me an excellent self-promotion brochure he created when he was just starting out. It made the most of the experience he did have, but also was strong on promises and benefits. The text began:

> Make no mistake. Your prospects may never know the benefits of your offer . . . unless you have copywriting that gets results! When you need that kind of copy . . . the kind that pulls in money . . . and generates leads, call Roscoe Barnes III.

Doesn't this sound confident, competent, and credible? It's so positive you don't even notice that Roscoe never actually says that he has done these things; he just says that he *can* do them, which is absolutely true. Keep in mind that a well-written brochure like Roscoe's is in itself a writing sample that shows what you are capable of. So make yours sparkle.

PUT YOUR BEST FOOT FORWARD

Many beginners make the mistake of telling prospects that they are beginners.

Although you may be new to this business, clients can't tell that by looking at you. Indeed, I've met some novice consultants/writers who, in their first presentations to new prospects, were far more polished and impressive than I've been on my best day during twenty-three years of commercial freelance writing.

Don't tell clients that if they hire you they will be your first (or second or third) client. Don't feel compelled to tell them that you are new to this business if they don't ask. Don't apologize for who you are or your lack of experience.

Instead, project an image of confidence. Let clients know that you are a reliable, talented writer who can get the job done for them. After all, it's the truth!

To some writers, the first assignment comes easily. Other writers have to work at it a bit. But it will come. That I promise. However, as a beginner you must try even harder to get clients and assignments.

Once you are established, it gets easier (although you can never stop marketing altogether). But the novice must write more letters, mail more brochures, make more telephone calls, and meet with more prospects in order to get the assignments.

Even though I am well established in this field and have many more projects than I can possibly handle, I still spend 10 to 25 percent of my time marketing my services, promoting my name, and selling my services to clients. That's because I know that if I don't plant the seeds for new clients today, I may not have any business six months from now.

When you're just starting out, you'll probably spend 25 to 50 percent of your time marketing. If you are not actively selling your services, advertising and promoting yourself just like any other business, you will not get the jobs. If you follow the marketing advice in this book, you will get business. And once you get your first few clients, others will see that you are successful and want to hire you. Success breeds success.

TRAITS OF THE SUCCESSFUL HOME-BASED SOLO ENTREPRENEUR

The primary characteristic that determines whether you will succeed as a freelance commercial writer is desire: If you really, really want it, you'll make it happen.

In an article in *SAP Connection,* Terri Lonier, author of *Working Solo,* says that successful solo entrepreneurs are self-starters, outgoing, lifelong learners, and optimistic. Don't worry if you don't have these characteristics in abundance. Exceptions are plentiful. Again, if you can write and are willing to do what it takes to succeed, you will.

An anonymous essay sent to me by motivational speaker Dr. Rob Gilbert gives this advice, which is extremely applicable to freelance writers: "What you achieve in your lifetime is directly related to what you do. You can choose your own direction. Everyone has problems and obstacles to overcome, but you can change anything in your life if you want to badly enough. Compete. If you aren't willing to work for your goals, don't expect others to."

An article in the newsletter "Creative Business" notes that freelancers:

- Enjoy working at home alone.
- Are somewhat motivated by money.
- Are not that interested in business details.
- Do not want to supervise others.

That last characteristic describes Don Hauptman, a highly successful freelance direct-mail writer. Don says he chooses self-employment over corporate employment because he does not like to be told what to do. And he has no staff or assistants because he dislikes telling other people what to do.

Keep in mind that writers seldom have all of Terri Lonier's characteristic entrepreneurial traits. Most writers are not outgoing. Many are downright introverted. Most writers do like to learn.

As for being a self-starter, that's helpful but not critical: As a freelance commercial writer, you'll be doing projects clients assign to you with specific deadlines. So your day will be somewhere between that of a classic entrepreneur and that of a nine-to-fiver: a mixture of scheduled, deadline work — with a great deal of flexibility concerning what you do when — and many hours of time to use as you choose.

Despite the fact that all the motivational speakers and self-help books say successful entrepreneurs are optimists, don't be worried if you're not. An article in the New York *Daily News* reports that unhappy people work harder, look deeper at situations, find more creative solutions, and do better work than happy people.

Cheerful folks who participated in the study, said the article, "overestimated their abilities, underestimated the complexity of the problems, and tended to opt for easy answers." In his book *Learned Optimism*, optimism enthusiast Martin Seligman admits that pessimists have at least one big advantage over optimists: They take a more realistic view of things, including business situations.

It really doesn't matter whether you are an optimist or a pessimist as long as you work diligently at your business. If you do, you will get results.

BUILDING A NEST EGG BEFORE YOU TAKE THE PLUNGE

Chapter 3 outlines the office equipment and devices you will need for your freelance High-Profit Writing business. Although freelance writing is still just about the least expensive business of any kind as far as start-up costs are concerned, the technology requirements have made it slightly more expensive to invest in than fifteen or twenty years ago.

When I started, I worked on an Adler electric typewriter from college, on a dining-room table I had picked up at a garage sale. A two-drawer file cabinet, costing $35, doubled as my night stand in a one-room studio apartment that served as both my residence and office. I had some stationery printed, paid $120 for a telephone answering machine, and was ready to go.

Today, with computers, software, modems, printers, fax machines, and voice mail, the initial investment can easily run you $1,500 to $3,500 or more. If cash is a problem, you can lease what you need, or buy used equipment inexpensively (you can get a decent PC these days for under $1,000).

Would-be freelancers should have at least six months' living expenses set aside, and should also try running their business part-time (moonlighting) before quitting a regular job. I advise having enough savings to live for six to twelve months without income.

Do I think you won't make any money during your first six to twelve months of freelancing? Quite the contrary. Although the first six months are indeed slow for many freelance High-Profit Writers, most seem to have first-year gross earnings of anywhere from half of to slightly more than the annual salary they were earning before they quit their full-time job.

Nevertheless, I recommend having cash equivalent to six to twelve months' income in the bank when you start your free-lance venture. The more cash you have, the more time you can allow for your business to build.

If you don't have savings or another means of support, you'll be under constant pressure to generate immediate revenue, which in turn can lead to some less than ideal decisions concerning which projects and clients you take on. This is something you want to avoid as much as you can.

On the other hand, when you have some significant personal net wealth, you are freed from the pressure to generate immediate revenue. This is particularly helpful if you have significant financial responsibilities such as car payments, a mortgage, and a spouse and kids to support.

The six- to twelve-month "stash" of cash is recommended for freelance writers whose writing income is their sole source of revenue. If you have a spouse or significant other who works full-time and can take over as the primary breadwinner for a spell . . . or a trust fund . . . or you live with friends or parents who are willing to support you while you make the transition from corporate employment to self-employment, you can probably get away with having a smaller nest egg.

3

SETTING UP YOUR FREELANCE WRITING BUSINESS

Okay. So you'd like to boost your income by getting high-paying assignments from commercial clients. This chapter shows you, step by step, what it takes to get started.

The first step is to decide what services you will offer your clients and the types of projects you will handle.

Some writers specialize, handling only direct mail or audio-visual scripts or annual reports. Others take on a broad spectrum of assignments.

Some writers work in only one or two specialized areas, such as fund-raising or high-tech or writing for political candidates. Others are generalists, serving clients in many different industries. The choice is up to you.

One way to get started is by focusing on areas where you've had previous experience. For example, if you worked on the public relations staff of a local hospital, you might specialize in public relations writing for the health care industry. As your client list and reputation grow, you can easily expand into other areas. The following list gives some of the different types of writing projects handled by freelancers serving commercial clients:

- Advertising
- Annual reports
- Application briefs
- Articles
- Booklets
- Brochures
- Business plans
- Case histories
- Catalogs
- CD-ROMS
- Circulars
- Data sheets
- Direct mail
- E-mail marketing
- Employee communications
- E-zines
- Flash presentations
- Fliers
- Instruction manuals
- Invoice stuffers
- Labels/packaging

- Landing pages
- Newsletters
- Posters and signs
- PowerPoint presentations
- Press releases
- Proposals
- Radio commercials
- Reports
- Sales letters
- Seminars
- Slide shows
- Software documentation
- Speeches
- Trade show display panels
- Training materials
- TV commercials
- Videotape scripts
- Web sites
- White papers

In chapter 4, I describe the tasks of the freelance commercial writer in more detail, focusing on those assignments that are either easy to get, or pay well—or both.

After deciding what types of services you want to offer, you must let potential clients know you are available for hire. I'll discuss the specialized markets for each type of writing and where to find directories and mailing lists in chapter 6.

9 MOST COMMON REASONS WHY CLIENTS HIRE FREELANCE COMMERCIAL WRITERS

If you are to succeed at selling your services, you must understand the reasons why clients hire freelance commercial writers.

This is not as trivial as it may sound. In my seminars, many beginning writers confess to me that they don't understand why an ad agency would hire a freelancer.

After all, don't they already have copywriters on staff? As for corporations, why would they hire a freelance writer when they have access to ad agencies, public relations firms, and writers on staff?

There are at least nine specific situations I can think of that generate a steady, substantial demand for freelance commercial writing services:

1. *The client is overworked.* The staff writers are busy with other work and don't have time to do the project. Or, they could do it, but not by the deadline. The freelancer is called in to help when the client's staff is overloaded.

2. *The client is understaffed.* There are busy times and slow times in every department. Rather than overstaff and have paid writers sitting around doing nothing in the off-season, most companies prefer to understaff and hire freelancers during busy periods. Some companies may not have any writers on staff and must depend on outside writers for all their writing.

3. *Quality.* In some situations, a freelancer may be able to do a better job on a specific assignment. One of the advantages of using freelancers is that you can pay for top talent on an "as-needed" basis, choosing the freelancer who is exactly right for that particular job. Joan Lipton, president of Martin & Lipton Advertising Agency, claims: "Freelancers are apt to be

even more talented than the permanent staff, and they can and do demand top dollar—and get it."

4. *Results.* Whether it's orders generated by a mail-order ad in a magazine, conversions on a Web site, subscriptions produced by a direct-mail package, or leads from an e-mail marketing message, the response can be measured. And when the response can be measured, the client may be on the lookout for new copywriters who can beat his current promotion, known in the direct response industry as the "control."

5. *Fresh perspective.* Staff writers can get bored writing about the same products year after year. For this reason, companies turn to freelancers for renewed enthusiasm, new concepts, a new point of view, and fresh ideas. Freelancers can approach a project with the sense of excitement and vigor the staff writers may have lost.

6. *The company or ad agency can't do the job themselves.* This happens when an assignment comes up that is outside the company's regular areas of expertise. A corporation that has never used direct mail before would benefit by hiring a writer with experience in this field. An ad agency that specializes in fund-raising and then acquires an account in computer software will probably look for a freelance copywriter specializing in high-tech. A fund-raising writer may not understand the ins and outs of the software industry as thoroughly as a writer who specializes in that field.

7. *The company is dissatisfied with its current suppliers.* For a variety of reasons, a company can become unhappy with the copy it is getting from its ad agency, in-house staff, or current freelance writer. If this displeasure continues, the company will shop around for a new writer. This is an opportunity for you to sell your services (unless the company doing the shopping happens to be your client!).

"There isn't a market for our services all the time," says freelance copywriter Bob Westenberg. "But you never know when someone just got disenchanted with a supplier, or received an overblown bill, or whatever. And suddenly they're ready to try someone else."

8. *The freelancer can do the job cheaper.* Most advertising agencies and PR firms shy away from handling one-shot projects, such as a single ad, brochure, or press release. PR agencies work on monthly retainers, which usually start at $3,000. Ad agencies expect clients to have an established annual advertising budget, with $100,000 a common minimum figure for small local agencies.

For the company with occasional rather than steady need for advertising and PR materials, freelancers are a cost-effective solution. Most freelancers are available to handle single projects on a fixed-fee or hourly basis.

9. *You are more flexible and accommodating than their other staff, freelance, and agency writers.* Sometimes you get a job simply because you say yes to certain conditions — specifically, deadline, fee, and working arrangements — that other writers say no to. There's nothing wrong with that, and it's a great way for established writers to fill a gap in a slow schedule or for beginning writers to gain clients.

Beginning and would-be freelance commercial writers in my seminars ask me, "Why would any client hire me when they can hire someone with a lot of experience?" For one thing, the experienced person charges more, and the job may not be worth that to the client. Or they simply do not have the budget. The veteran writer with a big workload may need three weeks to do the job, but you, with a lighter schedule, can turn it around in the four days the client is demanding.

When doubters in my seminars shake their heads in disbelief, I say, "Look at it this way: Every brain surgeon in practice did a first operation. That means the patients who had those surgeries hired a brain surgeon who had never done brain

peechwriter, a publicity writer, and a specialist in direct
or both fund-raising and political clients. Although I
primarily in business-to-business and direct mail, I'm
nown as a software copywriter. And I have developed
r subspecialty, promoting subscriptions to financial
tters.

key to having multiple specialties is to present yourself
ecialist in a particular field when pitching to clients in
ea. You might have three or four different resumés or
ach with a different cover letter highlighting your expe-
in a particular specialty.

idea of having different promotional materials aimed
erent segments of the market is known as "target
ing"—and it is practiced all the time by big corpora-
 client of mine in the software business has one ad
gn aimed at the hospital market and another com-
ifferent campaign aimed at manufacturers. By target-
ecific type of customer for a specific service, you have
 better chance of making the sale and getting the
ent.

 prospects need to pigeonhole you," writes Ilise Benun
arterly newsletter, "The Art of Self-Promotion" (no. 19).
h you hate it, let them do it; in fact, help them. Give
ox to put you in, and a label to put on your box. Your
 needs you to be a specialist. There's plenty of time to
 more later about your full range of services."

this mean you have to have a specialty right from the
our freelance commercial writing career? Not at all. If
 have specialized education or experience that would
ou toward a particular specialty, spend your first year
he business as a generalist.

end of your first year in business, do an analysis of
gnments. Although you took projects one at a time
riety of clients, you'll probably find that you've done

surgery before." If patients will trust their health to novice
brain surgeons, certain clients will give writing projects to
fledgling writers.

Trust me on this. Clients today are under pressure and on
short fuses. However unreasonable their demands, they dislike
hearing a vendor say no. At times, all of us must say no, to
avoid making a promise we can't possibly keep. Our "no" is an
opportunity for another writer to say "yes" and get the job we,
sadly, must pass up.

Wendy Ward, who ran a New York City agency that helped
match up freelancers with clients, says the outlook for freelancing is very positive: "The economy has dictated that the
freelance world is here to stay. Companies are operating with
very lean staffs, particularly in communications. They don't
want to pay benefits and so on if they can hire a freelancer and
use them just as long as needed for a particular project."

SHOULD YOU BE A SPECIALIST OR A GENERALIST?

Another question you might face early in your career is
"Should I be a generalist, a jack-of-all-trades, taking whatever
assignments come my way? Or should I specialize in a specific
type of assignment, client, or industry?"

My experience is that specialists almost always get paid better and are more in demand than generalists. The reason has
to do with the nature of the freelance business.

When companies or ad agencies hire a staff writer, they
don't care as much about his or her background or specialty
because they can always train the staffer in their type of writing. They are mainly looking for creativity and talent.

But when those companies or ad agencies need a freelancer,
it's for one specific project. They don't want to have to train the
writer or waste time "bringing her up to speed" in their businesses. They want a writer who can immediately step in, take

over, and do the job alone, without supervision—quickly, correctly, and competently.

They are looking for a writer whose background and expertise match the job at hand as closely as possible. They want specific skills and experience rather than overall creativity or brilliant writing. They want to hire a specialist, not a generalist.

For this reason, specialists are more in demand, and they can charge more. Time and time again—probably seven times out of ten—I've seen clients who, when faced with the decision about which writer to hire, will choose the specialist with experience in their type of project over the generalist.

Think about it. If you needed an advertisement to sell your new software program by mail, which writer would you choose, the one who does general consumer products, like soaps and shampoos, or the specialist who has a portfolio of successful mail-order ads for software? Most people want to go with a proven resource.

What are the specialties for freelance writers? Some writers specialize by type of industry: information technology (IT), telecommunications, retailing, financial writing, medical writing, fashion, and consumer electronics, nutritional supplements, defense and aerospace, chemical processing, publishing, and dozens more.

You can also specialize by type of assignment. There are specialists in direct mail, speechwriting, technical writing, software documentation, publicity, Internet marketing, annual reports, landing pages, white papers, and catalog writing, to name just a few.

All specialties are lucrative, but some pay better than others. The highest-paying specialties include:

- Direct mail and mail order
- Magazine and newsletter subscription promotion
- Financial services

- Medical and health care
- High-tech
- Speechwriting
- Annual reports
- Corporate communications
- Advertorials

In many cases, writers seem to dr
accident or circumstance rather than
a specialty. In my case, I had an en
industrial and high-tech writing was

I didn't set out to specialize in thi
happy to handle any work that ca
clients were eager to hire me becau
ground, while consumer accounts
much of a "techie." Also, all my wri
time jobs were technical.

My wife, who freelanced before
experience. When she became a fre
who hired her were trade associati
it just happened that way. As a resu
in publicizing and promoting trade

You may find the same thing
your first client is a bank, and yo
booklet explaining a new IRA. Otl
your work, or maybe you mail c
cover letter to advertising manage

Before you know it, you're kr
specialist. It isn't what you plann
the extra prestige and income. /
knocking at your door, instead of

What's more, there's no reas
than one specialty, or handle bo
ments. Richard Armstrong has s

groups of similar projects. Maybe you've done promotions for three different banks. On this basis you can begin to position yourself as a banking specialist.

To be a specialist, you don't need heavy credentials; experience with two or three good clients and a handful of projects under your belt will be enough to get you started. As you get additional clients in the specialty, your client list, portfolio, skill, knowledge, and market value grow, and you'll find it easier and easier to get clients and projects and charge higher fees.

Being a specialist doesn't mean you have to turn down an assignment outside your specialty. If one is offered to you — and it will be — go ahead and take it. Not every client is looking for specialists. So generalists can still get work.

"Diversification helps keep you creatively fresh," writes Cameron Foote in his monthly newsletter for freelancers, "Creative Business." "What you learn in one situation often helps clients in another. Only you can determine just how much or little specialization is appropriate for you."

In some situations, being a specialist can work against you, but this is rare. Recently, an engineering society asked several writers to bid on writing a direct-mail package to acquire new members.

I sent them a folder of engineering samples and in my correspondence highlighted the fact that I am an engineer. I didn't get the job. When I asked why, I was told they wanted the "non-engineering perspective" (which seems an odd thing to want when your audience is 100 percent engineers) and hired a writer with a general consumer background. The writer told me years later that his package bombed.

In most cases, however, having expertise or experience in a specific form of writing, technology, or industry will cause the client to prefer you to other copywriters being considered for the job. The marketing manager of a service firm asked me to send samples, specifically requesting examples of work in their industry, if I had any. I did, and I sent them. Weeks later, she called to let me know I had been selected to do the projects, and told me that seeing I had handled projects for another service firm in her industry was an important factor in my getting the job.

BUILDING YOUR PORTFOLIO AND SAMPLES FILE

A portfolio, mentioned in the previous chapter, is an oversized carrying case used to hold samples of your writing. The pages are clear plastic sleeves into which your samples are inserted. The portfolio is used to present your work to potential clients. Many prospects, especially ad agency creative directors, like to review a writer's portfolio before they hire her or him.

"But," you say, "I've never done any commercial writing before and I don't have any samples for my portfolio. What should I do?" I've found that even inexperienced writers usually have a few good samples to show clients.

Start compiling a file of your writings. Go into that file and see what looks good. Samples don't have to be exactly what the client is looking for as long as there is some relation to it.

For example, have you written a how-to book? Put it in your portfolio. If you're trying to get commercial assignments writing manuals, your book will demonstrate to prospects that you know how to write simple, clear, concise instructional prose. If the book is too bulky to fit in the portfolio, just put in a copy of the dust jacket and the first few pages.

Have you written any magazine articles? Clip and add them to your portfolio. Prospects that need PR services and want to get publicity will be impressed that you know how to get a story into print.

Did you write sales letters, press releases, bulletins, or sales sheets for any of your employers? Did you ever contribute stories to your department newsletter, company magazine, town newspaper, or church bulletin? Did you write copy as your homework in a marketing class or copywriting course?

All of these can serve as samples of your writing expertise. Put your best samples in your portfolio in any order you wish. The portfolio becomes a sample book you can take around and show prospects when you meet with them.

To use a portfolio you should have at least half a dozen samples. If you have only five or less, don't bother with a portfolio. Just include photocopies of these samples in letters you mail to prospects, or put them in a regular file folder and bring them with you when you meet with potential clients.

Don't panic if you don't have enough samples to fill a portfolio. Believe it or not, having a portfolio is helpful but not vital. Most clients are more interested in talking about their project than in looking through a bunch of samples. Most of the companies that hire me never ask to see my portfolio and I never show them.

A well-written sales letter describing your services is often all that's needed to convince the client you're a good writer. You may also want to enclose photocopies of two or three writing samples with that letter. But more than that is not required.

On the other hand, when you do have samples, don't hesitate to use them as a selling tool. They can be effective. If you have some great samples, send them routinely. If you have mediocre samples, send them only when a prospect requests samples, but send your better ones first.

The one exception is when you have samples that closely match the project at hand. Sending samples that are similar to what the client wants done can help you get the job, provided the samples are decent.

Save your samples. Build a sample library. Whenever you do a commercial writing project, try to get samples of the finished printed piece. If you can't get a copy of the finished piece, save a copy of your manuscript.

You can send these samples to prospective clients as examples of your work. If you only have one original of a printed piece, it's perfectly acceptable to send a photocopy. Remember, the prospect is interested in the written portion of the piece, not the graphics.

At first, keeping and sending samples is not a big issue, because you only have a few. But when you've been in the business for many years, as I have, you will accumulate a significant collection of samples.

The best way to manage this is to store the samples in hanging folders in a separate file-cabinet drawer (or, when the quantity increases, a separate file cabinet). In each folder, keep one original (which you never send out) and ten or so photocopies, so you can pull together customized packages of samples for various prospects quickly and easily.

A good idea I copied from freelance copywriter Sig Rosenblum is to put a sample database on my computer. The database contains a description of each sample and a sample number: for example, DM-12 is direct-mail sample number 12.

The hanging files are labeled with this code and stored in numerical order. When I need to send samples, I go through the database descriptions, pick out the samples I want to mail, make a note of their sample numbers, and then pull one copy of each sample from the files. This has dramatically reduced the time and effort required to fulfill inquiries.

Some writers who for some reason think it's bad to send photocopied samples (it's not) send their only originals with a reply envelope and a note asking the prospect to return the samples when finished with them. By creating extra work for the prospect, this becomes an annoyance and a turnoff.

Whenever I get original samples from a freelancer that have to be returned, I immediately put them in the return envelope, without looking at them, and have my assistant mail them back. I don't want to be responsible for someone's only originals, nor do I want to get calls from freelancers I don't even know asking me, "Did you send back my samples?" Your prospects feel the same way. So if you send originals, don't ask for or expect them to be returned to you.

SETTING UP YOUR OFFICE

More than 90 percent of the freelance commercial writers I know work at home. They do this for obvious reasons: When you work at home, you don't pay office rent, you have a commute of less than 60 seconds, and your work is always at hand, whenever you feel like doing it.

In an article on working at home, published in *The Sprint Business Resource,* Sprint Communications advises home-based entrepreneurs to set up a separate defined area of the home as an office. "Create an office that makes you comfortable," they recommend. "Don't pick out the darkest, ugliest room in the house, filled with cast-off furniture. Remember, you'll be spending most of your time there."

One aspect of freelance writing that is especially attractive to people with children is being home with them. But working at home with young children can be difficult, as they demand attention, make loud noises when you're on the phone, and do not realize that you're working and cannot be bothered. Although many freelance writers put up with this, it didn't work for me, and I rented an outside office shortly after the birth of my first son.

To my surprise, I discovered I like working at an outside office. The separation between work and home helps me relax and gives me a sense of privacy I wouldn't have if my business phone and fax were in my attic or basement instead of in a building two miles away.

I believe a comfortable writing environment increases productivity; space and solitude also help. In my rented office,

I write free of the distraction of my children, TV, and refrigerator. The quiet of an office away from the crowds—I'm on the third floor of a three-story building, so there's minimal traffic and noise—allows me to work uninterrupted.

Do not have a TV in your office. Do have a radio or stereo if background music helps you work, as it does me.

Plenty of desk space and file-cabinet storage also boost productivity. There's room to organize and store work materials so they're close at hand and easy to find. Having to search for a book or folder wastes time and can cause you to lose your pace when you're in a writing groove. I have three desks and a large table in my office, so there is plenty of surface space for various writing projects.

If you work at home, have two separate phone numbers, one for home and one for business. Make sure the business number is always covered by voice mail or an answering machine when you're away from your desk, and is always answered in a professional manner. At night, when you're done working, let the voice mail or machine pick up the business line, unless you're willing to stop what you're doing and talk with the client or prospect who is calling.

You also need a fax machine. Put your fax machine on a separate, third phone line. That's what real businesses do, and you are a business.

COMPUTERS

It should go without saying, but let me say it anyway to dispel any doubt: You must use a PC today to be a working freelance commercial writer. Manuscript produced on a typewriter is no longer acceptable.

Virtually every client today wants to receive your copy as an attached Word file via e-mail. If you can't produce a computer file to go with your manuscript, potential clients will be turned off. And, using a PC can dramatically increase your productivity; the more you embrace technology, the more you'll get done.

Get the best computer system and software money can buy. If you can't afford to buy, lease—the low monthly payments make computers affordable, and you can lease software as well as hardware.

Ask the computer salesperson to recommend a system configuration in terms of processor, memory, and hard-disk storage. Then get twice that, or at least as much above the recommendation as you can afford.

Reason? Whatever you buy today will cease being state of the art as soon as you learn to use it, so you can never have too much computer. Example: When I got a new system some years ago, I was thrilled to be buying "top of the line," a 486 machine. The instant it was delivered I read about the Pentium chip in the newspaper and realized I was already a generation behind.

Equip your computer system with as many productivity-boosting tools as possible. Hardware should include a high-speed fax/modem, a 3½-inch floppy drive, a CD-ROM drive, plenty of hard-disk storage, data backup, and high-speed laser printer.

You'll love the speed with which laser printers print manuscript; my HP LaserJet 4si does 19 pages a minute. No more wasting time waiting for your ink-jet clunker to crank out pages. As for hard-disk storage, my rule of thumb is: A working writer can never have too many megabytes.

A 56 Kbps dial-up connection to the Internet is too slow, and will waste too much of your time downloading files and Web sites. You must have a high-speed broadband connection like DSL, or a wi-fi hookup cable.

As for the PC (IBM-compatible) versus Macintosh question, do what works for you. Most ad agencies and graphic design firms use Macintosh but are capable of converting your PC files to the Macintosh format. In corporations, the majority of my clients seem to use IBM-compatible equipment and don't know how to convert a Mac file to DOS.

For software, I recommend Windows, Word, or WordPerfect word-processing software, and a contact-management program such as Act or Telemagic for maintaining a database of clients and prospects and generating personalized query letters. My preference for Word or WordPerfect is based on the observation that many clients like getting copy on disk in these formats. And they're good programs—they have lots of features and are easy to learn.

If you also provide business consulting services or just want to be more business-oriented, learn to use a spreadsheet. I have Excel and it meets my needs. It is also compatible with Word as part of Microsoft Office, as is PowerPoint. Most corporations and associations have standardized on Microsoft Office PowerPoint for creating presentations.

If your corporate clients haven't asked you to write in PowerPoint for them yet, they probably will soon. It pays the freelance commercial writer to own and learn this program; you'll be able to say yes to some nice assignments you would otherwise have had to turn down.

Traditionally, clients have sent source material—background information for writing projects—to their freelancers via FedEx and Express Mail. Then, with the introduction of the fax, it became standard practice to fax source materials unless there were too many pages, in which case they'd be sent via an overnight delivery service.

Today clients may want to send you source documents via e-mail. And many will want you to deliver your copy drafts the same way. With e-mail, you save time in submitting your work to clients.

Instead of having to print and mail a manuscript and transfer files to a floppy disk, you simply hit a button and instantly "download" your copy to your client's e-mail address. I submit virtually 100 percent of my assignments in this fashion, including book manuscripts, and I love it. You can send copy for a full-length brochure in five seconds. You also save a considerable amount of money by eliminating postage and FedEx charges.

Your Internet service provider (ISP) will supply you with a Web browser such as Netscape Navigator or Microsoft Explorer. With this simple software, you can surf the Web, which means you can easily get onto various Web sites. When you begin a project and ask the client for background information, many will say, "Look at my Web site."

All this computer stuff can be acquired and learned gradually, as time and budget permit. Don't feel you have to load up on a complete set of high-tech gear before you start soliciting business. As long as you have basic word processing, e-mail, and Internet access, you're ready to go. Upgrading, if necessary, can be done within a few days, as computers and software are readily available for lease, rental, or purchase.

Here are a few helpful computing tips from Verbatim Corporation, a diskette manufacturer:

- Keep your PC away from dust, sunlight, heat, vibrations, and physical impact.
- Have enough office insurance to replace the entire computer system.
- New viruses are always being developed, so you need to update your anti-virus software every three months.
- Save your work to your hard-disk drive every 5 to 10 minutes.
- Install a surge protector and uninterruptible power supply system.

- Back up your files. Store at least one copy of your backup media off-site.

BUILDING A REFERENCE LIBRARY

Every freelance commercial writer should start building a reference library of books on the subjects he or she most frequently writes about. If you are a medical writer, for example, buy books on health care and medicine. If you specialize in travel, collect the Fodor's guides. It's not essential to have a complete reference library when you're starting out; building one is something you can do gradually.

As a writer, you can improve your productivity tremendously by having the information you need at your fingertips. If you have to run to the public library or spend hours on the Internet to get missing facts, you will waste an enormous amount of time . . . time that could be spent writing.

In commercial writing, the client supplies the writer with extensive background information on most projects. But sometimes a piece of information is missing. Or you may decide you can write a better piece of copy if you know certain facts the client has not provided. A good reference library puts these facts at your fingertips.

Doing research on the Internet is fine, but you have to be able to document your information. In some instances the items you read online are not credited to a source. That's why, in addition to Internet research, I also rely on my library of reference books and my file of clippings for reference use.

For example, I specialize in computers, so I have more than twenty books about computers. I also have a lot of books about business, chemistry, energy, and investing because I do a lot of work in these fields.

The best way to acquire a good library without spending a lot of money is at used-book sales sponsored by local libraries. Here you will find incredible bargains. I purchased the 950-page *Encyclopedia of Banking and Finance* for 50 cents and the 20-volume *American People's Encyclopedia* for $20. Granted, you won't get new editions or mint-condition books at these sales, but older editions are fine for your purposes. I also bought last year's *Books in Print* for only $1 per volume.

Become familiar with your local secondhand bookstore; often the proprietor will locate items for you if they are not in stock. You can also get thousands of used books online at such sites as www.amazon.com and www.alibris.com.

Keep your reference library small and up to date. Every year or so, go through the books. If a book is outdated because the information in the field has changed, throw it out. Also get rid of books you haven't looked at over the last few years; chances are, you'll never open them again.

You should start a clipping file of articles related to the industries and subjects you write about. I have thick files labeled CHEMICAL INDUSTRY, COMPUTERS, TELECOMMUNICATIONS, ENERGY, HEALTH CARE, CAREERS, and FINANCE because I regularly handle assignments in these areas. My files include article clippings, booklets, ads I've torn out of magazines, and brochures I've collected at trade shows and conventions.

I also keep extensive files for each one of my clients. These files include the client's ads and brochures as well as ads and sales literature produced by their competitors. Be sure to update such files regularly. Otherwise you risk extracting information from them that is out of date, which can introduce errors into your copy.

Build your article file as you build your book library. Keep organized clipping files on all subject areas in which you write. Spend at least 20 minutes a day scanning newspapers and magazines. Look for pertinent articles; clip and file information you can use in articles and books.

Stay in this scanning mode; avoid the trap of getting caught up in miscellaneous reading during work hours, which can cut into your productive hours. Always jot the source (magazine or newspaper name, issue date, and page number) on clippings. This saves time tracking sources later on.

4

TASKS OF THE FREELANCE COMMERCIAL WRITER

In chapter 3 we briefly touched on the various types of projects you can write for clients. Actually, the list will never be comprehensive because new types of assignments and special requests are coming up all the time.

In this chapter we look at some of the most common types of assignments you are likely to be asked to write. I'll tell you what the assignment entails, what types of clients need this copy written, and how to estimate your fee, and I'll alert you to any special problems or conditions. A summary of the fees for these assignments appears in appendix G.

ADVERTISING

Ad agencies and corporate clients need ads (known as "print ads" or "space ads") for magazines and newspapers. Contact the advertising manager at corporations; creative directors at ad agencies.

"How much would you charge to write an ad?" is a common query. Fees vary widely, ranging from $1,250 to $3,500 for a full-page ad, and $750 to $1,000 for a fractional (partial-page) ad.

Since ads are everywhere, it's fairly easy to study the form. Read magazines and newspapers. Pay attention to the ads. Start a clipping file of ads you think are effective. Feel free to adapt any techniques or ideas that would work for your assignment. To become a master ad writer, read the books on advertising by Ogilvy and Caples listed in appendix B.

ADVERTORIALS

An advertorial, also known as an advertising supplement or special section, is a section within a magazine that looks like an article but is in fact a paid advertisement. Companies pay to have their ads put into this advertising section. As a bonus, they get coverage in the main article that forms the core of the "editorial" portion of this section.

That big article, known as the advertorial article, is typically written by a freelance writer hired by the magazine in which the advertorial will appear. The magazines come up with the ideas for advertorials and produce them as a special promotion to get more advertising.

Whenever you open a magazine and see a special section on a single topic, with the word "Advertisement" printed at the top of each page, you are looking at an advertorial. An advertorial can range from 4 to 16 pages or even longer.

Advertorials always have a theme focusing on a specific topic, market, technology, or industry, such as home decorating, automobiles, personal computers, or mobile communications. The promotions director at the magazine will create the theme, then look to hire a writer to do the copy. Advertorials mostly appear in large-circulation business and consumer magazines, although some smaller specialized publications do them.

Promotions directors will hire advertising copywriters as well as journalists to do advertorials. The rationale behind hiring a journalist is that the reporter can produce more objective, less blatantly promotional copy—more in line with the editorial look and feel of the special section—than an ad writer. The perceived negative is that journalists are too objective, more interested in getting a good story than in incorporating the major points each advertiser wants to get across. Most journalists are trained to be objective and therefore do not know how to sell. Advertisers expect favorable coverage in the advertorial and usually have the right to review, change, and approve the copy.

Advertising copywriters, trained to take directions from clients and communicate their messages, often produce advertorials that are more pleasing to the advertisers. The problem they sometimes have is that their advertorial reads more like a sales brochure and less like an article for that particular magazine, which is how it's supposed to sound.

Advertorial writing is a limited field, since there are thousands of individual ads produced for every one advertorial written. It does pay well: $1,000 or more per page of advertorial, with about 400 to 500 words per page.

ANNUAL REPORTS

Writers don't do annual reports for glory or fame or to obtain literary and artistic fulfillment. They perceive, quite correctly, that annual reports are a well-paying area for which freelance writers are frequently hired, and they want to get their share of the loot.

Fees range from $8,000 to $15,000 or more per project. Larger companies, such as those in the Fortune 500, usually create more elaborate annual reports and pay higher fees than smaller publicly held companies. Several years ago a writer told me he had been paid $20,000 to write the annual report of a Fortune 500 food company.

The fees quoted here include revisions, and there are nor-mally lots of revisions on this type of assignment. The advantage of large assignments such as annual reports is that if you get a few assignments, you are well on your way to making your income goal for the year.

If a corporate writer does half a dozen annual reports per year, those six assignments alone could bring him $50,000 to $90,000 in fees. If you can do one, two, or three annual reports for clients, and do them annually, that's a solid base from which to build a profitable freelance writing income.

In an article in *Writer's Digest*, annual-report writer Stephanie Ferm of SM Communications notes, "Today's typical report encompasses more than the obligatory chairman's letter, product reviews, and financial highlights. Many now include lively company histories, employee profiles, or features on corporate philanthropic commitments. Some major conglomerates have recently added proactive reports that reinforce corporate initiatives on such social issues as the environment, health care, and education. The most innovative of the lot are experimenting with videos, newsletters, newspaper formats, and computer disks to supplement or enhance their financial reports. For the past two years, Marvel's annual report has been in the form of a comic book."

Annual reports are produced by public companies; privately owned corporations are not required to file them with the Securities and Exchange Commission. The best annual report assignments come from the Fortune 1000 companies, whose reports are long and lavish. Contact the director of corporate communications to find out whether they use freelancers and what it would take for you to be considered for the assignment. Keep in mind this is a lucrative but limited market: A company may produce dozens or even hundreds of brochures and sales sheets, but puts out only one annual report every year.

BOOKS

Some clients may want to promote their firms, causes, technologies, or methodologies by writing and publishing a book on the topic. For example, a management-consulting firm can gain prestige, visibility, and new clients by having staff members publish a book on its unique management methods.

Corporate staff members seldom have the time or inclination to write a book-length work, so occasionally you may be asked what you would charge to ghostwrite a book. Again, this is a decent paying but limited market. A corporation may commission dozens of articles a year, but a book only once a decade, if that.

Fees vary, but most ghostwriters charge by the book page; typical ghostwriting fees are $125 to $175 per book page; a book page contains approximately 300 to 400 words. For a 200-page book, figure $20,000 to $30,000. But you won't always be in this range. I have been offered less than $10,000 and more than $50,000 to ghostwrite books for various clients.

If the client is a celebrity, or you feel the book will be a bestseller, you can offer to waive your up-front fee in exchange for a percentage, usually 40 to 50 percent of all advances and royalties the book earns when sold to a publisher. Usually, though, a flat fee is best—most clients doing books for marketing purposes write on a narrow topic that won't sell large quantities, and some even privately print the book and distribute it only to potential customers.

Some clients may ask for a book proposal to present to publishers in the hope of getting a commitment from the publisher before paying you to write the book. You can charge $2,000 to $3,500 for a book proposal, which may also include a brief sample chapter.

BOOKLETS

An alternative promotion that is quicker, easier, and less costly and time-consuming than producing a book is a booklet. Advertisers offer how-to and informational booklets to promote usage of and preference for their brand or product category.

Unilux, a company that rents strobe lights to TV production companies, offers an informational booklet on how to get the best effects with strobe lighting. Fala Direct Marketing, a letter shop specializing in producing large volumes of personalized direct mail, has produced a pamphlet on the pros, cons, and usage of personalization to increase direct-mail response rates.

Most promotional booklets are designed to fit a number 10 business envelope, measuring approximately 4 by 9 inches. Most are brief—4 to 12 pages—for a total length of 1,500 to 3,000 words. Fees for booklets can range from $1,500 to $2,500 or more, depending on topic, length, and complexity.

BROCHURES

Almost every organization uses brochures. Hotels have brochures they make available in the lobby and mail to potential lodgers who request more information. Museums give away brochures providing detailed information on the background of specific exhibits. Product manufacturers and service providers need brochures to sell their products and services to potential customers.

Brochures pay fairly well, and it's a big market. Even in the Internet age, almost every company produces brochures, and some do many pieces each year. For example, a major chemical manufacturer counted all the brochures, data sheets, fliers, and other promotional pieces it did in a 12-month period and found the total to be over 700. That's enough to keep you and me busy and profitable for the year!

For a full-size brochure, with a page size of approximately 7 by 10 inches, the page will not be solid text, but text mixed with graphics. Copy length is around 400 words a page. Writers charge by the brochure page—anywhere from $750 to $1,000 a page.

Some brochures are not full-sized but are designed to fold and fit into a number 10 business envelope. These are known in the trade as "slim jims." The typical slim jim is made by folding a letter or legal-size piece of paper two or three times vertically to fit the envelope or a display rack. Fees for slim jims range from $1,500 to $2,500 or more.

Often, when a client does not want to spend the money for a full-scale brochure, he will ask you to write what is called a spec sheet or data sheet. This is product information on both sides of an unfolded letter-size sheet of paper, usually in one or two colors. Commercial writers charge anywhere from $1,000 to $2,000 per data sheet, with a 10- to 15-percent volume discount if the client needs multiple data sheets on a line of related products.

BUSINESS PLANS

There are consultants who specialize in writing business plans, but some clients may ask you, their freelance commercial writer, to write their plan for them. If you get such an assignment, go to the computer store and buy one of the software programs that are used to help businesses (and writers) create business plans on their PCs. This will save you time and give you a better-quality finished product.

Depending on the size of the company and the level of detail in the business plan, you can charge anywhere from $2,000 to $10,000. The $2,000 would cover editing an existing manuscript into smooth prose, while $5,000 to $10,000 would be charged to create a complete business plan from scratch.

CASE HISTORIES AND APPLICATION BRIEFS

A case history is a product success story. It tells about a company that had a problem and solved the problem using your client's product or service. Case histories can be published as articles in trade magazines or printed by the client as promotional sheets. Typically, case histories are written to fit and are printed on a single sheet of letter-size paper. Word count runs from 500 to 1,500. Most case histories follow this outline:

1. State the problem the company had.
2. Describe their criteria and search for a solution, including solutions they looked at but rejected.
3. Describe the solution the advertiser provided: what it is and how it works.
4. Outline the results, especially the benefits achieved, when the solution was implemented.

An application brief is a specialized type of history focusing on the use of a product in a specific application or niche industry, e.g., a stock brokerage that protected its corporate network by using a certain brand of firewall. Companies use applications briefs to market their products to potential customers in specific industries or vertical markets.

Freelance writers generally charge $1,500 to $2,500 for case histories, depending on length and complexity. The client may supply a copy of a taped or transcribed interview with the subject of the case history, or you may be asked to do this interview over the phone.

CATALOGS

Unlike a brochure, which typically describes a single product or product line in depth, catalogs give briefer descriptions of a number of products. Typically, clients supply background material—old catalog pages, spec sheets, ads, brochures— from which you get the information to write the catalog description. Fees for catalog copy range from $750 to $1,000 or more per catalog page. You can also charge from $200 to $250 per item, depending on copy length and complexity.

DIRECT-MAIL PACKAGES TO GENERATE SALES LEADS

A direct-mail package used to generate sales leads usually consists of an outer envelope, business-reply card, one- or two-page letter, and possibly another insert such as a small slim jim brochure. Fees for writing such a package vary widely, from $2,000 to more than $5,000. Clients who mail large quantities of direct-mail packages, have expensive products, or are dependent on sales leads to generate business will pay toward the upper end of the scale. Clients who mail small quantities (under 5,000 pieces), have slim profit margins, and don't rely on direct mail for most of their new business inquiries tend to pay toward the low end of the range.

DIRECT-MAIL PACKAGES TO GENERATE MAIL ORDERS

Direct-mail packages designed to bring back an order rather than a lead are usually more involved and complex. Typical elements include an outer envelope, four-page letter (or longer), second short letter (known as a "lift note"), color brochure, order form, business reply envelope, and possibly one or two other small additional inserts.

Fees for writing a direct-mail package to generate mail orders depend on the client, the volume mailed, the price of the product, and the market. Fees for such assignments "are all over the lot," as freelancer Sig Rosenblum observes, ranging from $2,500 or less to $10,000 or higher.

I recently wrote a direct-mail package to solicit membership in a professional society for scientists, and the $6,000 I charged was a perfect fit for the client's budget. A business publisher for whom I wrote a direct-mail package to sell a $295-per-year monthly business newsletter indicated that my $7,500 fee was right on target, while a publisher retaining me to write a direct-mail package to sell subscriptions to a financial newsletter for consumers often pays more than the $9,500 I charged them. So fees are indeed all over the lot.

E-MAIL MARKETING

E-mail marketing messages range in size and format.

The shortest format, a "teaser" e-mail, consists of perhaps only a few paragraphs of text. It is designed to drive the readers to a microsite, or landing page (described elsewhere in this chapter), where they can-order a product or request more information. A reasonable fee is $1,500 to $2,000, though I know writers who do these for less.

A "lead-generation" e-mail is similar to the teaser e-mail, but slightly more detailed, equivalent in length to a one-page sales letter. Fee range is $1,500 to $2,000.

A "long-copy" e-mail is designed to sell a product directly by driving the recipient to a landing page where he can order the item. Copy length is equivalent to a 2- to 3-page sales letter; fee range is $2,500 to $3,500.

An "online conversion series" is a sequence of e-mails sent

as follow-ups to someone who has visited a Web site or landing page but did not place an order. These series typically have five to seven efforts, and I charge $1,000 per effort.

FEATURE ARTICLES

Small businesses, public relations firms, and corporations routinely hire freelance copywriters, article writers, and journalists to ghostwrite articles under the bylines of their executives and technical staff. They then place these articles in appropriate publications to generate publicity for the company and its products, services, or capabilities.

Ghostwriting an article for a corporate client is actually less work than doing it for a publication, since the corporate client provides the background material and makes its staff experts available as resources to you. Also, you are dealing with one information source, the corporate client, rather than having to interview many companies or individuals.

The length of ghostwritten articles ranges from 1,000 to 3,000 words. Fees vary widely, with writers and PR counselors charging clients $1,000 to $4,000, depending on length, topic, and complexity.

INFOMERCIALS

An infomercial is a half-hour TV commercial produced to resemble a TV show rather than a promotional spot. In fact, infomercials often have conventional one-minute commercials integrated within them! Most infomercials are designed to sell mail-order products, but occasionally an infomercial advertiser uses the format to generate sales leads. Fees for writing infomercial scripts range from $4,000 to $10,000 or more.

LABELS/PACKAGING

Any product you see that has copy on the box, bottle, package, or label probably was the result of an assignment given to a writer to create that copy. Obviously, the definition of "package" encompasses a wide range of projects, from a few bullet points on a tiny package to many lines of copy for a product sold in a large box. Small assignments may pay only $500 to $750, with larger projects commanding fees of $1,500 to $2,500 or so.

LANDING PAGES (MICROSITES)

A landing page, or microsite, is a specialized type of long-copy Web site dedicated to selling a single product such as a newsletter, e-book, or conference. It is the online equivalent of a 6- to 8-page sales letter, and when you click on any of the links on the landing page, you are brought to a simple form where you can order the product using your credit card. Depending on length, complexity, product sold, and the client (mom and pop operator vs. major direct marketer), fees for landing pages range from $3,500 to $7,500.

MAGALOGS (DIRECT-MAIL PIECE IN MAGAZINE FORMAT)

Did you ever get something in the mail that at first glance looked like a color magazine but turned out to be an elaborate promotional mailing to sell a book, vitamins, newsletter subscription, or other mail-order product?

These are known in the trade as "magalogs," indicating a cross between a magazine and a catalog. I think a more accurate term would be "magamail," because these promotions are really a hybrid of magazine and direct-mail package.

Magalogs, which have a slightly smaller page size than a

regular magazine, are generally 16 to 24 pages long, though some run to 40 pages or more. They can be extremely effective when selling consumer newsletters in the financial and medical areas, as well as related health products.

Novice copywriters may charge as little as $7,000 for a magalog; I know a top magalog writer who gets $25,000 per project. The average is around $12,500 to $15,000, making magalogs a large and lucrative assignment.

MANUALS

Writers who can produce clean, clear, easy-to-follow instructional prose for user, operating, installation, and maintenance manuals for business and consumer products are in demand.

Manuals are handled primarily by technical writers on an hourly or per diem basis. Technical writers who work as independent contractors charge anywhere from $25 to $70 per hour on freelance assignments. A fee of $400 a day is pretty common.

MULTIMEDIA PRESENTATIONS: VIDEO, SLIDE PRESENTATION, OR OTHER AUDIOVISUAL SCRIPTS

Corporations, small businesses, and other clients often need scripts for promotional videos, slide shows, and multimedia presentations. Promotional videos are usually brief, with running times of 5 to 20 minutes. For a typical 10-minute sales video, the scriptwriting fee might be $3,000 to $3,500. Another way to figure it is by the minute, with fees ranging from $150 to $350 per minute.

Unlike videos, which are linear, CD-ROM presentations are interactive, with user-controlled branching from topic to topic. Some companies distribute their catalogs, brochures, sales presentations, and other promotional materials on CD-ROM to supplement or in some cases replace paper promotions. You can get CD-ROM assignments from corporate clients or from interactive multimedia producers specializing in this medium. Script fees range from $100 to $300 per minute of presentation.

NEWSLETTERS

Many companies use promotional newsletters as part of their marketing communications program. Newsletters can be 2, 4, or even 8 pages or longer. Most are quarterly, meaning they are published approximately four times a year.

The client typically provides a list of articles to be written and appropriate source material. Short blurbs can be written directly from these materials. For feature articles, you may be required to conduct some telephone interviews with the company's employees or customers. For newsletter writing, writers charge anywhere from $500 to $1,000 per newsletter page, with each newsletter page containing 400 to 500 words.

An e-zine, also known as an e-newsletter or online newsletter, is a promotional newsletter distributed online, typically as a text or HTML e-mail. They are considerably shorter than print newsletters, and therefore your fee would be considerably less: perhaps $1,500 to $2,500 for a short issue.

ONLINE ADS

Clients may ask you to write small ads promoting their products. These ads typically run in e-zines and consist of approximately 100 words or so of text plus a link to a URL (usually a landing page, Web site, or order form). I charge $500 for such an ad.

Banner ads are ads that appear on Web sites and consist of a few words and an HTML design. I also charge $500 to write a banner ad and sketch out a rough design.

POSTCARDS

Postcards are a cost-effective promotion, particularly for small businesses on a limited budget. Fees for writing postcard copy range from $500 to $1,500 or so.

Do not underestimate the amount of work or creativity that goes into writing an effective postcard. Just because the copy is necessarily short because of space limitations doesn't mean it's easy. In fact, writing for limited space — e.g., a quarter-page ad instead of a full-page ad — is often more difficult, because you have very little room to communicate all the key selling points.

PRESS RELEASES

A press release is a short news or feature story the company mails to the mass media to generate press coverage for its event, product, cause, or idea. Most press releases are one to two double-spaced pages. Some clients value good publicity writing and will pay a decent fee for a well-crafted press release that can get them a lot of publicity. Others view it as a low-level writing job for which they want to pay low-level wages.

Fees for writing a single press release range from $500 to $1,000. My book, *The Copywriter's Handbook* (listed in appendix B), contains instructions for publicity writing with sample press releases you may be able to adapt to fit your assignment.

PROPOSALS

Many companies generate proposals as part of their selling process. Proposals are sometimes outsourced to freelance commercial writers, who typically charge $65 to $95 an hour for doing such work. The amount of time and total fee vary tremendously, as proposals can range from 2 or 3 pages to 500 pages or longer. (When I was at Westinghouse, our proposals for major system bids were reprinted and bound in large three-ring binders.)

Another type of proposal is the grant proposal. This is a document an organization submits to apply for a grant. Fees vary. You can charge by the hour, from $65 to $95 per hour, or by the proposal page, from $100 to $250 per page or more. Or you could base your fee on a percentage of the grant awarded to the client, except you would get nothing if the client does not win the grant.

RADIO COMMERCIALS

Radio commercials are typically 30 or 60 seconds long. Freelance radio copywriters I know charge $400 to $800 a commercial.

This is a tough market for freelance writers who want to charge such a fee, because many radio stations will write the sponsor's copy at no extra charge as part of the advertising program. You can contact radio stations and see if they need help writing radio commercials. But because they're not charging the sponsors, they won't want to pay much. Advertising agencies and some radio advertisers who run more elaborate and sophisticated commercials may be willing to pay your asking price for a commercial script.

REPORTS

Corporations that generate a lot of paperwork sometimes outsource the writing of reports to freelance writers.

Another situation in which you may be asked to write special reports is for a newsletter publisher or other client who wants to offer the report as a premium, a free bonus given as an incentive to buy a product. For report writing, freelancers charge between $50 and $85 an hour.

RESUMÉS

Corporations rarely hire freelance writers to write resumés for employees. The exception might be a corporation that is downsizing; the human resources department might hire a writer to produce resumés as part of its outplacement package for the downsized employees. More often, the company will go to a consulting firm specializing in outplacement and get the resumés as part of a total package.

Once in a while corporate employees will ask you to write resumés for them. This is not a well-paying assignment, and even though the fee is modest, the employee will find it a lot of money to pay (since it is coming out of his or her pocket, rather than a corporate budget) and is likely to be fussy, putting you through many agonizing revisions and rewrites for a small sum, typically $150 to $300 per resumé.

One reason to do this work is as a favor to a valued client on whose good side you want to remain. The American Writers and Artists Institute (www.awaionline.com) sells a basic resumé writing course that includes software with templates for different resumés.

SALES LETTERS

Some clients do not want a complete direct-mail package but will use a simple one- or two-page sales letter to generate leads. For such a lead-generating letter, freelance copywriting fees range from $750 to $2,500. The fee usually includes copy for a simple reply card.

SELF-MAILERS

As an alternative to a traditional direct-mail package consisting of a letter and reply card in an envelope, advertisers may use self-mailer formats to generate leads and even mail orders. A self-mailer is any direct-mail piece that can be sent without an outer envelope.

The most common format is the trifold self-mailer. This is a letter- or legal-size piece of paper folded twice horizontally to form a self-mailer; the bottom panel is often used as a business reply card. Fees for writing a trifold self-mailer range from $1,500 to $2,500.

Another format that has become popular in recent years is the double postcard. This is a regular promotional postcard with a tear-off business-reply card attached. The most popular application of the double postcard is in promoting magazine subscriptions. Fees for writing a double postcard range from $1,000 to $2,500.

SPEECHES

Public relations firms and corporate communications managers routinely hire freelance commercial writers to write speeches for executives to deliver at customer meetings, user conferences, and industry events. Since most speakers talk at a rate of 100 to 120 words a minute, the typical 20 minute speech is 2,000 to 2,500 words.

Speechwriting is one assignment where the client may require you to do research on the subject matter to supplement the source materials provided. You can charge anywhere from $2,000 to $4,000 to research and write a 20-minute speech for a corporate executive or business manager.

TV COMMERCIAL

Television commercials are usually 15, 30, or 60 seconds, but late-night TV commercials selling mail-order products can be two minutes. Most advertisers do not hire freelance copywriters directly to write TV commercials. Instead, they give the assignment to write and produce the commercial to their ad agency, which in turn has a staff or freelance writer do the copy. Again, fees vary widely, from $1,000 for a cable TV spot for a local advertiser to $2,500 or more for a sophisticated, slick commercial for a national advertiser.

WEB SITE CONTENT

A Web page is a section of a Web site with copy and graphics devoted to a particular topic, such as a service, product, or application. Although Web pages can be any length, for estimate purposes, define a Web page in your client proposals as having a maximum length of 400 to 500 words. I charge $750 to $1,000 for most Web pages, and double that for a Web site's home page.

WHITE PAPERS

A white paper is a promotional piece in the guise of an informational article or report.

Just as many infomercials convey the look and feel of an informative, unbiased TV program rather than a paid commercial, a white paper attempts to convince the reader that he is being educated about the issue or problem your product addresses (e.g., computer security, improving customer service, managing your sales force, saving for retirement), rather than being sold on a specific product.

The white paper serves the same sales purpose as a brochure—to sell or help sell a product or service—but reads and looks like an article or other important piece of authoritative, objective information.

Unlike a sales brochure, a white paper must contain useful "how-to" information that helps the reader solve a problem, or make a key business decision (e.g., whether to install a new firewall or build a facility instead of leasing).

A typical white paper is 4 to 10 pages, with each page containing approximately 300 to 400 words of text. Fees for white papers range from $2,000 to $7,000 or more, depending on the complexity of the topic and the experience of the writer. Of the more than 500 white paper writers surveyed by www .whitepapersource.com, 41 percent charge between $2,000 and $5,000 per white paper.

5

SETTING YOUR FEES

One of the toughest questions both beginning and experienced freelance business writers wrestle with is "How much should I charge?"

Charge too little and you diminish your prestige and importance in the eyes of your clients. You also diminish the perceived value of your service and dramatically reduce your own income potential. Worst of all, you work harder and earn less.

Charge too much and you may price yourself out of the market and lose out on jobs to other writers who charge less. This chapter is designed to help you determine how much you should charge for your time and services.

How much do freelance copywriters earn? Copywriter Chris Marlow surveyed 289 freelance copywriters to determine the answer to this question. According to Chris's 2004 Freelance Copywriter Fee and Compensation Survey, 50 percent of freelance copywriters earn between $40,000 and $100,000 a year, and 25 percent earn more than $100,000 a year.

PROJECT VS. HOURLY FEES

Professional commercial writers generally charge according to one of two methods: by the project or by the hour.

Writers who charge by the project quote a flat fee for writing a specific piece of copy: so much for an ad, so much for an article, so much for a brochure. For example: "I will write your sales letter and flier for X dollars."

Writers who charge by the hour tell the client, "My fee is X dollars an hour for working on your project, for as many hours as it takes." Or, "My fee is X dollars an hour, and I estimate it will take Y hours to complete this project. If I spend less time, I will bill you for hours actually worked. If I think it will take more time, I will tell you so and give an estimate of the additional hours required."

Which method should you use? Ed Buxton and Sue Fulton, coauthors of *Advertising Freelancers* (New York: Executive Communications), conducted a survey of freelance advertising writers to find out how they charged. The results showed that 74 percent charge a fixed fee per project. Only 26 percent use an hourly or day rate. Chris Marlow's survey showed that 64 percent of copywriters charge a fixed fee.

At first glance the project-fee arrangement seems riskier. After all, if the job is more complex than you originally anticipated (and it almost always is!), then it will take longer. Yet you can't charge more, so you are not making as much profit per hour. The writer takes all the risk; the client is assured of getting the job he wants at the price he agreed to. For this reason, many clients prefer a fixed-fee price quotation, which makes it somewhat easier for you to sell to them.

From the writer's point of view, the majority of freelancers prefer a fixed-fee arrangement because it is usually (not always) more lucrative. Let's say a client needs a marketing brochure for a new software product. You think the job is worth $3,000. To the client, $3,000 seems a reasonable sum to get the brochure they need. So they will not blink an eye when you quote this figure.

Now, let's say you tell the client you charge by the hour. How do you arrive at a price of $3,000? If you say that the job will take two days, or 16 hours, you must charge $187.50 per hour. Even though you may be worth this, clients may balk, because they think that a writer's hourly charge should be less than a lawyer's, consultant's, or other independent professional's fee. So the client says, "$187.50 per hour . . . for writing? Ridiculous!" And you lose the job.

On the other hand, if you say your fee is a reasonable $45 per hour, and you want $3,000, you must tell the client that you estimate spending 66.7 hours on the job—more than eight solid days. The client finds it difficult to believe the work will take so long, and tries to get you to lower your fee based on their (perhaps mistaken) perception of how long it should take to write a brochure (which, in their mind, is a simple matter, even though you and I know better).

And that is the problem with writing on an hourly basis. To get the really big fees, you either have to quote a high hourly rate, which many clients may find unacceptable, or say that the job will take many hours, which clients will not understand. An hourly quotation makes both your hourly earnings and your working methods (amount of work you get done per hour) visible to the client, who may find either or both unacceptable.

The fixed-fee project method makes your fee somewhat of a mystery. After all, if you say the fee is $3,000, the client doesn't know (and shouldn't care) what it involves or how hard you must work for it. You are saying, in effect, "I will guarantee the result you want for an amount you can afford to spend." Frequently, clients find this much more palatable than an hourly quotation. People understand a single price for a single product, which is how most things in this world are sold.

DOES AN HOURLY RATE EVER MAKE SENSE?

As you can see, I prefer to quote the client a fixed fee for a given project. However, there are situations in which it may be better for you to quote an hourly rate.

• *When you're at the top of your profession.* When you are able to command an hourly fee of $100 or more, you can probably make a good profit on jobs handled on an hourly basis. If your fee is less than $100 an hour, you will probably make more quoting a project fee.

• *When the job cannot be estimated accurately.* There are times when it is difficult, if not impossible, to give an accurate project estimate. For example, if a client doesn't know what he wants, how can you tell him what it will cost? The same holds true when the client thinks he knows what he wants but isn't sure and may change his mind. It is also difficult to give an accurate estimate for a project that is in its early planning stages, where the specific elements have not yet been clearly defined.

In these situations, the best you can do is tell the client that you will work on an hourly basis until such time as the specifications of the assignments are more precisely defined. At that time, you can elect to continue billing on an hourly basis or present the client with a fixed-price proposal for taking each element to completion.

• *When the job is too small to be given a project price.* For very small assignments, such as cleaning up the language in a short instruction sheet, or rewriting an existing booklet or brochure, the project may be so small that the client would balk at any project fee. In such a case, you can simply inform the client that you will do the work for a fee of X dollars an hour but can only give a rough estimate of exactly how long the work will take.

• *For work other than writing.* Even though you are a writer, clients will ask other things of you. They may ask you to consult on marketing strategy, edit written documents, proofread, work with art directors, attend meetings, suggest ideas, come up with names for a product, or supervise production. For these non-writing tasks I prefer simply to say I will perform them for a fee of X dollars an hour.

Should you have different hourly rates for each task or charge one uniform hourly rate? My own preference is to charge my regular fee, my current hourly rate, for all work.

This sends a message to clients that says I am a highly paid professional, and if they need something as trivial as editing or proofreading, they ought to hire people who do that level of work. If you charge $65 an hour to write copy, and then turn around and tell the client you will do proofreading for $15 an hour, you are saying, in effect, that your time is really worth $15 an hour, not $65.

Having said that, I must point out that I know several writers who disagree with me and happily and productively charge several different rates to the same clients. I suppose this works if you want to do a lot of lower-paying assignments, such as proofreading, editing, or desktop publishing, but my advice is to stick with the high rate and try to do only the work—writing—that you love and that pays best.

DETERMINING YOUR HOURLY RATE

Everyone should have an hourly rate. Writers who charge by the hour need to set the rate they will quote to clients. But even writers who charge by the project need an hourly rate. If you charge by the project, much of your estimate for a project will be based on multiplying the number of hours the job will take by the hourly rate you want to earn.

The difference between the fixed-fee project writer and the

hourly-rate writer is that the hourly-rate writer quotes the hourly fee to the client; the fixed-fee writer does not. But both know what they want and expect to earn per hour.

According to the Chris Marlow survey, 32 percent of freelance copywriters have an hourly rate of $51 to $75; 20 percent charge between $76 to $100 an hour; and 12 percent charge more than $150 an hour, with the top rate exceeding $300 an hour.

Of the copywriters Marlow surveyed, 24 percent charge $50 an hour or less. If you are getting $20 to $50 an hour, you're in the novice range, but that's still not bad. Established freelance commercial writers charge between $75 and $100. Top pros in high-paying specialties—corporate communications, speechwriting, annual reports, direct marketing, and medical—may go up to $150 or higher. Writers who also provide expert advice as part of their service, such as those who are marketing consultants in a specialized field, can sometimes get $150 to $250 an hour, but that's pushing the top of the range.

Here are the steps in determining your hourly rate:

1. Determine how much you make per hour now (if you are currently employed) or, if you are not employed, how much you made per hour on your last job.

2. To calculate hourly wages, divide your annual salary by 2,080 (52 weeks a year x 5 days a week x 8 hours a day):

$$\underset{\text{(annual salary)}}{\underline{\hspace{3cm}}} \div 2,080 = \underset{\text{(dollars per hour)}}{\underline{\hspace{3cm}}}$$

NOTE: This assumes your full-time job is similar to the work you plan to do on a freelance basis. If this is not the case, for "annual salary" you should put the salary you think you would be earning if you were employed as a full-time writer in your field.

3. Next, determine your minimum hourly rate. This is the absolute minimum fee you should be charging clients, and represents the minimum acceptable per-hour profit you will accept on any job.

4. To calculate this minimum hourly rate, multiply your "on-the-job" hourly rate by 2.5. We pick this factor because someone who is independent should be earning more per hour than someone who works as a full-time employee.

Why? To compensate for lack of benefits (health insurance, vacation, sick days, expense account, all of which must be paid out of the freelancer's pocket), the expense of running one's own business (home office, computer, accountant's fees, etc.), and also to compensate for the risk being taken, and the lack of a steady paycheck.

$$\frac{\qquad\qquad}{\text{(full-time hourly rate)}} \times 2.5 = \frac{\qquad\qquad}{\text{(freelance hourly rate)}}$$

Is this necessarily what you should charge per hour? No, it is simply a starting point, the minimum fee you must earn for your freelance business to be profitable. If you are not earning this fee, you are probably not charging enough.

If you do not earn this minimum figure and are absolutely convinced your clients would balk if you raised your rates, then they do not perceive your service as valuable. In that case, you need to work for better clients, or you should enhance the services you offer so you can charge more. Just how high you can set your hourly rate above the minimum figure calculated depends on several factors.

First, what is the competition charging? You can find this out by calling them and requesting their literature. If you are shy about doing this, have a friend in a business office call your competitors and ask their rates. Then you charge somewhere within the going range of rates.

Once you begin quoting your rate to potential clients, you will quickly get a sense of whether it is too high, too low, or just right. If you lose a lot of jobs because prospects tell you, "Your price is too high," you may have to adjust downward.

On the other hand, if clients accept your price without even blinking, you might consider raising your hourly rate $10 or $15 and seeing what effect this has on your ability to get business.

The important thing to remember is that you are not locked into an hourly rate because you quoted it to one client. You can experiment with different rates until you find the right range for your service and your market.

BONUSES AND ROYALTIES

A common question that comes up is "The client says my fee is too high. He asked me if I would charge a lower fee up front in exchange for a percentage of profits or sales if the promotion I write for him makes money. Should I take it?"

In most instances, no. Small businesses routinely try to get writers to lower their fees in exchange for a bonus or royalty. They even try to persuade you to take the offer based on guilt, telling the writer, "If your copy is really any good, and you have confidence in it, you will stand by your confidence by taking part of your compensation as a performance-based bonus." If you refuse, they may say, "Why? Doesn't your copy work?"

Sorry, but this is pure baloney. As I spell out for my clients in my standard contract (see appendix F, under Results, p. 359): "There are many factors in your marketing—product, market, price, list, demand, consumer preferences, major events—that Bob cannot control. Therefore, while he can and does guarantee your satisfaction with his copy before you test it, he does not promise and cannot guarantee specific results."

Do I ever work on a royalty or bonus arrangement? On occasion—and 31 percent of the copywriters surveyed by Chris Marlow also say they accept bonus arrangements for some assignments.

But the bonus or royalty in such arrangements is not in lieu of my full project fee, in most instances. Instead it is to give the writer an incentive to periodically update and refresh the winning promotion—without an additional fee—if the promotion makes money.

For instance, if you are getting a royalty on a promotion, and the client tells you, "We need to update some of the figures or we can't keep mailing it," your ongoing royalty is your payment, and the client does not have to pay a separate project fee.

One client told me, "The reason we pay a royalty is to get you thinking about our product and your promotion on a regular basis." When you're getting a royalty, it's in your best interest financially to make sure your promotion continues to outperform all other test promotions. Therefore, you have a financial incentive to come up with new headlines and "tweaks" to the copy on a regular basis. Your ongoing royalty is the compensation for that effort.

Although most clients who offer bonuses are small, I only accept royalty arrangements from large direct-marketing clients. These clients have a mechanism in place for tracking royalty payments, so you know their bonus checks will be accurate and on time. Smaller companies may promise a bonus, but then conveniently "forget" to track the results, and somehow you never see the bonus you were promised.

Several different bonus and royalty arrangements are possible. One can be a fixed-dollar bonus based on specific performance. For instance, once I agreed to write a direct-mail package for $6,000, and the client and I agreed that if my mailing beat their current mailing, I would get an additional $6,000 as a one-time bonus, which I did.

The most common arrangement when writing direct mail for large-volume mailers is a "mailing fee." You write the mailing for a flat fee, which entitles the client to test mail it in a quantity you specify, typically 50,000 pieces.

If the mail piece performs successfully in the test, the client will want to keep mailing it, and that's when your mailing fee, which is typically 1 to 3 cents per piece mailed, kicks in. If the mailing fee is 2 cents per piece mailed and the client mails 250,000 additional pieces after the test, your royalty payment would be $5,000.

For online promotions, the royalty is typically 2 to 3 percent of gross sales, which is defined as revenue generated minus cancellations and refunds.

HOW TO SET YOUR PROJECT FEES

As you know, I prefer to quote a fixed project price for each copywriting assignment I accept from a client. Usually, this is stated as a fixed amount, e.g., "$2,500 for a two-page sales letter."

However, if there is a great deal of uncertainty as to the scope, complexity, or length of the project, I might quote a range instead of a single number, e.g., "$3,500 to $4,000 for an 8- to 10-page white paper." This way, I can charge what the job is worth and give my clients a price break if the job turns out to be simpler than expected.

The formula for determining project rates is similar to but not exactly the same as the formula for calculating your hourly rate. Here it is:

Take an educated guess as to how much time the project will take, then multiply by your hourly rate. Example: a client wants you to write a brochure.

You estimate the research, writing, editing, and rewriting will take four or five days, but you're not exactly sure. Your hourly rate is $50, which translates into $400 a day for an eight-hour day. On the basis of an estimate of four to five days, you should quote the client a range of $1,600 to $2,000.

As you did when determining your hourly rate, call competitors and ask what they are charging for a brochure, press release, mailing, or whatever. Many will be glad to tell you. For some reason, writers in this field are very open and sharing with other writers.

If they will not tell you, try to at least get your hands on a copy of their fee schedules so you can see how they structure their pricing. Have a friend pose as a potential client, call your competitors, and ask for this information. Some freelance writers post their fee schedules on their Web sites.

Based on your analysis of competitor fees, set your own rates accordingly. Be aware that the range of fees for a particular type of project may vary enormously. I find that a writer's fee for a one- or two-page press release ranges from $200 to $1,000; I charge $700 to $850, depending upon degree of complexity and subject matter.

As you quote fees to potential clients, you will get a sense of what they expect and are willing to pay for your services. In the New York City area, among clients who are knowledgeable in direct mail, I find that some clients expect to pay $750 for a lead-generating sales letter while others are willing to pay $2,000. But no one expects to pay less than $500 or is willing to go much beyond $3,000. So the range for a sales letter is $750 to $2,000.

FOUR FACTORS THAT AFFECT FREELANCE FEES

As I stated earlier, setting fees for freelance services is a challenge. You want to charge enough so that you are making good money, but not so much that your fees are out of line and force prospects to turn to other, less expensive writers.

How much should you charge? It depends on four factors:

1. Your status—whether you are a beginner or an old·pro, and how good you are
2. The going rate for your type of service—what the market will bear
3. The competitors and what they are charging
4. Financial need—how much you need the business

The first factor, status, says that experienced writers can generally command higher fees than beginners. But talent is even more important, and a highly talented novice is worth more to clients than a hack, no matter how long the hack has been working. Still, as a rule, beginners set their fees at the low end of the scale, old pros at the high end.

The second factor is the market value of your service, i.e., what are clients willing to pay for a press release, sales letter, TV commercial, ad, or speech?

Unlike such professions as law or medicine, there are virtually no restrictions, standards, or guidelines for freelance writing fees. As a result, fees are "all over the lot," as freelancer Sig Rosenblum has said. Copywriting fees for a direct-mail package range from a low of $750 to an amazing $25,000 and more.

The variation in freelance fees is tremendous. However, by talking with a few prospective clients, you quickly get a sense of the upper and lower limits for projects in your specialty, your industry, and your geographical location.

You may find, for example, that some clients expect to pay $600 for a brochure, while others regularly pay $2,000; but no one expects to get it for $200, and no one is willing to go to $4,000. After a few initial conversations and meetings with potential clients you'll get a good idea of what the market will bear.

The third factor to consider in setting fees is the competition in your area. Call some other freelance writers (perhaps they are running ads in local newspapers, business magazines, industry trade journals, or the advertising journals) and ask what they charge for an ad, letter, or press release. Most will gladly tell you. Finding out the competition's fees is a real help to the beginner. You learn just where to price yourself in relation to other writers. You'll also benefit by asking these writers to send you their resumés, brochures, or other background materials on their freelance services.

The fourth factor is your own financial needs. This shouldn't be a consideration, but it is. If you've got a million bucks in the bank, or dozens of top corporations are knocking at your door begging you to make space for their projects in your hectic writing schedule, then you obviously don't need the work, and this helps at the bargaining table. If the job isn't right, or the client gives off bad vibes or haggles over your fee, you can happily walk away without regrets.

If, on the other hand, the rent check is three weeks overdue, and you haven't had a phone call or an assignment in the past two months, you may be willing to take on a less-than-ideal project or client who, if he senses that you can be made to bargain, may be able to force down your price.

Ideally, you should negotiate each project as if you didn't need or want the work. But when you're hungry and just starting out, that isn't always possible or even wise. Sometimes you need the ego boost that comes with landing a project or being busy with work. For the writer, "psychic" wages can be as important as the green, folding kind.

The tendency of beginners is to set their rates in the lower range of fees, reasoning that they do not have the experience or portfolio to justify higher rates. This is the strategy I used myself when starting out, and I suppose it makes sense.

However, clients will probably take you more seriously if you put your fees in the medium to medium-high range. I have found that the less a client pays for a piece of copy, the less he or she respects the work and the person who produced it.

One beginner I know charged during his first year fees that it had taken me four years to get up the nerve to charge, and he had absolutely no trouble getting them, despite the fact that he was young and lacked significant experience. So I may have lost a lot of money by charging too little for too many years. I hope you don't make the same mistake!

A general fee schedule showing the range writers are charging for various projects is presented in appendix G.

TERMS AND CONDITIONS

When you and the client agree on your fee, you should also come to an agreement on the terms and conditions of the assignment. For example, if you are charging an hourly rate, is there an estimate of how many hours the job will take to complete? What happens if the job takes longer than anticipated? If you are charging a fixed project fee, does this include revisions? To what extent?

What does the client receive for the fee? For example, does your fee cover time spent in meetings with the client? If so, how many meetings? Unlimited?

What is the dollar amount of the fee and when is it due? Upon completion of the manuscript or approval by the client?

What happens if the client doesn't like the copy?

My solution is to describe my terms and conditions in the material I send to prospective clients and then review these points thoroughly with the client before taking on the assignment.

My terms and conditions are the following; yours may be different:

- My fees are for copy only.
- Assignments, unless otherwise stated, are handled primarily by mail, e-mail, fax, and phone.
- The copy I write is based primarily on material provided by the client.
- There are no additional charges to the client other than those agreed to in the purchase order.
- I absorb the cost of local phone calls, photocopies, postage, and other incidental expenses, and do not bill clients for these expenses.
- The client pays out-of-pocket expenses, primarily overnight shipping or messenger if required. (My rationale for charging for FedEx and messengers is that I have e-mail, and it is easy enough for the client to have e-mail, too. E-mail eliminates the need for FedEx and messengering of hard copy or disk files. Therefore any client can eliminate these costs simply by getting online, and most are.)
- My copywriting fee for new clients is payable 50 percent in advance, with the balance due upon receipt of copy.
- We do not begin work until we have the deposit.
- Revisions are free provided they are (a) assigned within 30 days of receipt of copy; and (b) not based on changes in the assignment made after the copy is submitted.
- A purchase order or letter of authorization is required for all jobs.

You may be uneasy about presenting a list such as this up front. It should be done with tact; you don't want to scare off clients or seem as if you're more interested in your fees than in helping your clients.

However, many disputes between writers and clients occur because terms, conditions, fees, and working arrangements were not discussed prior to giving the writer the assignment.

By being clear about your working and billing methods up front, you ensure mutual understanding and prevent problems later on.

I often get calls from writers who tell me, "The client keeps asking for revision after revision, and I am losing money on this job. When I told him I would have to charge more, he refused, saying we had already agreed on a price."

"How many revisions did you agree to make for that price in your contract?" I ask.

The writers often reply that they either didn't have a written agreement, or they had an agreement but the issue of how many revisions the client is entitled to for the fee stated was not discussed in it.

"Then you're screwed, and you have to make as many changes as the client wants without additional fee," I tell the unhappy writers. Reason: Whenever there is any ambiguity or gray area in an agreement between a vendor and a client, it is the vendor, not the client, who is responsible.

PRESENTING YOUR FEES AND RATE STRUCTURE
TO POTENTIAL CLIENTS

One of the key concerns a client has when looking over your materials is "How much is this going to cost me?" Introducing the matter of fees and fee structure into the sales presentation at the right time is critical. Bring it up too early, and you may scare off good potential clients.

But if you are too evasive, clients become suspicious and uncomfortable. Don't you like to have some idea of what something is going to cost you before you get too far into the sales pitch? Your clients feel the same way.

If you are meeting with the client in person, then handling the matter of fees is somewhat easier than if you are dealing by mail. In a personal meeting, you can tell from feedback when the client is ready to discuss fees. Usually this will come as a direct question such as "How much do you charge for a press release (or ad, or whatever it is the client needs)?" Or, "Can you give me an idea of how much you charge?"

When the client asks, answer directly and factually. State how you charge (hourly or by project), what your fees are, and, if appropriate, give the reasoning behind why you charge the way you do. Do not be shy or apologetic about fees, as so many freelancers are. You offer a professional service and the client expects to pay a professional fee for it.

But what about a prospect who telephones or e-mails?

Once I have determined that I am interested in working with the prospect, my next step is to tell him or her that I will send detailed information about my services. The material I send includes a one-page fee schedule (see appendix C) listing my charges and the terms under which I do business. I also keep the fee schedule as a PDF file on my computer so I can e-mail it to clients who want to see it right away.

I like a fee schedule because it gives the prospect what she wants (an idea of what I charge) and also proves that I am an honest professional who is so open about his fees that he publishes them. In addition, the fee schedule gives me a firm position when I am quoting a fee. For example, if the client wants an eight-minute script for a videotape and I quote $2,000, she sees that it is within the range I said and that I am not pulling the figure out of a hat.

The one disadvantage of a fee schedule is that it locks you into a fixed price, which may be too low for handling this particular assignment from this particular client. The solution is to list a broad range of fees for each item on your fee schedule rather than a single dollar figure. Then, for a specific project, you can quote a price within that range, either high or low, that reflects the difficulty of the job and the amount of work involved.

When presenting your fee schedule, be sure to note on it that the prices are not quotations but merely "rough guidelines" for pricing, and that each job must be estimated and quoted on individually. The quote should be within the range indicated on the fee schedule, unless there are some extraordinary conditions (e.g., the client wants you to fly to Alaska), in which case your quote must acknowledge these conditions and show the extra charges.

Many, many writers do not have published fee schedules. In one survey of seventeen top direct-mail copywriters, nine said they did not have a published fee schedule. If you don't, you ought to give the client a rough indication of your fees either over the telephone or in an e-mail.

For example: "For the project we discussed, my fee would be in the range of $500 to $1,000 for a 1- to 2-page letter, plus $750 to $1,000 for a booklet folded to fit a no. 10 envelope. I can quote an exact project fee once I review the background material you are sending me by Express Mail today."

I think it is a mistake to give no indication of fee in the initial package you send out. The fee is one of the client's key concerns; the majority of prospects, although they won't necessarily buy the lowest-priced writing service (indeed, the opposite is often true), want to get a feel for your fee structure fairly early on in the buying cycle.

PRICE QUOTATIONS AND FEE NEGOTIATIONS

Although you may have a schedule of fees or an hourly rate, don't be totally inflexible about your fees. Often the fee schedule is a starting point for negotiation, not the final word. Whoever said "Everything is negotiable" was certainly correct. Everything *is* negotiable. How many times have you actually paid the full sticker price for a new car, or accepted the first offer from an antiques dealer or flea market operator?

There will be many instances in which new clients accept your fees without protest. In other situations, however, prospects might try to negotiate a lower fee with you. Should you play?

It depends on several factors. How busy are you right now? How badly do you want or need this assignment? If things are slow and the project fits nicely into an empty slot on your schedule, you may come down on your price slightly to accommodate the client.

Is the assignment a big project that would put a lot of money in your pocket? Or is the client asking for a discount for giving you several assignments at once? You might consider giving a volume discount to clients who spend a certain amount of money with you. One writer who charges $800 for a single radio commercial will reduce the price to $700 per commercial if the client hires him to do six or more spots at one time.

Do you especially want this assignment because it would look good in your portfolio, or because you want to add a prestigious name to your client list? You might submit a lower bid to ensure getting the assignment.

Is your best client asking for a break on a particular project where his budget is not so high? Good clients are a freelancer's most valuable asset, and it doesn't hurt to do your client a favor now and then.

The real question that decides whether you will stand firm by your fee schedule or negotiate is this: Do I want or need this assignment so much that I am unwilling to risk losing the project by refusing to budge on my fees when asked? Only you can answer that question in the specific situation.

Every writer has a slightly different approach to fees. Some are vague about fees and encourage negotiation as a normal part of doing business. I prefer to make my fee schedule available in printed form to anyone who asks. And I stick to these

rates except as a favor to current clients or on large assignments where I will give volume discounts (in the range of 5 to
15 percent off). Otherwise, clients generally pay a similar fee
for similar services. This seems fair to me and to my clients.

When you are a beginner, or when business is slow and you
need the work, the temptation to quote a low price to get the
work is overwhelming. Steve Howard, president of the Act
Group (Phoenix, Arizona), gives 12 reasons why you should resist this temptation and not undercharge (as quoted in the
newsletter "Words from Woody," Summer 2005):

1. When you cut price, you cut or eliminate profits.
2. You undermine future profits. Low prices lock you in to
   a vicious cycle of more low prices.
3. You work twice as hard for the same money.
4. Clients lower their expectations of you. Price is visual evidence of value. Most people are aware of the old adage
   "You get what you pay for." Low prices create fear, uncertainty, and doubt about you.
5. You offer no differentiation. When all else is equal,
   people buy the lowest price. But when given a choice,
   most people will pay more for your service if it provides
   wanted benefits no one else offers. Being different and
   better is your greatest advantage.
6. You buy expensive clients. When you sell price, you get
   price-buyers. Their greatest joy is grinding you down.
7. You get stressed out. Most price-buyers are irrationally
   demanding. They want something for nothing. When
   you sell price, you buy stress.
8. You get disloyal clients. People who always buy the lowest price are disloyal. Next time they have a need, they'll
   buy it from whomever has the lowest price.
9. Good clients may be driven off. It is impossible to sat-
   isfy price-buyers. Those folks take so much of your time

complaining and asking for concessions, you don't have time to take care of your good clients, so you lose them because of simple neglect.

10. You eliminate the price floor. If you cut your price once, people expect you to do it again and again.

11. You can lose trust and credibility. A $1,000 price cut may send a message to the client that you were overcharging them $1,000 in the first place.

12. The goal of business is not creating work, it is creating profits. Firms that sell price are the busiest the day before they go bankrupt. More than 80 percent of your potential clients will pay more for additional benefits, faster results, and superior solutions to their problems.

SHOULD YOU EXTEND CREDIT?

Anyone who does not get paid in advance for his or her services (or upon delivery of products) is extending credit to clients and customers.

In the freelance writing business, it is customary to extend credit to clients. Few writers can demand and get full payment in advance. Few clients will pay the full fee in advance. Many writers get partial payment up front (usually one-third to one-half of the total fee), with the balance payable and due upon completion of the assignment.

Joan Harris, a Long Island–based freelance copywriter specializing in direct mail, gets a $1,000 retainer up front before beginning any project. Other writers are content with no advance and send an invoice upon completion. Thus most writers extend credit for all or part of their fee.

Whenever you extend credit, you take the risk of not being paid. This doesn't mean you are going to be burned by a client; many freelancers never face the problem of a client who doesn't pay a bill. But the majority of freelancers I know have, at one time or another, been faced with a client who wouldn't or couldn't pay his or her bill.

If you extend credit, you can't eliminate the risk of this happening. But you can minimize it. The best way is to follow my suggestion of spelling out your fees and terms up front, then putting your agreement in writing and getting the client's signature on the agreement before you begin the project. My personal preference is to ask clients to issue a company purchase order for me.

Getting all or part of your fee up front, at least on the first few jobs you do for any new client, also helps weed out the deadbeats. In an article in *Advertising Age*, freelancer Charles J. Sass offers the following 10-point checklist for making sure you are not stiffed by your clients:

1. Handshake contracts don't count, ever.
2. Demand a third of your money up front, or don't do it.
3. Remember that everything takes longer than it should, costs more than expected, and goes wrong in the most unlikely of places.
4. Assume nothing, expect nothing, and trust nobody.
5. Don't believe for a moment that right is might.
6. Possession of your money by the client is nine-tenths of the law.
7. Find out why a little operator like you got this wonderful opportunity; why not a big operator?
8. Check the client's reputation; has this happened before?
9. If you don't have time for up-front checking, run away.
10. Think like a lawyer, or an accountant, or the IRS. Don't think like a creative genius. Have an official-looking statement of policy or an agreement form . . . and get somebody to sign it . . . or walk away. A nod's not a signature.

You need to protect yourself most when dealing with an organization you haven't done business with before. It's especially important to be careful with smaller and out-of-state companies.

If the job is from a company who has hired you before, you don't have to go through the items in Sass's checklist. Large corporations and local clients can also be taken on by you with less vigorous checking than Sass recommends.

Some clients would object to paying an advance by telling me, "It takes us weeks to process such a check request. I will begin the process, but can't you start the job without it?" I now reply, "You can put the deposit on a credit card," and I accept MasterCard, Visa, and American Express. By accepting credit cards or Pay Pal, you eliminate the client's excuse of not being able to pay you a timely deposit because of the corporate paperwork involved in issuing checks.

6

FINDING YOUR MARKETS

Once you decide what type of services you want to offer and what you will charge for these services, you must find clients who need this type of service performed. If you're a medical writer, do you know who hires medical writers? Doctors? Hospitals? Pharmaceutical companies? Medical advertising agencies? You need to know where to direct your sales and marketing efforts to get clients.

The six major markets for freelance commercial writers are corporations, small businesses, advertising agencies, public relations agencies, graphic design studios, and audiovisual producers. Many freelancers work in two additional markets, associations and the government (federal, state, and local).

The first three markets—corporations, small businesses, and ad agencies—are the biggest and probably account for 90 percent of the work assigned in this field. Let's take a look at these markets: who they are, where the buyers are, how to reach them, and what they buy.

CORPORATIONS

Corporations are the biggest employers of freelance commercial writers. Manufacturers, utilities, distributors, insurance companies, banks, management consultants, service companies, and professional organizations need just about every type of written material you can imagine, from ad campaigns and annual reports to sales literature and speeches for executives, to technical writing and trade show displays.

There are many departments within a corporation that regularly use the services of outside writers. The advertising department needs copywriters to turn out brochures, sales bulletins, and new product announcements. The employee communications department may hire you to write an employee newsletter or a series of booklets explaining a new benefits program.

The public relations department needs someone to help with news releases, press kits, and feature articles. The technical publications department may hire outside writers to put together proposals, reports, manuals, and other technical documents. The corporate communications department may tap your services for a speech or annual report.

A single corporation may produce enough print and online material to keep you, me, and dozens of other writers busy on a full-time basis. There is plenty of work to go around, and not enough writers to handle it. This is why good commercial writers are in constant demand.

Within the corporate market there are many submarkets. One way to characterize the market is by the specific department within the company that hires you, which could be advertising, public relations, corporate communications, or one of the other departments outlined above.

Another way to look at the corporate market is by industry. One writer might specialize in writing for banks, insurance companies, and other companies in financial services, while another writer might serve the computer hardware, software, semiconductor, and electronics industries.

A third way to characterize the corporate market is by size

of company. You can work with big companies, with sales in the hundreds of millions or billions of dollars; medium-sized companies, with sales in the tens of millions of dollars; or small businesses (see next section), with sales less than two to three million dollars or perhaps no sales (start-up ventures).

Most writers prefer working for medium-sized and large corporations. Big companies can give you a lot more work, are able to pay better, and are usually more professional to deal with.

A good directory of corporations is the *Standard Directory of Advertisers* (see appendix B). This directory, which is three inches thick, lists 17,000 corporations. Each listing gives the name of the company, address, phone number, annual sales, number of employees, products, and key management personnel (which usually includes people in charge of advertising, marketing, and sales, as well as the president and chief executive officer). The *Standard Directory* is published annually and is available in most local libraries.

You might also want to take a look at *Thomas Register,* a huge directory of American industry that lists more than 140,000 companies. In 2006, Thomas Publishing ceased publication of the print edition of *Thomas Register;* new editions are available online only.

Whom do you contact when seeking work in this market? At large corporations, target people with titles such as advertising manager, marketing communications manager, marketing manager, director of corporate communications, media relations manager, public affairs director, public relations director, technical publications manager, and investor relations manager.

At medium-sized corporations, you can contact the owner or president, general manager, director of sales and marketing, or marketing manager. In small companies, aim your promotions at the owner, president, or manager.

Writers who work for large corporations like to think of that corporation as "their client." Actually, these corporations are so diverse and have so many hiring managers within them that your client isn't really XYZ Company or ABC Construction; it's John or Betty or Stuart—whoever hired you at XYZ or ABC.

With rampant downsizing, corporations and their staffs are less stable today than twenty-three years ago when I started in business. Even the companies themselves lack stability. For example, only 29 of the top 100 companies in the first Fortune 500 list, published in 1956, can still be found in the top 100 today. During the 1980s, 230 companies disappeared from the Fortune 500 list—46 percent of the total.

When your contact leaves, or the company restructures, you may lose the account, as the corporation as an entity has no contractual obligation or long-term loyalty to you. But don't take this as a given. Contact the new person and see if there is work for you. At the same time, follow your old client to his or her new position; perhaps he or she can hire you to write for the new employer.

SMALL BUSINESS

You may hear the term "SOHO" to describe the small business market. SOHO stands for "small office/home office." It indicates a company so small that the owner, with perhaps an employee or two, works from her home. Or, the next step up, works in a small office building with maybe half a dozen employees or so.

Some writers prefer the challenge and excitement of dealing with small businesses. One advantage of writing for a small company is that you may get to work directly with the top decision makers, whereas at a large company your client is a manager who must get approval from higher levels before okaying your copy.

However, many small firms operate on tight budgets and may not be able to afford the fees of a top professional writer. Also, their projects may be few and far between, as they just don't generate that much printed material.

"Bigger companies produce an enormous amount of marketing communications materials," observes successful corporate freelance writer Anne M. Phaneuf in an article in "Assignments" newsletter (formerly "Writing for Money"). "Smaller companies invest their entire sales and marketing efforts in one or two brochures."

Here is another key difference in working for large corporations versus small businesses. When you write copy for a large corporation, they are generally looking for copy only. They know what to do with your copy—how to design a Web site, or produce a direct-mail campaign—and don't need you to advise them.

Therefore, large corporations are the ideal market for copywriters who, like me, prefer to write copy only and do not want to have to explain marketing—and what to do with our copy— to our clients. As my friend direct-mail writer Don Hauptman phrases it, "I like working with a client who knows where the indicia goes on the envelope."

Small businesses, by comparison, often need a lot of marketing help, not just copy. Therefore, small companies are good clients for copywriters who see themselves as "marketing consultants," not just copywriters, and are eager to dispense marketing advice to their clients. Just be sure that you are paid a separate consulting fee for dispensing that advice, and are not giving it away free when you write copy for these small clients.

ADVERTISING AGENCIES

Another major market for freelance writing services is advertising agencies. Surprisingly, writing ads and TV commercials is only a small part of what an ad agency may hire a freelancer to do. Other tasks ad agencies frequently farm out to freelancers include catalogs, direct mail, sales brochures, labels and package copy, dealer promotions, radio commercials, newsletters, slide presentations, videotape scripts, slogans, concepts, on-line copy, and campaign strategies.

I've worked for both the big agencies (J. Walter Thompson, Grey, Doremus) and some medium-sized and small agencies you've never heard of. Be wary of the many "mini-agencies," extremely small ad agencies that usually consist of the owner-president and one or two partners or employees.

These mini-agencies come and go quickly, have a hard time staying solvent, and suffer from severe cash-flow problems. As a result, they tend to pay freelancers and other suppliers only when (and if) they get paid by their client—which is the wrong way to do business.

If in doubt about an agency's ability to pay, make it clear that your invoice is payable and due in X number of days, and payment is not dependent on whether the agency gets money from its client. Better still, get half your fee in advance; this tactic always separates the sincere from the deadbeats.

Although there are many published directories of ad agencies, the best is the *Standard Directory of Advertising Agencies,* also known as the "Red Book." The Red Book lists 4,400 advertising agencies in alphabetical order and is indexed by city and state.

Each listing gives the agency's name, address, phone number, specialties (if any), number of employees, year founded, billings (gross income), breakdown of billings by media, key personnel (including the names of creative directors and copy supervisors who hire writers), and major accounts. The book is updated and published three times a year, and most libraries have a copy.

How does freelancing for ad agencies compare with working for clients directly? Some observations:

• First of all, freelancing for ad agencies and freelancing for corporate clients are not mutually exclusive. Most freelance commercial writers have both corporations and ad agencies as clients. However, when you are freelancing for an ad agency, never approach their clients and offer to work for them directly. It's unethical and will hurt your reputation.

• Ad agencies are usually in more of a rush than corporate clients. If the average corporate client gives you X days to do a given type of project, the average ad agency will generally have a deadline that is half that number of days. After all, they need time to review — and have you rewrite, possibly several times — the copy before they show it to their client.

• When you work for agencies, you effectively double the review and approval process for your copy: First the agency has to like it, and then their client has to like it. When you work for clients directly, you eliminate this intermediate agency approval.

• Agencies have more variety and potentially more assignments for you. If you work directly for Acme Widgets, the advertising manager is only going to give you Acme Widgets assignments. If you are hired by Acme Widgets' ad agency, not only do you get Acme Widget assignments but they might also hire you to work on some of their other accounts, multiplying your workload from them many times over.

• Since the agency wants to make a profit or at least not lose money when they hire you, they put a markup on your services when billing the client. As a result, the fees paid by agencies to freelance writers are typically (but not always) around 20 to 30 percent less than you would get if you billed the client directly. Some agencies offset this by acting as liaison between you and the client, reducing the number of phone calls and meetings required for "client contact," therefore saving you (in theory) time spent on the job.

• Agencies provide a wide range of services that cover a lot more than just freelance writing—everything from photography, illustrations, and graphic design to printing, media placement, HTML and Flash programming, and video production. So a client who demands full service from a single vendor is often best served by an ad agency providing all the services under one roof, usually from a combination of staff and freelance resources.

• Agency people, most of whom focus on campaigns, put somewhat more of an emphasis on creativity than most freelancers, who generally focus on individual projects and therefore put somewhat more of an emphasis on utility and results. Working with a good agency and getting the agency's input on a project can get you working at a level of creativity and freshness a step higher than your norm, which can be a fun change of pace.

• Most freelancers present ideas to clients as memos, outlines, or rough drafts. Agencies present ideas, concepts, and project progress much more visually, using sharp-looking graphics and computer-generated layouts. Your work looks better, and therefore may be received more enthusiastically by the client, when the agency enhances it with graphics and layouts for presentation.

PUBLIC RELATIONS FIRMS

Public relations firms hire writers to write press releases, feature articles, speeches, and newsletters for their clients. Many provide other marketing services for clients and also need writers to produce annual reports, advertisements, brochures, and direct mail.

The problem with this market is that there are a huge number of PR agencies that are really one person: a freelancer like yourself working from home or a rented office and calling herself a company. These mini-PR firms, like their mini-ad agency counterparts, usually don't have much money. Be careful when dealing with them. Again, getting half the fee in advance is a good way to separate the payers from the paupers.

Public relations firms generally pay fees equal to or lower than ad agencies. Many smaller PR firms typically work on a monthly retainer ranging from $2,000 to $5,000 or more. If the monthly retainer is $3,000, you can understand why it's hard for the PR firm to pay a freelance writer $2,500 to write a single feature article that is only one of many items covered under the retainer for that month. Public relations managers at corporations have larger budgets for project work, and a high fee for a speech, article, or newsletter is generally not a problem for them.

The best directory of PR firms is *O'Dwyer's Directory of Public Relations Firms,* published by J. R. O'Dwyer and Company, Inc. The book lists 1,700 firms and their addresses, phone numbers, key executives, numbers of employees, and areas of specialization.

O'Dwyer also publishes *Directory of Corporate Communications,* which lists in-house PR people at 3,100 companies and 500 trade associations. Your library may own a copy of both of these books, or you can buy them from the publisher (see appendix B).

ASSOCIATIONS

There are thousands of professional, business, and trade associations in the United States. A recent magazine article commented, "America is association-crazy." In an association, people with a common background, profession, industry, or goal network with one another for mutual benefit. *The Encyclopedia of Associations,* published by Gale Research and available in most local libraries, is the best guide to associations. What do associations buy from freelance commercial writers? Articles for their newsletters and magazines. Direct mail to sell subscriptions, sign up new members, or get existing members to renew membership. Mailings and brochures to sell life insurance, medical benefits, meetings, seminars, annual conferences, and other member benefits. Press releases that keep the business world and general public up to date on the organization, its activities, and all the good things the industry or profession is doing in the world.

In most cases, you cannot make money doing work for local associations or local chapters of national associations. Your contacts should be executives at the association's national headquarters. Titles to target can include director, executive director, communications director, marketing director, meeting and conference planner, publications manager, or editor.

Pay scales vary widely. The bigger and wealthier associations pay freelance writers fees close to or even equivalent to what business clients do. Smaller, cash-strapped associations may pay as little as half this amount, which can still be decent money and make the association a profitable client. Most freelance commercial writers target their sales efforts at corporations and ad agencies, so the competition in the association market may not be as keen.

AUDIOVISUAL COMPANIES, MULTIMEDIA PRODUCERS, AND INTERACTIVE AGENCIES

Many audiovisual firms use freelancers to write scripts for slide shows, films, videotapes, TV commercials, CD-ROMs, and multimedia presentations. Audiovisual producers are listed in the *Interactive Multimedia Sourcebook* (see appendix B), updated annually.

Obviously, only those writers who have done audiovisual scripts or are interested in doing them should target this market. Audiovisual producers generally won't hire writers who do not have scriptwriting experience and a reel (a sample tape of produced presentations they have scripted).

If you haven't done video and want to break in, start by getting print assignments from ad agencies or corporate accounts. Many of these clients, if they like the print work you do for them, will ask you to do an occasional video or commercial. If they know your work and feel you know their business, they will hire you even though you lack experience in audiovisual media. After doing a few of these jobs, you can put together a reel and target audiovisual production companies directly.

Interactive multimedia is a growth area, in which CD-ROM presentations and Web sites are the biggest opportunities for freelance commercial writers. Multimedia producers who can hire you to do such work are also listed in the *Interactive Multimedia Sourcebook.*

Again, a CD-ROM producer or Web design firm is unlikely to hire novices who haven't worked in these media. But don't worry. The experience is easy to get. Inevitably, your ad agency and the corporate clients who hired you for print work will ask you to do a CD-ROM or Web pages for them. Build a portfolio of interactive work that way, then go back and approach the multimedia producers armed with these samples and experience.

GRAPHIC DESIGN FIRMS AND ART STUDIOS

Graphic design firms produce brochures, annual reports, invitations, folders, and other printed graphic material for their clients. When a client asks for copy as well as design and production, the design firm obliges by hiring a freelance writer to handle the editorial portion of the job; the overwhelming majority do not have writers on staff. Local graphic design firms can be found in the Yellow Pages under "Graphic Arts Studios," "Design," or "Art Studios."

The upside of working for graphic design firms is that they sometimes control the hiring of freelance writers on large, lucrative projects such as annual reports and corporate capabilities brochures. They can get you projects you would not have been able to get on your own. Often these are plum assignments that are large and pay exceedingly well.

The downside is that occasionally you will find a graphic designer who views your copy as merely another design element and is more concerned that you keep it short than that you produce effective copy. This was quite common when I started freelancing in the 1980s, but is less so now.

GOVERNMENT AGENCIES

According to the late Herman Holtz, a prolific freelance writer who spent decades handling writing projects for government agencies, there are 34,000 U.S. government offices and other facilities throughout the country. The U.S. government contracts out $14 billion a year for editorial projects to freelance writers and other communications specialists.

Says Holtz, "The government, with its hundreds of agencies and thousands of offices, is a multibillion-dollar market for every kind of writing conceivable, and most of it is done under contract by private organizations and often by individuals." Government agencies hire writers to prepare reports, manuals, proposals, training programs, audiovisual scripts, video scripts, lecture notes, speeches, brochures, articles, newsletters, technical manuals, books, pamphlets, and other documentation. Government agencies hire freelancers to write publications designed for both internal consumption and the general public.

The military is one of the largest government clients for freelance writing. They require technical manuals and other documentation to be used for training military personnel, for day-to-day systems operations and maintenance, and for the bidding and system acquisition process.

The contact at a government agency would be the contracting officer or the head of the public information office. Write to them and request information about their procurement procedures. Some key government agencies that hire writers include the Small Business Administration, the General Services Administration, the Department of Energy, the Environmental Protection Agency, the Department of Transportation, and the Department of Labor, all based in Washington, D.C. The General Services Administration also has a major office in Denver and branch offices in Boston, Chicago, Seattle, New York, Atlanta, Houston, Los Angeles, Philadelphia, Fort Worth, San Francisco, and Kansas City, Missouri.

Many bids and proposal opportunities are listed in the newspaper *Commerce Business Daily* (see appendix B), published by the U.S. government. State and local governments advertise their requirements in the local classified columns under "Bids and Proposals." You can also call on procurement offices in your state capital, county seat, and city or town hall.

NONPROFITS

Another market for freelance writing services is nonprofits: churches, religious organizations, political candidates, political parties, museums, colleges, and cause-related organizations such as United Cerebral Palsy, Covenant House, North

Shore Animal League, and the Sierra Club. These organizations need a variety of materials, such as member newsletters and public service announcements, but their biggest writing assignment is direct mail for fund-raising.

With few exceptions, there is little or no money in writing copy for local nonprofits; these organizations are simply too small, and they rely on volunteers for writing their materials. You might volunteer to write a fund-raising letter for a local nonprofit whose cause you support as a way of getting some experience and a sample for your portfolio. National nonprofits can pay decent fees to freelance writers, though these fees are generally half of what you would get writing material of similar length for a corporate client.

ONLINE JOB MARKETS

A variety of Web sites are promoted as a way for freelance writers to get assignments through the Internet. The most well known of these is www.elance.com, which can help not just writers but programmers, Web designers, and many other professionals find freelance assignments.

I advise you to completely avoid www.elance.com, www .guru.com, and all other Web sites promising to find writers work online. They are a complete waste of time. Clients who put jobs up for bid on these sites are, almost without exception, all price-buyers: They are shopping for the low bid, and are not looking for quality, experience, credentials, or any other advantage you may offer.

Therefore, if you respond to bid requests on www.elance .com, you will be outbid every time if you charge your normal rates, and will consequently never win any job. You can only win jobs by being the low bidder, and we discussed in chapter 5 why underpricing yourself to win jobs is a terrible strategy for building a successful freelance writing practice.

7

PROSPECTING: GENERATING SALES LEADS

For most writers handling commercial assignments, prospecting—looking for and generating sales leads—is an essential activity. Just as General Motors must advertise if the company expects to sell cars, so too you must advertise and promote yourself and your freelance writing business if you expect people to call you with assignments.

A sales lead is an inquiry from an individual at an organization that is a potential client for your freelance commercial writing services. The inquiry can come via phone, e-mail, fax, or postal mail. In essence, an inquiry is a prospective client saying, "We may be interested in hiring you; please tell us more about who you are and what you do." This is an essential step in the selling cycle; chapter 11 shows you how to follow up on these leads and convert them to paying contracts for writing assignments.

How much of your time will be spent marketing and selling your services? Most established freelancers probably spend 10 to 25 percent of their time on self-promotion, whether it's giving seminars and speeches, sending out mailings, or networking at association meetings. For a beginner, even more effort must be devoted to establishing a reputation, getting clients, and making your name known to the local business community.

How do you promote yourself? Does direct mail work for freelancers? Does it pay to advertise? How can you get people to hire you? I'll show you what techniques can work for you, including:

- Cold calling
- Testimonials
- Direct mail
- Personal letters
- Advertising
- Networking
- Premiums
- Telephone hotlines
- Sales literature
- Follow-up (covered in chapter 11)
- Using the Internet (this is so important we've added two new chapters to cover it, chapters 9 and 10)

COLD CALLING

A "cold call" is a phone call to a prospect you don't know, asking for business. Many freelancers generate business by calling up potential clients on the telephone in a cold call and asking these prospects whether they need freelance services.

"Calling on the phone every day really does work," says Steve Brown, a freelance graphic designer and illustrator. "You just have to make lots of calls, and keep calling back. Do this in every area where you have expertise and samples to show."

When you cold-call prospects, do not give them a sales pitch. Instead, ask them a series of questions that qualifies them as a decision maker and sets up the next step in the selling process. Here's how it works.

First, when the prospect answers the phone — "Widget Manufacturing Company, Betty Jones speaking" — introduce yourself:

> YOU: Ms. Jones, this is Joan Smith calling. Am I catching you at a bad time?
> PROSPECT: No, Joan. How can I help you?
> YOU: I'm a freelance copywriter specializing in widgets. May I ask you a question?
> PROSPECT: Sure.

At this point you want to find out whether you are speaking to a decision maker, what the company's needs are, and whether they use freelance writers.

> YOU: Are you the person in charge of producing your company's catalog?
> PROSPECT: Yes, I am.
> YOU: Do you hire freelance copywriters from time to time to produce catalog copy for your widget line?

If the person says no, she is probably not a good prospect: You want to target businesspeople who buy copy and, when they do buy it, hire freelancers.

If the person says yes, ask the following question:

> YOU: What would it take for me to be considered to do a project for you?

The prospect will tell you whether there's a chance of your getting an assignment, and if so, what you have to say, do, or send to be considered for the job. The selling process continues on from there.

The American Writers and Artists Institute, an organization

that offers a wide variety of training programs for writers (www.awaionline.com), recommends the following as a script for making cold calls to market your freelance writing services (their model is tailored for direct-mail copywriters, but you can modify it to fit your market):

"Good morning (Mr. Smith) my name is (Donald Mahoney), and I'm a direct mail copywriter. I'm calling you today because I think I can help you boost your sales dramatically.

"Honestly, I think I can beat the control you're mailing. I have a unique formula for evaluating sales copy, and when I applied it to your control, I found several critical weaknesses. Do you mind if I just point out a couple to you?"

<Pause for response>

"Well, just to give you an idea, I found (summarize three weak points found in analysis).

"Now, that was just a small part of my evaluation. The point is, that I think I can DOUBLE the response of your current control. Would that be of interest to you?"

<Pause for response>

"Then let me make a proposal to you. Let me mail you a brief analysis of your control, and show you what I think the weak points are. I'll also include an outline of how I would approach a promotion for your product.

"Then, if you're interested, we can discuss my fee for a test package to go against your control. And let me say this: I think you'll find my offer quite reasonable. And even if you're not interested, you'll have gotten a FREE critique of your control.

"Does that sound fair?"

<Pause for response>

"Thank you very much (Mr. Smith). Let me make sure I have your mailing information correct. You're at (etc.)."

<Pause for response>

"Would you like me to e-mail the critique to you? If so, can you give me your e-mail address?"

\<Pause for response\>

"Thank you again for your time. You should hear from me in about one week. If you don't mind, I'll call you about a week afterward, to make sure you received everything."

\<Pause for response\>

"Thanks again (Mr. Smith). Have a good day. I will speak with you soon."

\<Hang up\>

Mail your critique and outline promptly, within three days after the call. Include a cover letter reminding Mr. Smith of who you are and how you intend to help him.

TESTIMONIALS

Many self-promotions—including brochures, direct mail, ads, press releases—can benefit from the addition of testimonials. A testimonial is a statement from a satisfied client praising you and your services. A typical testimonial might read:

> Thanks for the great job editing our EASYFILER user manual, Linda. We're already getting feedback from users saying that the manual is the best they've ever seen!
> — Steve Sagan, Marketing Manager, Bi Level Software, Inc.

Some testimonials are received unsolicited; for example, a client might send you a letter thanking you for a job well done. Naturally, this makes a good testimonial. But before you use it, get the client's permission in writing. Otherwise, the client may become angry if he sees himself quoted in your next ad or brochure without his consent, and you will have damaged your relationship.

Getting permission is easy. When I want to quote a client, I send a standard permission letter, reproduced in appendix F. The client simply signs it and sends it back to me, allowing me to show the testimonial to other companies. I always send the client a self-addressed stamped envelope and two copies of the letter. This way the recipient doesn't have to make a copy of the letter or address and stamp an envelope.

"But what if clients don't send me nice letters?" you may ask. That's okay—most clients won't, because most people don't bother to send notes and thank-you letters nowadays. However, this doesn't prevent you from asking satisfied clients to endorse your services with a testimonial. Appendix F includes a letter I have used to solicit favorable comments from clients. If you send this to five clients, you'll probably get two or three good testimonials to use.

Here's an Internet shortcut to getting great client testimonials: When you finish a copywriting assignment, send a quick e-mail to the client saying, "I just want to make sure you got the final copy, and that you're pleased with everything."

Many clients will reply along these lines: "Got it. You did a great job! We love the copy!"

Then you reply and say, "Thanks for the kind words. Would you mind if I used them as a testimonial to promote my services?"

Most clients will say yes. At this point, print out the whole e-mail exchange and save it for your records. To be safe, also have the client sign the testimonial permission letter shown in appendix F.

DIRECT MAIL

When other writers ask me, "What is the most effective self-promotion for you?" I answer without hesitation: direct mail. An effective sales letter can be quickly written and mailed to prospective clients. It is a relatively inexpensive promotion. And it gives you great control over cost, since you can mail as few or as many letters as you wish.

Direct mail can be as simple as a one-page letter or as complex as a multi-component package with see-through windows, color brochures, order forms, reply envelopes, computer-personalized letters, and other inserts. It can be produced using only a PC with Word, or you can add color, glossy stock, photographs, drawings, pop-ups, and three-dimensional objects.

Cameron Foote, a Boston-based freelancer who specializes in annual reports, sends a self-mailer to corporate communications directors at large public companies. The message begins: "Is writing your annual report an annual headache?" The sentence has a nice ring to it, but also goes to the heart of the need Cam's service addresses.

In my experience, cheap and simple is best for freelance writers who mail limited quantities on a limited budget. My standard package consists of a one-page letter (a typed form letter with printing on one side) and a reply card mailed in my regular number 10 business envelope.

Although I could personalize each letter using my computer, I prefer a form letter because it's faster and easier to produce and mail. If I personalized, I could only mail letters when I wasn't using my computer for writing copy. A form letter can be pulled off the shelf and stuffed in an envelope at any time, in seconds.

If you need a lot of leads, you can mail in large quantities. I like to test any new letter by mailing to 100 prospects. If the letter generates a good response, I use it in larger quantities — say, 500 or so at a time. If the letter fails to produce any replies, I go back to the PC and try again.

Also, there's no law that says you have to mail in large quantities. Whenever I learn of a potential client — say, an ad agency with a new account or a company launching a new product — I can look up the client in a business directory, type an envelope addressed to the appropriate person, and drop a form letter in the mail. This is much quicker than writing a personal letter from scratch, and allows me to reach many new prospects I might not otherwise have time to contact.

I was lucky in that the first sales letter I mailed was successful, generating a 7 percent response. This letter is reproduced in appendix F. You can either adapt my letter to suit your needs, or write your own letter from scratch. If you want to write your own letter, here's an outline you can use:

1. *Begin with an opening statement that grabs attention.* You can promise a benefit, as I do in my headline, "How an engineer and former ad manager can help you write better ads and brochures." Or, you might get attention by stating a fascinating fact, quoting a statistic, or asking a provocative question. One freelance PR writer began his letter: "Is 'freelance' a dirty word to you?"

2. *Next, identify the reader's problem.* Then offer your services as a solution. I do this in the three opening paragraphs of my letter.

3. *Elaborate on your background,* showing why you are uniquely qualified to solve the client's problem. Explain why your services are superior, or why you have the best qualifications for the job. In my letter, this section follows the sentence, "Here are my qualifications."

4. *Call for action.* Ask the reader to phone or write or mail back a reply form. Offer a reason for the reader to respond, such as free information, a free consultation, a free meeting, a free analysis of his current ad. Tell readers the specific action you want them to take and spell out the benefits they will receive if they respond now.

The advantage of having a tested sales letter—one that will generate a certain percentage response every time you mail it—is that you can quickly produce as many sales leads as you need, whenever you need them. For example, if your letter generates a 3 percent response, mailing 100 letters will, on average, produce three inquiries. If your goal is to get 10 sales leads, you will need to mail 300 to 400 letters. As a rule, you'll get the majority of responses to your letter within one week or so if you send it First Class mail.

Letters should include some kind of reply card. The front is addressed to you and asks the reader to put a stamp on the postcard. The back has a space for prospects to fill in name, address, and phone number. It also lets them indicate the type of copy they need and how they want you to respond to them (see sample in appendix F).

Always include a reply card in your mailings. Without a reply card your response rate will drop dramatically, possibly to zero. Get your mailing list from prospecting directories that cover your target markets (see appendix A) or contact a mailing-list supplier (also listed in appendix A).

New directories can be expensive, but any directory more than a year or so old is in danger of being badly out of date. That's because business addresses change so frequently— according to an article in *Target Marketing* magazine, 1.7 million businesses move each year.

PERSONAL LETTERS

If you have the time, and feel that direct mail is too impersonal for your taste, you could write personalized letters targeted to specific prospects. The key is to personalize not only with the person's name but with specific details that show your knowledge of the business, industry, products, and goals.

For two months in 1981, I tried to start a small ad agency in New York City. One freelance writer sent me a letter that began, "Dear Mr. Bly: Congratulations on your new business.

May you have great success and pleasure in it." I found this opening effective because it (a) flattered me; and (b) showed me that the writer knew something about my company.

One way to personalize without writing a brand-new letter each time is to write a basic "boilerplate" (standard) letter that you can then tailor to a particular reader by adding a few details. If you write an entirely new letter to every prospect, you may get a good response but you won't be able to get many letters in the mail. The overall effect may be a reduction in total leads produced instead of an increase.

Milt Pierce, a successful New York writer specializing in mail order, came up with a clever promotion. He suggests that you study a potential client's current advertising campaign or direct mail program, then send a letter along the following lines:

Ms. Jean Blake, President
Gourmet Delights, Inc.
Anyplace, U.S.A.

Dear Ms. Blake:

Thanks for sending me your recent direct-mail package on the "Home Cook's Recipe File" collection of recipes.

After studying this promotion I've come up with a list of 14 ways you can improve your mailing package and boost response.

I'd be delighted to meet with you to go over the list in person. No cost. No obligation.

I'll call next week to arrange it.

Regards,

This letter could work well if your goal is to set up a meeting with the prospective client. Of course, there's always the danger that the person receiving your letter wrote the copy you are criticizing, and he or she might take offense at your suggestions. But try it and see for yourself.

You can base your letter on one of the letters reprinted in this book, or try something totally different. The important point is that you are not committed to your first effort, nor will one bad sales letter ruin your reputation. At worst, it simply won't get any response. The important thing is to try a variety of approaches and learn which works best for you.

The easiest way to ensure a solid response to your sales letter is to offer a "bait piece," which is a free booklet, special report, or other information-based premium the recipient gets when he replies. For instance, if you are a speech writer, offer a booklet, "7 Ways to Make Your Next Speech More Memorable and Persuasive."

This sounds like a gimmick, but it's important: Simply adding the offer of a bait piece can double the response to your mailing! Therefore, I advise you to think of, write, and produce at least one bait piece right away, and offer it in all your promotions.

ADVERTISING

Another way to get people to call and ask about your services is to advertise in newspapers, magazines, and directories.

While your own experience and judgment may suggest where to run your initial ads, you can't really predict which publication will work best. As with direct mail, you should test your ads—both the content and where you place them. Only by testing do you know which ad and which publications will get the best response.

Although I have run larger ads, I found that small classified and display ads work best for me. In any case, I recommend that you test small versions of your ad first. If the smaller ad gets good results, you can do a larger version based on the same theme. If the ad flops, rewrite and try again before spending more money on a bigger version.

Where should you advertise? Obviously, in publications read by your prospective clients. And which are these? It depends on your business, on the services you offer, and on the market you want to reach.

Since I'm primarily an advertising writer, I have gotten the best results from two advertising magazines, *Adweek* and *Advertising Age*. I've also advertised, with varying degrees of success, in many other publications, including *Direct Marketing* and the now-defunct *High-Tech Marketing* and *Business Marketing* (which actually morphed into *BtoB*).

A useful reference for people who advertise is the *Standard Rate and Data Service* (see appendix B), which contains comprehensive listings for all magazines and newspapers, plus advertising rates for each publication. *SRDS* is available at most local libraries. However, common sense and experience are at least as useful as *SRDS* in planning your advertising. What publications do other freelance writers in your area advertise in? What publications are your clients reading? What publications do you read?

Don't neglect small local publications, such as the newsletters of local business associations or bulletins produced by professional groups and associations. Once, for two dollars, I placed a 35-word ad in *IABC Employment Letter*, a newsletter published by the local chapter of the International Association of Business Communicators. The first (and only) call I received resulted in an immediate $5,000 assignment to write a small annual report.

Once you have been in business for a time, you will begin to receive many solicitations in the mail asking you to advertise in a variety of professional directories. If you decide to try an ad, insist that it be placed in a separate category, "Freelance

Writers." Don't allow your ad to be lumped in with ad agencies and other companies. Try a small ad or listing first. If you get a good response, you might consider a larger ad in next year's edition.

Some business publications have separate sections for classified and display ads offering freelance writing and related business services. People turn to these sections when they are looking for a service, so your best bet is to put your ad in that section under the appropriate category. However, you might also want to test an ad outside the special section.

My advertising strategy, when I advertised years ago, was to run small (one-inch) ads in the special services sections of *Adweek* and *Advertising Age*. These ads ran continuously all year long. That way, people could always find my name when they turned to the section to look for a writer. I also developed ads for other publications that I ran periodically when I wanted to increase the flow of new business leads.

NETWORKING

Networking is a new name for an old activity that has been going on for a long time: doing business through personal contacts. The purpose of networking is to meet as many people as possible who can in some way help advance your career. And the reason these other people are networking is to find someone—perhaps you—who can help them.

Writing in *Success*, Steve Fishman defines networking as "the single-minded pursuit of useful contacts at every convention, seminar, or neighborhood barbecue. To the networker, every stranger represents an opportunity, the chance to find prospects, reach targets, or meet friends."

Is it necessary to network? I'm living proof that it isn't. I have served well over one hundred satisfied clients, and not a single one has come to me through networking, meetings, or social contacts (most are through direct mail, publicity, referral, my Web site, or word of mouth). I used to tell beginning writers, "Don't bother with networking; you don't need to do it and it's a waste of time."

Now, however, I'm starting to "come out of my shell" (as some of my colleagues have observed) and am making much more of an effort to meet people, make contacts, and join and participate in professional societies and informal groups, even though I'm shy and an introvert by nature.

Why? There are several benefits. First, writing is a solitary activity, and loneliness can be a problem. One way to cope with isolation is to force yourself to get away from the keyboard every now and then. It can be mentally stimulating and refreshing to have lunch with a group of writers or attend an evening lecture sponsored by a local business club. You meet new people, make friends, and exchange ideas.

Forming a network, a group of people you know and who know you, can open up many new doors for you. For instance, at one luncheon I met a man who recently opened his own printing business. We established a good rapport, and he now does most of my printing for me, paying closer attention to my jobs than other printers I had found through local Yellow Pages ads.

Networking builds a base of "people resources" you can count on to help you with many situations. Now I can turn to my card file and find artists, writers, printers, photographers, lawyers, accountants, and many other professionals who can be of service to me or my clients. I know I'll get immediate attention from these people because we've already established a personal relationship, no matter how brief.

Often I will refer one person in my network to another person who can help. For example, an audiovisual producer called and asked if I knew someone who could direct an industrial film for her. I was able to give her the name of an independent director I had met. The referral ended the producer's search and put some money in the director's pocket. And, although I've never asked for it, I'm sure both of these people would be glad to return the favor someday.

Some people keep their resource network a carefully guarded secret, doling out the names as if they were casting bread upon the waters. I don't keep my network secret, and share my resources readily with anyone who asks; in fact, I even post my network on my Web site for all to see and use (go to www.bly.com and click on "Vendors").

Networking can also lead to more business for you. Most often, someone you meet through networking may keep your card and someday give your name to a prospective client. Or, sometimes you meet a potential client directly.

In either case, the more people who know your name, the better. The advantage of networking over advertising is that people you meet through networking are more likely to remember you because of the face-to-face contact.

Before I got involved in networking, I kept an eye on the "Meetings" section of several advertising trade journals and promised myself I'd go . . . when I had the time. As it turned out, I never had the time, and never went to any meetings.

So, what if you are not a networker? What if you are an introvert, like I am? Get over it. You are not ruled by birth, genetics, upbringing, beliefs, or attitudes. You can change yourself and your life to suit your purposes and goals.

You don't have to entirely transform your life into a whirlwind of networking, but you probably should do more than you do now. If you are at home or in your office all the time, you're not meeting people, and it is other people who make our success.

If you're like me, a good way to get started in networking is to join several clubs or associations. Paying the membership dues somehow makes me feel as if I should at least attend a meeting or two to get my money's worth. (I am currently a member of the Business Marketing Association and the Newsletter and Electronic Publishers Association.) Another way to force yourself to go is to call up a friend and invite him to a luncheon or evening meeting. Do it several weeks in advance. Making the commitment early helps to prevent you from backing out at the last minute.

Some additional ideas for more effective networking:

- Always bring a handful of business cards. Exchange cards with everyone you meet.
- Don't be a wallflower. Try to walk over to people and make conversation.
- Get a drink from the bar and hold on to it, even if you don't drink. Having a glass in hand can help shy people overcome nervousness.
- Do not sell while networking. Your purpose is to make contacts, not to get a client to sign a purchase order.
- If you've never attended a meeting of a particular group before, go with a friend who can introduce you to people in the group.
- Dress in proper business attire. Your comfortable, well-worn "writing clothes" are not appropriate for a business gathering.
- The best way to make friends and get people talking is to ask them questions. Instead of telling all about yourself, ask other people about what they do.
- When you get home, follow up by sending people a short note that says, "It was a pleasure meeting you. Let's keep in touch." You might also enclose another business card, a brochure about your services, or a reprint of a recent article you wrote.

- Keep a "contact file" of business cards, organized alphabetically or by type of business.
- When making referrals, think of people in your contact file first. Sending some business to a person is a good way of cementing the relationship between you.
- Wear your name tag on your right shoulder. When someone shakes your hand, his line of sight is to your right shoulder.
- Make sure your name tag has big letters.
- Eat early. It's hard to eat and mingle. Get your fill when you first arrive so you are free to shake hands, talk without spitting food, and work the crowd effectively.
- Do not smoke unless you're speaking with another smoker and are in a room full of smokers.
- If you attend a meeting with a friend or associate, split up. It's a waste of time to talk, walk, or sit together.
- If you know nobody, stand in the food or bar line. That way, you'll always have at least two people to talk to — the one in front of you and the one in back of you.
- Don't be afraid to go up to another lost soul, extend your hand, smile, and introduce yourself.
- Be happy, enthusiastic, and positive. Don't grumble or lament your tough day. People want to do business with a winner, not a whiner.
- Don't butt in. Interrupting can create a bad first impression. Stand close by, and when a pause or opening appears, jump in.
- Know when to cut bait — don't hang around someone who is of no possible use to you. Move on to the next person.
- Stay until the end. The longer you stay, the more contacts you make.
- After the meeting or event, follow up good contacts with a letter or phone call immediately. Otherwise, you will have wasted your time.

PREMIUMS

A premium is a free gift item you distribute to prospects and customers. Most premiums are inexpensive items ranging in price from $1 to $10 and imprinted with the advertiser's logo, company name, address, phone number, and possibly a short slogan or descriptive phrase.

The purpose of giving away premiums is twofold: first, to create goodwill by giving people a gift, no matter how small or inexpensive; and second, to serve as a constant reminder of you and your services.

My dad was an insurance agent. Each year he mailed an attractive wall calendar, imprinted with his company name, address, and phone number, to his clients. Posted on a wall at home or in the office, the calendar put my father's name in front of his customers the whole year-round. An advantage of premiums is that people keep them—unlike advertisements and sales letters, which are read once and then thrown away or filed out of sight and out of mind.

Typical premiums include coffee mugs, key chains, pocket tool kits, golf caps, T-shirts, umbrellas, note pads, golf balls, pocket sewing kits, memo pads, pens, pencils, windbreakers, watches, clocks, balloons, and tote bags. But don't just pick an item out of a premium catalog. The best premiums are ones that are original or unusual or that have a strong tie-in with the product or service you are offering.

Jim Prendergast, president of his own ad agency, uses a stuffed teddy bear as a premium. In fact, the Prendergast teddy bear has become somewhat famous among New York's direct-response advertising community.

Writer Chuck Lebo created a full-sized wall poster as his premium. The poster contains a photo of Chuck along with an essay he wrote about good advertising. The essay, which is a delight to read, makes the poster worth keeping.

I've had great success using my books as premiums. When I want to impress potential clients, I give them a copy of one of my books on advertising or writing, usually *The Copywriter's Handbook* or *Power-Packed Direct Mail*.

The books work extremely well because, for some reason, in the average person's mind a "real" writer is someone who writes books. Even though clients are hiring me to write ads, not books, they are often more impressed with my book and with talking to a real live "author" than they are by the fact that I have a track record of writing winning ads and direct-mail campaigns.

Everyone is curious, and some folks even get sidetracked into asking questions about publishers, literary agents, advances, royalties, book proposals, and related publishing topics. I don't mind, since it is flattering to be asked, and the conversation helps to establish a rapport.

Even if people don't actually read your book, they will give it a prominent place on their bookshelves, especially if you autograph it. I put a sticker with my address and phone number on the title page so that the prospect always knows how to reach me.

Sometimes an idea for a premium just strikes your fancy and seems right. Many years ago, I received a promotional mailing for an item called the Big Clip. The Big Clip is an oversized (five inches long) plastic paper clip that can be imprinted with any message.

Since I always used a big paper clip to hold together the pages of the finished manuscripts I mailed to clients, the Big Clip was a natural for me. I ordered 250 Big Clips imprinted as follows (it helps to know that at the time I specialized in industrial copywriting for machinery, equipment, and chemical manufacturers):

For "industrial-strength" copy . . .
BOB BLY (201) 385-1220

Whenever I finished an assignment, I mailed the copy attached to a stiff piece of cardboard with a Big Clip. One client commented: "Your oversized clip really stands out in my desk drawer. Every time I look down I see your name!" (I eventually stopped ordering the clips, and now transmit copy to all my clients as an attached Word file via e-mail.)

Try a premium yourself. Don't give people the same old coffee mug or golf cap or ballpoint pen that everyone else does. Think of something unusual, original, unique—something that ties in nicely with your sales pitch.

TELEPHONE HOTLINES

Here is an interesting lead generator that can work for you: Create and promote your own telephone hotline. Offer free information to callers. Although most callers will just be calling for the free hotline information, some will be prospects, and this is an excellent way to let them know about you and what you do, and to get them to request details on your services.

Example: Years ago, I created the Advertising Hotline, a nationwide telephone hotline to provide free advice, information, and tips on advertising, direct mail, publicity, and other marketing techniques to ad agencies, large corporations, and small businesses.

Callers who phoned the Advertising Hotline heard a taped "mini-seminar" on an advertising-related subject, such as "Seven Ways to Improve Your Direct-Mail Results," "Ten Ways to Stretch Your Advertising Budget," and "How to Write and Publish a Trade Journal Article." Each week the tape was changed so callers could hear a new seminar. The seminars averaged three to five minutes in length.

Setting up and promoting the hotline was easy and cost about $500. First, I installed a new phone line in my basement, bought an answering machine to take the calls, and wrote and recorded the first taped seminar.

Next, I printed 1,000 Rolodex cards with the hotline's number and a description of the service. I also mailed 200 press releases (with Rolodex cards) announcing the hotline. Response to the press release was excellent. Over a dozen editors called to interview me so they could feature the hotline in their publications.

To spread the word, I included hotline Rolodex cards with all my outgoing correspondence and direct mail. I also mailed the cards with a cover letter to 500 or so key creative directors and advertising managers in the New Jersey–New York area.

How did the hotline benefit me? In several ways:

- Editors wrote articles about me and the hotline in the trade press. This publicity resulted in several new assignments.
- At the end of the hotline, I gave my regular business phone number and encouraged people to call me with specific questions and problems. In this way, the hotline served as a lead generator for my freelance writing business.
- Another message at the end of the tape advertised inexpensive products the caller could buy from me through mail order. These products included transcripts of the hotline mini-seminars, article reprints, copies of my books, and other informative publications dealing with advertising and marketing. In this way the hotline generated a small but steady additional income beyond my regular freelance services.

I discontinued the Advertising Hotline many years ago, when I became too busy to keep up with it. But hotlines are a good promotion. They work. Try it!

SALES LITERATURE

According to studies done by Thomas Publishing, it is extremely difficult to sell a product or service to a business without some type of sales literature describing the product or service and its features. Yet I am constantly amazed at the number of professional freelance writers who have no such literature describing their services.

When someone calls and asks for more information about your service, how will you respond? Perhaps at first you'll want to visit everyone who calls. But you'll soon find that this isn't practical. Some clients are too far away.

Sometimes you'll be too busy handling writing assignments to make sales calls. And, unfortunately, many inquiries come from brochure collectors and tire-kickers who will just waste your time, or from people who for one reason or another will not end up hiring you.

With a brochure, you can quickly and easily respond to all inquiries with solid information and a well thought-out sales pitch. A brochure serves to whet the appetites of those who represent genuine prospects and discourages those who are not serious about hiring you. For example, by presenting your fee schedule up front, you don't waste time talking with people who can't afford you.

Some freelancers use a single brochure to tell their entire story. Ben West, a New Jersey freelancer specializing in financial copy, had a brochure that described the benefits of his services, listed the types of products he had experience in handling, and included a tear-off reply card the reader could use to request an appointment.

Veteran writer Joe Sacco offered prospects a 26-page booklet, "The Professional Copywriter," which contained two lengthy but informative articles on copywriting. It made for fascinating reading. And it was pure information, not promotion.

The only sales pitch was on the back cover, with a brief biography and description of Mr. Sacco's most famous ad campaigns.

Brochures, like the one used by Ben West, look like brochures — they are designed and typeset by professional artists. An alternative to the brochure, used by such successful freelancers as Peter Howard, Richard Neukranz, Sig Rosenblum, Rene Gnam, Luther Brock ("The Letter Doctor"), the late Burton Pincus, Leo Bott, Jr., Wayne Hepburn, and David Powers, is the "package."

Instead of telling their stories in one piece — one booklet or one brochure — these writers send a package of materials consisting of a half-dozen or more different sheets of letter-size paper printed on one or both sides. Some sheets may be typeset, but most are produced using a PC or Mac.

What are the advantages of a package versus a single booklet or brochure?

- The package looks more impressive than a single piece when it arrives on the recipient's desk.
- The package is more easily updated because it is modular and inexpensively printed in small quantities from a typed original.
- In addition, a package consisting of several elements has a greater chance of making an impression on those readers who only glance at mail before throwing it away. As John Caples explains in his book *Tested Advertising Methods* (Prentice Hall):

> If your entire advertising message is contained in a single circular or single booklet, the prospect will devote a few seconds to it, and if it doesn't arouse his interest, he will throw it away. On the other hand, if your envelope is stuffed with half a dozen different pieces, the prospect will probably glance at each piece before throwing it away. Therefore, your six different inserts give

you six opportunities to catch the interest of the prospect instead of only one.

I have been using a package to respond to inquiries about my services for more than two decades. My package, which I promote as a "free information kit," contains the following elements:

- Four-page cover letter, written in question-and-answer format. Thanks the reader for interest in my services. Covers such topics as my qualifications, background, experience, types of assignments and clients I handle, fees, deadlines, revisions, how to order copy from me.
- One-page fact sheet elaborating on my background and experience.
- Client list.
- Testimonials from satisfied clients.
- At least three photocopied samples of my work. I usually send samples similar to the type of work the prospect needs.
- One-page fee schedule. Gives estimated fees for typical projects and lists my terms and conditions.

I like to send a comprehensive package because it answers all questions before they are asked and tells prospects everything they need to know about me to make an intelligent decision about hiring me. My goal is to get people to hire me by mail, without a meeting. The key elements of this package are reprinted in appendix E.

You may not want to send detailed information and may prefer instead to encourage prospects to ask for an appointment. If getting an initial meeting with the prospect is your goal, send less material than I do, not more.

I also recommend posting these materials on a Web site.

Creating a Web site for your freelance writing business is discussed in detail in chapter 9.

KEEPING TRACK OF SALES LEADS

When I first got started, I received relatively few inquiries, so keeping track of them was no problem. Whenever a potential client called, I packed up my portfolio and went running to her office. After the meeting, I pinned the client's business card to my bulletin board, then followed up with calls and letters and waited for the phone to ring.

But now I get many calls and letters every month, and I simply don't have time to meet with all the people who contact me, much less take them all on as clients. Instead, I send my sales literature. When someone does call, it helps me to have a record of who she is and when I mailed my package. A filing system for leads is also helpful for follow-up.

My filing system is simple. For every inquiry I record basic information about the prospect, including:

- Date of inquiry
- Source of inquiry
- Method of response (e-mail, phone, fax, mail)
- Name
- Title
- Company
- Phone number
- Fax number
- E-mail address
- Web site URL
- Street address or P.O. box number
- Mail stop, floor, or suite number
- City
- State

- Zip code
- Industry (or, if an ad agency, type of accounts handled)
- Type of projects they assign to freelancers

You can maintain records of these sales leads on your PC with various software, including mailing-list programs, database managers, or contact managers such as Act or Telemagic, all available from your software dealer (see appendix A).

Or, you can record sales leads on a lead form as shown in appendix E. The forms are punched and kept in a three-ring binder. When I did this manually before switching to contact management software, I used section dividers to separate the forms by several categories:

- Projects pending—for prospects who have a hot project and are likely to become clients within the next few weeks.
- Projects possible—for prospects who might give me an assignment but are not as definite as "projects pending."
- Leads to follow up—the largest section, this contains the files of everyone who inquired about my services within the past year but did not have an immediate project in mind. Most of the prospects in this section requested my literature to keep on file for future reference, in case a project comes up.

Today in my office, we use Act, a contact management software program. Act allows you to organize your lead database by any criteria you choose. And it automatically alerts you when it's time to recontact a lead.

Prior to Act, I had a separate notebook in which I kept forms for leads that were more than a year old. This notebook was divided into two sections:

1. Past clients—companies that have used my services in the past but haven't hired me recently.
2. Old leads—people who requested my package a year ago or more but did not hire me.

The filing system described here, whether implemented manually or on computer, allows you to promote yourself to your best prospects again and again, while keeping good records of every promotional activity.

For example, if I write an article on "How to Sell Insurance through Direct Mail," I can look in my files and send a reprint of the article to advertising managers at insurance companies who previously requested information on my services.

Sometimes this type of follow-up can reawaken the interest of a prospect who received your literature but has forgotten about you. It has resulted in many additional sales for me. Any follow-up of this type is noted under the "Contact Record" section of my form.

As I mentioned earlier, a few years ago I switched from the paper forms and notebooks to contact-management software. Such software offers a number of advantages over paper, a key one being that you can tell the software to automatically remind you to follow up with selected prospects on specific days. Every so often, make a hard-copy printout of your sales-lead database, and also back it up on floppy disk or tape, so that if you have a hard-drive problem, your precious sales leads aren't lost.

ONLINE CHAT GROUPS AND FORUMS

There are many specialized groups and forums on the Internet, including online services that deal with writing, marketing, advertising, public relations, and other business topics. Many writers regularly spend time in these groups and forums having e-mail "chats" with other visitors to these areas. Many of the visitors are your fellow freelance writers, but some are potential clients looking either for advice and help in general or services in particular. By responding to their queries with helpful suggestions, you can establish a dialogue that may lead to the person's hiring you for a project. At some point, go beyond e-mail and reach out with regular mail, phone, and fax to discuss the details and confirm the assignment with the prospect.

Some of the prospects who come to these forums looking for general advice, not specifically for services, will become interested in knowing more about you and, eventually, hiring you when they see how informed and helpful your e-mail replies to them are.

The overall philosophy of the Internet is one of information exchange rather than sales and marketing. You generate leads in forums by participating in online conversations and giving helpful advice, and casually mentioning what you do for a living. If you go online and blatantly pursue sales leads or hype yourself, it won't work and your messages may be blocked.

E-MAIL MARKETING

When you build your database of sales leads, get e-mail addresses as well as physical addresses. By doing so, you build an e-mail mailing list to which you can inexpensively send a promotional e-mail whenever you want.

An alternative method is to do what I do: Scan your e-mail prospect list periodically. When you see the name of a prospect or client you haven't talked with in a while, send a little e-mail just to keep in touch. This periodic greeting reminds the prospect of you, which in turn may prompt him or her to call you to discuss an upcoming project.

In addition, publish a monthly online newsletter with marketing advice and copywriting tips, and distribute this free of charge via e-mail to your clients and prospects. Creating, writing, and publishing your own e-newsletter is discussed in detail in chapter 10.

WEB SITE

Building a Web site won't by itself produce a lot of leads. But you can generate leads by building a Web site and then promoting that Web site in your ads, mailings, literature, and publicity.

By talking about all the good information on your Web site, you encourage people to visit the site. Once they're on it, they can contact you directly if they want to talk about using your services. Have an enrollment page on your site and give people a reason for registering (such as access to a certain secure portion of your site or a free monthly e-mail newsletter).

As people enroll, build a lead database that includes e-mail addresses. Some people who might not call or write will visit Web sites; if they like what they see on yours, they can become good leads for your services.

As a freelance writer, you'll want to put basic information about your services and yourself on your Web site. You might also want to scan some samples of your writing and make them available on a "portfolio" page of the site. This is especially useful when prospects come to you from sources other than the Web, request information, and are in a hurry. In addition to mailing or faxing information, you can give them the option of checking out your Web site, which allows them to immediately check out samples of your work.

If you do business under your own name, register a domain name for your Web site that incorporates your name. If you use a made-up company name, incorporate that in the domain name you register. See chapter 9 for more information on how to write and design a successful Web site for your freelance writing business.

THINK OUTSIDE THE BOX

Don't feel you have to limit yourself to the self-promotion tactics I've listed here. Yes, direct mail, advertising, promotional newsletters, free premiums, and Web sites are all time-tested ways to generate new business. And they work. But you can be even more successful if you go beyond my list and think of new promotions that are truly original.

If inspiration strikes and you get a great idea, try it! Too often we file ideas away for future consideration, then lose interest or enthusiasm. Try something new every once in a while if it can be tested at a reasonable cost. New methods of prospecting—like my Advertising Hotline, described earlier in this chapter—can be fun and exciting, and they can also raise your level of enthusiasm for self-promotion.

8

SELF-PROMOTION: BUILDING YOUR REPUTATION AND VISIBILITY

In the previous chapter, I outlined prospecting methods you can use to generate immediate inquiries about your services. They are blatant pitches to get new business. And they are hard-sell direct response, designed to produce a result on the spot.

In this chapter, I present some "soft-sell" promotional techniques you can use in conjunction with those hard-sell direct marketing methods. Not only do soft-sell promotions — articles, publicity, speeches, seminars — generate immediate response, they also build your reputation and visibility over the long haul. They position you as a qualified expert in the commercial writing field while making large numbers of prospects aware of who you are and what you can do for them.

Nicholas Evans, author of the novel *The Horse Whisperer*, was quoted in the New York *Daily News* as saying, "One of the things I learned about horse-whisperers is that if they want to catch a horse they don't run after it, they let it come to them." That's how public relations and other soft-sell promotions work — potential clients hear or read about you and they come to you, rather than you calling on them.

When people ask me what it takes to market and promote

themselves, I answer, "You can do it if you are willing to invest money and a little time, or a lot of time with minimal money, but you have to put in a substantial amount of one or the other —time or money. You can't do it without spending either."

Direct hard-sell marketing, such as advertising in business magazines, takes minimal time but more money. The soft-sell approaches in this chapter will cost you almost nothing in cash, but you have to put in the time to do the activities.

If you have time and money, you can accelerate your progress in building your freelance practice. If you are unwilling to spend money and don't have the time to do it yourself, you're in trouble and must rethink your priorities.

ARTICLES

A full-page ad in a business publication can cost $2,000 to $8,000 or more. But how would you like to get that space for free? That's what article writing can do for you.

Next to direct mail, writing articles for the trade press is the most effective self-promotion I have used. Articles that have appeared under my byline include "31 Ways to Get More Inquiries from Your Ads" (*Business Marketing*), "10 Ways to Improve Your Trade Show Direct Mail" (*Exhibitor*), "How to Write Business Letters That Get Results" (*Amtrak Express*), "Why Engineers Can't Write" (*CPI100*), and "10 Ways to Stretch Your Advertising Budget" (*Business Marketing*).

These articles have several things in common. To begin with, they are all short. When writing an article for publication, I try to limit the length to 1,500 words so that it can be reprinted on one or two sides of a single letter-size sheet of paper using my office copier. However, if the subject deserves a more comprehensive treatment, I'll write a longer piece.

Second, most of the articles are written in list form, i.e., 22 rules, 10 tips, 31 ways. List articles are easy to organize, easy to write, and easy to read. I can write a short list article in less than an hour. Yet editors tell me that of all the articles I publish, these list articles are the most popular with their readers.

Third, the articles all deal with subjects related to my freelance services. This is intentional. The best way to prove your expertise in a subject is to write and publish an article about it. For instance, if you specialize in writing film scripts and slide presentations, you can impress clients by sending them a reprint of an article you wrote on the topic of audiovisual presentations.

Here are titles for some articles you might write. Feel free to use any or all of them:

- "6 Questions to Ask before You Hire a Freelance Writer and the Answers"
- "10 Ways to Improve Your Business Writing"
- "Why Executives Can't Write"
- "8 Ways to Drive More Traffic to Your Web Site"
- "6 Secrets of Writing Effective E-Mail Marketing Campaigns"
- "7 Steps to Producing Better Brochures"
- "Speaking before Groups with Clarity and Confidence"
- "How to Promote Your Product on a $10,000 Budget"
- "The Do-It-Yourself Sales Letter"
- "The 8 Most Common Mistakes in Employee Communications"
- "How to Get People to Read Your Annual Report"
- "15 Ways to Get Your Name in the Newspapers"
- "Does Radio Advertising Have to be Funny to Sell?"
- "10 Secrets of Successful Fax Marketing"
- "9 Ways to Build a Better Web Site"

Sit down now at your PC and generate a list of article ideas that relate to your particular business and specialties. Print out and pin this list to your bulletin board, and make an effort to get at least one of these articles published within the next two months in a trade magazine your potential clients read.

I use reprints of my articles as supplementary sales literature. If a client asks me about public relations, I send my article on technical publicity. If a client wants me to write a speech, I'll send a reprint of my article on how to give a good presentation.

If a client calls and asks, "What do you know about catalog marketing?" I'll send reprints of columns I wrote on catalog copy for "The Business-to-Business Catalog Marketer." I also post my articles on my Web site, www.bly.com.

Another way to get the most out of your articles is to enclose reprints along with your regular direct-mail letters. You can send the article with your regular direct-mail letter. Or the article itself can be the focus of the mailings.

In one mailing, I sent reprints of an article to 100 clients and prospects, each with a handwritten note that said, "Hi, Jim [or Jane or Joe]. Here's an article you might find interesting, and (I hope) helpful. Regards, Bob." This is a great way to keep in touch with clients or impress prospects. People in business need information and respond well to it.

For small quantities of article reprints, you can photocopy. If you need 100 or more, have them offset at a local print shop. For quantities of 500 or more, the publication may be willing to sell you reprints on glossy stock. Be sure your name, address, and phone number appear on every article reprint and every other promotion you send out.

Which publications should you target? There are three basic types:

1. *Publications dealing with advertising, public relations, marketing, sales, and communications.* Examples include *Business Marketing, Direct Marketing,* and *Advertising Age.* Articles aimed

at these publications naturally deal with such topics as advertising, publicity, effective writing, and marketing.

2. *Trade journals dealing with specific industries that you handle.* For example, I have a number of clients who manufacture chemicals, so I have promoted myself by placing articles in *Chemical Engineering* and *Chemical Engineering Progress.* Many technical publications have monthly columns dealing with nontechnical subjects, such as personal improvement, career advice, or business skills. They will accept articles on communications skills (e.g., technical writing, public speaking, telephone skills, writing a report, writing a memo) as well as general management topics (time management, stress, resumés, career advice, getting along with people).

3. *General business publications, especially regional magazines such as* Crain's New York Business *and* NJ Biz. These magazines are looking for articles on all aspects of business, including communications, marketing, and advertising. Several directories list magazines by category (advertising, sales and marketing, writing, business) and by industry (chemical, pulp and paper, food processing, construction). Two of the best, listed in appendix B, are *Bacon's Publicity Checker* and *Writer's Market.*

But an even better place to start is with the magazines you now read, because you're already familiar with their editorial style and content. For example, if a local business magazine has a monthly column written by a different person each month, write to the editor suggesting an idea for the column.

If you've written for magazines before, you already know the procedure for proposing an article. If you haven't, take a look at *Writer's Market,* which contains some helpful guidelines. The best book I've ever read on how to publish magazine articles is *The Freelance Writer's Handbook* by Gary Provost (New American Library). Others are available; check your local bookstore.

The best approach is to send the editor a brief letter outlining your idea. Tell her the title of the article, the major points you will cover, why this information is important to readers, and your qualifications for writing the piece. In appendix F you'll find a query letter that got me a writing assignment from *Amtrak Express*. I think it's a pretty good example of this type of letter; the magazine even paid me $400 for the article!

Always enclose a #10 self-addressed stamped envelope with your query. If you don't hear from the editor within ten weeks, write a follow-up. If you still don't hear, write another letter saying you are withdrawing the article from consideration. Then try another publication.

If you get an assignment to write an article, and, after you submit it, the editor calls or writes to say that he liked the article, be prepared to suggest another article you can write for her publication. An editor who is enthusiastic about your writing is your best prospect for future article sales.

Once you write several articles for an editor, you may get to the point where you don't need to write query letters. If you have a good relationship with an editor, you may be able to call him or her, give a quick outline of your idea, and get an immediate go-ahead over the phone. It's a real advantage to have at least one editor who will publish your articles on a regular basis. This way, you always have a forum for getting new ideas into print.

A big question freelance writers ask me is "Should I get paid for my articles?" Unlike consumer and general interest magazines, which pay high rates for articles, many trade journals do not pay. And those that do pay offer small fees, called honorariums, which typically range from $50 to $100 per magazine page.

One reason trade journals don't pay is that they figure you are writing the article to promote yourself. Therefore, they are giving you free publicity in exchange for your article. Naturally, if a trade journal offers to pay for your article you should accept gladly. But should you insist on payment from magazines that don't regularly pay for articles? It depends on your goals.

When I started freelancing, I didn't care if I got paid for a trade journal article. The important thing, I reasoned, was to get publicity and reprints for self-promotion. My procedure was to ask what the magazine paid and accept that rate; even if it was zero.

Of course, if you feel strongly that writing articles is a paid activity, then you can try to negotiate a payment. Some editors may agree to it; others will refuse. One strategy that has worked well for me is bartering: I write the article and take a free ad in the magazine instead of a cash fee.

TIP: Run your ad in the same issue in which your article appears. Ads get better responses when you also have an article in the magazine. Why? Because many people who read your article may become interested in knowing more about you. When they see your ad, it becomes easy for them to get in touch with you.

LETTER TO THE EDITOR

If you don't want to invest the time to write an article, but still want visibility in the business and trade press, an easier way to gain visibility is to write a letter to the editor.

Letters to the editor are one of the best-read sections of most publications, so it's likely your letter will get noticed. And you can write a letter in minutes.

What do you write about? Most letters to the editor are written in response to articles that have appeared in the magazine.

You can write to agree with an article, express admiration for it, or express an opposite point of view. I find the latter gets you the most mileage as far as visibility goes. As F. Scott Fitzgerald said, "The cleverly expressed opposite of any generally accepted idea is worth a fortune to somebody."

And it's easy to do. As you read, you'll undoubtedly see something that strikes you as wrong. Dash off a letter to the editor expressing your disagreement and explaining the reason for it, backing up your opinion with a few choice facts. Occasionally this will spark a rash of letters to the editor from both sides, giving you even greater visibility.

PUBLIC SPEAKING

Another great way to build your reputation and get your name around is by giving lectures.

If you've written articles or books, or have gained a reputation locally as an authority in business communications, it is inevitable that at some point someone will invite you to speak. And if you're not invited? Then invite yourself.

Write a letter to the program chairpersons of local business organizations. In the letter, propose a topic and offer yourself as a speaker. Feel free to copy the model pitch letter in appendix F.

Most talks are given at lunch or dinner meetings of local advertising clubs, trade associations, professional societies, or business groups. I have spoken before dozens of groups, including local chapters of the Women's Direct Response Group, Business/Professional Advertising Associations, the Publicity Club of New York, the Financial Advertising and Marketing Association, the American Chemical Society, the Society for Technical Communications, and Women in Communications, to name just a few.

The best place to speak is at any function where potential clients will be in attendance. If you get invited to speak, don't hesitate to ask the person about the meeting. How many people will attend? What companies are they from? What are their titles? Giving talks to people who are not in a position to hire you may be fun, but it won't build your business.

Your topic should be directly related to your business. If

you specialize in writing subscription promotions, and you are addressing a group of circulation managers, one possible topic might be "The Six Most Common Mistakes Made in Subscription Promotion and How to Avoid Them."

The talk should not be a sales pitch for you or your services, however. It should provide the audience with interesting and helpful information on the topic. By giving your audience good advice, you establish yourself as an expert whom they may want to use for further consultation on a paid basis.

Don't feel obliged to be entertaining or funny when you speak. Instead, concentrate on giving the clearest, most informative presentation you can. Speak in a relaxed, natural manner. Just be yourself.

Most luncheon and dinner presentations run 20 to 60 minutes, with extra time for a question-and-answer period. Practice your speech at home and make sure it fits the time limit allotted for your presentation. The speaker who does not rehearse until he knows his material "cold" is inviting disaster.

When you give a talk, bring typed copies of it. Or, if you are using a PowerPoint presentation, you can bring a hard-copy printout of your slides.

Let people know that copies are available at the beginning of your speech. But don't hand them out until after you've finished. If you distribute the speech in advance, people will read it and ignore you.

An alternative to making copies of your speech is to distribute a handout summarizing key points or a recent article you've written on the topic of your talk. All handouts and reprints should have your name, address, and phone number printed on them so people can get in touch with you.

Or, at the conclusion of your talk, say, "If you would like a copy of this presentation e-mailed to you as a PowerPoint, just give me your card." This is a great way to collect business cards from qualified prospects sitting in the audience.

A big advantage of public speaking versus writing articles is that speaking allows you to make contact with people on a more personal level. Speaking at a small- or medium-size gathering, you make more of an impression as people get to see you, hear you, meet you, and shake hands with you. Mixing with the crowd before and after your talk, exchanging handshakes and business cards, is a good way to make contacts for new business.

A disadvantage of public speaking is that you reach far fewer people with your lecture than with an article. A speech on how to write more clearly might be heard by thirty people at a luncheon. An article on that same topic, published in a business magazine, might be read (or at least glanced at) by tens of thousands of readers.

Yet the speech takes at least as much time to research and write as the article. And it must also be rehearsed a number of times. This is why I personally prefer articles to speeches, although I use both types of promotion.

One thing to keep in mind is that a speech can always be turned into an article, and vice versa. You should recycle your material whenever you can. It saves time and gets your message across to the broadest audience possible.

And what about money? Some groups will offer a small honorarium for speakers; most expect you to give them your wisdom for free. If you're doing it for the publicity, then don't worry about the pay. However, if you feel strongly that you should be paid for your time, then by all means ask the program sponsor for a fee. The worst they can do is say no.

TEACHING

Way back in the early 1980s, I taught an evening class in advertising copywriting at New York University. The class, which met from six to eight P.M. Tuesday evenings, ran ten weeks every semester. Although my official rate of pay from NYU was

$26 an hour back then, when you add up the time spent commuting to and from New York, grading homework, and preparing for class, my real take-home pay was closer to $10 an hour.

Friends asked, "Why do you teach the course for ten dollars an hour when you are earning many times that in your writing business and already have a full schedule?"

One reason is that teaching a college-level course is in many ways another form of self-promotion. Saying that you teach a college course in writing, business, or communications is a very impressive credential to parade in front of potential clients.

After all, the product you're selling as a freelancer is you. Doing things like writing articles, giving speeches, and teaching college courses enhances your professional reputation, thus increasing your value in the marketplace. So in that sense teaching is a business builder.

A secondary benefit of teaching, in terms of promotion, is that occasionally prospective clients will call you and tell you they got your name from the course catalog or as a recommendation from the dean's office. I didn't get many leads this way. But a few clients did come to me as a direct result of my teaching at NYU.

Another reason why I taught is that I enjoyed it. It's fun to teach your craft to other people, to encourage beginning writers, to see people improve their writing, advance in their career, or go freelance and succeed at it. Plus, teaching is educational. I learned a great deal about advertising as a result of preparing lectures and teaching the class.

"When I first started as a freelance writer, I taught a lot of writing workshops and classes to find more clients," says Houston-based copywriter Joe Vitale. "I've learned that people like to do business with people they already know. Somehow I had to get people to know me. Workshops are a great way to do that, as everyone felt they knew me after hearing me speak."

How do you get a teaching gig? Some people are lucky enough to be asked to teach. If not, you can always write a letter to the head of the appropriate department at your local community college.

The college already has staff for its existing courses, so your best bet is to propose a new course. For example, NYU has an extensive program of copywriting courses, so my proposal for a specialized course in business-to-business copywriting was a natural extension of their curriculum.

Your letter should also outline your qualifications for teaching the class. If you get turned down, try another department or another college. Small community colleges, especially those with evening classes for adult education, are more likely to be receptive than Ivy League colleges and universities.

You might also try contacting adult community education programs sponsored by local high schools. These programs frequently offer introductory courses on business, communications, and writing-related subjects.

Teaching is one self-promotion activity that you should be paid for. The college is making good money from tuition paid by students attending your class, and can afford a modest salary for you. Hourly rates ranging from $20 to $45 are common for businesspeople teaching evening courses for adults.

SEMINARS

Another alternative to college teaching is to get into the seminar business.

One way to break in is to write to organizations that sponsor and market seminars and offer them your services as a seminar leader. Check newspaper ads and your mailbox for promotions from seminar companies that give courses in your area. The Learning Annex, the American Management Association, Fred Pryor, and CareerTrack are a few of the many seminar organizations that hire seminar presenters, albeit at extremely modest wages.

Another method is to create your own seminar and give it on your own. In this case you would have to market the seminar as well as teach it.

Not only does being a seminar leader get your name around in your industry, but it also can be profitable in its own right. Seminar leaders hired by big companies earn anywhere from $400 to $2,000 a day and up. And if you run your own seminar business, your income can be tremendous, depending on how many people attend your program. I know several writers who found the seminar business so lucrative that they made it their main activity and now do writing only as a sideline!

Gary Blake, a friend of mine who gives writing seminars to managers and support staff at Fortune 1000 companies, came up with a very clever promotion. Although his full twelve-hour seminar program costs thousands of dollars, Gary sent out letters inviting key prospects in the New York area to attend a two-hour mini-version of the full seminar at no charge.

The idea, of course, was to sell these people on hiring Gary by allowing them to sample his methods and techniques in the free seminar. And the promotion worked beautifully. With a 10 percent response to his letter, Gary had no trouble filling the free promotional seminar. At least one attendee has already hired Gary's firm.

OFFER AND PROMOTE A FREE BOOKLET OR SPECIAL REPORT

A few years ago I wrote a short article, published in *Business Marketing*, "31 Ways to Get More Inquiries from Your

Advertisements." I then reprinted the article in booklet form and distributed it widely throughout the local area by sending out a press release and a direct-mail letter.

The body copy of the booklet presents my 31 tips—pure information, no promotion. However, the back cover had my picture and a brief biography, as well as my phone number and address. You could also include in such a booklet a tear-off reply card the reader could use to request more complete information on your freelance writing service.

Printing and distributing information booklets and reports gives you a nice blend of soft sell (giving pure information) and hard sell (offering details on your services). If you've published a good article that people will find helpful, you may be able to get extra mileage out of it by reprinting it in booklet form. Somehow, a folded booklet or pamphlet seems to have more value to people than a regular 8½ by 11 reprint of the article.

Of course, you can publish an original piece of writing in booklet form without first having it published in a magazine. But saying that the booklet's text is reprinted from an article published in a respected journal adds a degree of credibility to the information you're offering.

One way to increase your booklet's distribution is with a press release. Freelancer Richard Armstrong recently sent out a press release to the editors of advertising magazines. The release was about a new booklet he published, *Six Questions to Ask before You Hire a Freelance Copywriter.*

The release, reprinted in appendix E, quotes extensively from the booklet and offers a free copy to readers who write or phone Richard. The booklet includes a tear-off reply card recipients can use to request more detailed information on Richard's freelance writing services.

How did it work? "Mentioned in two publications; thirty-five inquiries received," says Richard. "So far, directly responsible for at least one nice, plum assignment, a three thousand – dollar direct-mail package."

A short informative booklet or report offered free to generate leads for a service or product is called a "bait piece." Today, bait pieces do not have to be printed. You can design your bait piece as a PDF document. Prospects can download it for free from your Web site in exchange for giving you information you require, such as their name, phone number, company, and e-mail address.

NEWSLETTERS

A number of writers and consultants I know use a newsletter to promote themselves and keep their name in front of potential clients.

"A successful marketing program requires that you be consistently visible to your existing clients and prospects, in addition to making them aware of your capabilities and accomplishments," says Jack Miller, a consultant to the construction industry. "Newsletters are an excellent way to achieve that."

Self-published newsletters, mailed regularly, are a powerful way of building your reputation and awareness of your name with a select audience (the people receiving the newsletter) over an extended period of time. And nowadays, newsletters go beyond mere image building.

Many newsletters are mailed with a business-reply card, encouraging the reader to send for more information on products and services offered by the newsletter publisher. Rhu Lund, an independent management consultant based in Oregon, once told me, "For years, I have mailed my simple monthly newsletter published on two sides of an 8½- by 11-inch sheet of paper to seven hundred key corporate decision makers in Oregon. It contains helpful tidbits of information and advice based on my experience or excerpted from recent books, journal articles, and other sources of management information that cross my desk.

"The advantage of a newsletter is that it gets people to come to you, rather than your going to them. I constantly get calls from people who say, 'I've been getting your newsletter for some time. Now I have a problem. Can you help me?' In fact, it has been so successful that it is the only marketing promotion I use."

The newsletter is Rhu's only promotion. Other self-employed professionals who use newsletters say that it is only one part of a comprehensive marketing program.

Should you use a newsletter? As for everything else in this chapter, I say, "Try it and see." It may work for you. If not, you can always stop publishing.

A simple format is best. A promotional newsletter can be produced directly on your PC and duplicated at a local quick-print shop. No need to typeset or hire a professional artist. In fact, it's better to make your newsletter look cheap. A typed newsletter looks like real, hot-off-the-press news, while a fancy design, photography, typesetting, and glossy paper stock can give the newsletter an undesired "promotional" rather than "newsy" look and feel.

How long should the newsletter be? Two sides of a sheet of typing paper is fine. Four pages is also a good length. Longer than that isn't needed. People won't read a longer newsletter unless the content is exceptionally informative or provides exclusive information.

David Wood, a freelance commercial writer in Weare, New Hampshire, has had great success mailing an eight-page promotional newsletter, "Words from Woody," to prospects and clients. The newsletter is mailed quarterly to more than six

hundred companies as a reminder to clients and prospects
that Woody is available. "The kinds of things we do are needed
on an ongoing but irregular basis," says Woody. "Having clients
be aware of you and thinking of you when the job needs to be
done are two different things."

Bob Westenberg, a freelance copywriter in Sedona, Arizona, has a unique format: a newsletter printed on the back
of a postcard. Bob has been sending his postcard newsletter
to a list of 165 clients and prospects monthly for seven
years. "Nothing I've tried has produced more business," says
Bob. "Referrals come regularly; one resulted in fourteen
thousand dollars in freelance work. Existing clients ask
for additional work as a result of the postcard's monthly
nudge."

How often should you publish? Four to six times a year
seems ideal. If you publish more frequently, writing the newsletter may interfere with your other work, or you might run out
of fresh material. On the other hand, people tend to ignore
newsletters that come out less than once a quarter.

What about content? Your newsletter should provide solid
information, tips, and advice on topics related to the professional services you sell to your clients.

For instance, if you write sales-training programs for companies based in Silicon Valley, your newsletter might be titled
"The Silicon Valley Sales Reporter." Articles would provide tips
on how to sell high-tech products.

Having said this, I must confess that I have never used a
newsletter to promote my own business until a few years
ago, when the Internet made it extremely easy and cost-
effective to distribute a newsletter electronically via e-mail.
Prior to that, I always felt that if I was going to write something, I may as well publish it as an article so that it reaches
a wider audience. And because my schedule is fairly hectic,

I didn't want to commit myself to a regular publishing schedule.

But thanks to the Internet, you can now write and distribute a regular online newsletter to thousands of clients and prospects at virtually zero cost. No printing or postage. This is discussed in detail in chapter 10.

9

CREATING A WEB SITE FOR YOUR
FREELANCE WRITING BUSINESS

When it comes to Web sites for freelance writers, the first question to answer is "Do I even need a Web site?"

Well, if you intend to freelance in the business world, the answer is, you can probably get away with not having one. But you're better off with than without.

Reason: All other considerations aside, writing Web copy is a major source of revenue for most freelance copywriters today.

If clients ask, "What is the URL for your Web site?" and you say, "I don't have one," they will be reluctant to hire you for online copywriting assignments. After all, if you don't even have your own Web site, they'll think, how much about online marketing can you really know?

And since online writing is becoming a larger and larger percentage of all copywriting work, cutting yourself off from these assignments will have a significantly negative effect on your revenue. What's more, many copywriting clients are looking for a writer who can handle both their online and offline work. So being perceived as a writer lacking Web savvy might even cost you regular offline writing assignments!

Also, when potential clients can find your Web site on the Internet, it creates the perception that you are a "real" freelance commercial writer committed to the business, and not an unemployed individual looking to earn a few bucks on the side until you find another staff job. Says copywriter Peter Bowerman, "Having your own Web site lends an aura of legitimacy that you may not deserve."

7 STEPS TO CREATING A WINNING WEB SITE

Okay. So you're going to bite the bullet and put up a Web site for your freelance copywriting business. Here are 7 tips that can help you get more bang for your Web buck:

1. *Register a branded domain name.* Avoid domain names that are plays on the word *writing* such as www.writeworks.com. As a writer your brand is your name, so build your domain name around it: My Web site is www.bly.com.

Domain names are inexpensive today, around $10 a year or less. You can register one in literally a minute using one of the many online services for domain name registration. One of the most popular is www.godaddy.com.

Let's say your name is Tom Smith. You go to register www.tomsmith.com and find it is already taken. You could try a domain other than .com, such as .org, but Internet marketing expert Fred Gleeck has another suggestion: Register your name with "the" in front of it, for example, www.thetomsmith.com. "This makes clear that you are the real Tom Smith, and the other guy is an 'imposter,'" says Fred.

2. *Design your Web site to cater to the interests and needs of potential clients,* not casual Web surfers. Don't post content just because it's fun or amusing. Everything on the Web site should work toward a single goal: convincing potential clients to hire you for a writing assignment.

3. *Organize your site so your potential clients can find what they are looking for quickly and easily.* Keep the layout simple. Go to www.bly.com and you can see that all the content is available from a menu of choices on the left side of the screen, clearly labeled (e.g., "Testimonials," "Books").

4. *Think about what your potential clients ask you for when considering whether to hire you, and then provide that on your Web site.* In my case, as a freelance copywriter, the two most frequent questions I am asked are "Who are your clients?" and "Can I see some samples of your work?" So I have a "Clients" page that lists clients in alphabetical order by category (e.g., "Banks," "Ad Agencies").

5. *Make your online portfolio—samples of your work the prospect can view and read with a few mouse clicks—the most important selling feature of your Web site.* On my portfolio, I show a wide selection of samples, organized by category (e.g., "Ads," "Direct Mail").

When you click on the category, you see a list of samples within that category, labeled according to the name of the client. Click on a sample label, and you see a screen filled with thumbnails of every page of the sample. You can then click on each page to blow it up to a size where you can read the text.

6. *If you have written articles, allow visitors to read, print out, or even download them.* This adds tremendous value to your site and may prompt visitors to return periodically. Do not charge visitors for the privilege of reading your articles. The Web is a medium where offering free content is an effective marketing strategy. And it costs you nothing to post your articles and offer them for viewing.

7. *Have a page on your site with pictures and descriptions of any books you have written.* Link these descriptions to www.amazon.com so the visitor can buy the book online with a mouse click. Join Amazon as an affiliate, and you will get a small commission on each sale.

One other point: By offering site visitors something free in exchange for their e-mail address—either a free subscription to an online newsletter or some free content, such as a special report available as a downloadable PDF—you can quickly build a database of site visitors.

By sending the people in your database your regular online newsletter, as well as solo e-mail messages with special offers— an invitation to a speech you're giving, an announcement about the publication of your new book—you can quickly convert Web visitors into paying customers. For the freelance writer who wants to make money, this is the primary reason to have a Web site in the first place.

MAJOR SECTIONS OF YOUR WEB SITE

There is no standard model for creating freelance commercial writer Web sites, and everyone seems to do it differently.

Having said that, certain sections are probably a good idea for you to have. These are outlined briefly below, and you can go to my Web site, www.bly.com, to see an example of each.

- *Home page*—This is the first page you see when you click on the Web site address. I have a short introductory positioning statement about my copywriting services on my home page. Some other writers have long, aggressive, hype-filled sales copy on their home pages. I believe my approach attracts larger, more serious clients. My guess is that a hype-style home page would attract smaller, more entrepreneurial clients.
- *Registration box*—Prominent on my home page is a registration box where the visitor can sign up to receive a free subscription to my monthly online newsletter by providing an e-mail address.

- *Privacy statement* — A link on my home page goes to a brief privacy statement assuring visitors that I will not sell or share their e-mail addresses with anyone else.
- *Services* — A description of the services you provide (e.g., industries served, areas of specialization, types of projects handled).
- *Portfolio* — In this section, you scan and post samples of your copywriting work. When the visitor goes to the portfolio, she sees thumbnails of each page of the promotion. By clicking on any thumbnail, she can make the image large enough to read the copy. Portfolios can be organized by type of project (e.g., direct mail, ads), industry (e.g., pharmaceuticals, electronics), or product (e.g., magazine subscriptions, software).
- *Bio* — A one-page biography of you including your photo.
- *Clients* — Your client list in alphabetical order, organized by industry if it is large.
- *Testimonials* — Favorable client comments about your copywriting services and the results your copy has achieved.
- *Articles* — Any articles you write for self-promotion (see chapter 8) should be posted on an "Articles" page.
- *Books* — Either books you have written or books you think your prospects should read, with a link to www.amazon.com. Contact Amazon to join their affiliate program so you get a modest affiliate commission on every sale.
- *Contact* — An online form the visitor can fill out and submit to inquire about your copywriting services or get a price quotation for a potential assignment.
- *FAQs* — Frequently Asked Questions. On your FAQ page, present a list of questions you are frequently asked by potential clients about your copywriting services, along with

the answers. This saves you and your prospect the time and trouble of having to discuss these points over the phone.

- *Links* — A page of links to Web sites that may be of interest to those who visit your site. When you link to someone else's site, ask them to put a link from their site to yours in return. Reason: The more sites that link to yours, the higher your rankings in the search engines.

I also have some pages on www.bly.com that are fairly nonstandard:

- *Vendors* — A list of mailing-list brokers, graphic designers, and other resources I recommend to my clients, organized by category.
- *Methodology* — Answers the common client question, "How do you work?" Outlines my methodology for writing copy, selling products online, and other services I perform.

A few other Web site design tips for freelance writers:

- Have your key contact information — e-mail address and phone number — prominent on every page of your Web site, not just your home page.
- Keep your content fresh. Periodically update your portfolio with new samples. Add every new article you write to your "Articles" page.
- Be clear about who you are and what you do. It's fine to talk about your marketing philosophy, unique approach, or the results you achieve. But keep in mind the visitor is looking for a writer. So if you are a copywriter, for example, make the word *copywriter* prominent on your home page; don't substitute other terms.

GETTING YOUR WEB SITE UP AND RUNNING

The steps to putting up a Web site are as follows:

1. Register the domain name.
2. Create the site architecture.
3. Write the copy.
4. Design the site.
5. Get the site hosted.
6. Appoint a webmaster.

Let's take a look at each step in a bit more detail:

1. *Register the domain name.* Earlier, we discussed domain name selection and registration. I told you why I think using a domain name that is your name makes the most sense, but it's up to you.

2. *Create the site architecture.* "Site architecture" refers to the structure of the site: what the major sections are and how they are organized.

We've already reviewed the major sections. My architecture at www.bly.com is standard and simple, and I recommend it to you: Have each major section available by clicking on a link. These links are a series of labeled buttons in a vertical column to the left of the home page. We call this the menu.

Use standard language the visitor is familiar with when la beling the buttons in your menu. For instance, use "frequently asked questions" or "FAQ," not "What you want to know." Your bio button should say "Bio" or "About Jim," not "The Man behind the Words." You get the idea.

3. *Write the copy.* Since you are a writer, you will write your Web site copy yourself. Visit the Web sites of other writers for inspiration, ideas, and to get a feel for the tone and style. Here

are a few you can check out, and of course there are dozens of others, all worth looking at:

www.bly.com	www.overnight-copy.com
www.collindayley.com	www.peterfogel.com
www.eileencoale.com	www.russphelps.com
www.jdamico.net	www.sigrosenblum.com
www.jedblock.com	www.steveslaunwhite.com
www.levison.com	

4. *Design the site.* Once you have the copy written, you need to put them into a design that can be posted on the Web. There are three options here:

- Inexpensive services on the Internet allow you to quickly put up your Web site using their templates. These are simple, standard-page designs into which you simply insert your copy. One such do-it-yourself Web site building service is available online from Network Solutions (www.netsolwebsites.com).
- Buy and learn how to use one of the various programs for designing and programming Web sites. Two of the most popular are Dreamweaver and Front Page.
- Hire a freelance Web site designer. I think it makes much more sense. There are plenty around, and it's quite affordable. You can find freelance Web site designers online at www.elance.com.

5. *Get the site hosted.* You need to get your Web site hosted. All Web sites consist of code stored on a computer known as a server. A hosting service is a company that stores your Web site on a server they own and manages all aspects of connecting to the Internet for you.

As with domain names, hosting services have gotten cheaper and cheaper over the years. You can expect to pay a nominal sum, around $10 to $20 a month, for the hosting of your Web site. There are numerous hosting services including Network Solutions (www.netsolwebsites.com) and Coastal (www.coastalwebhosting.com). For a comprehensive directory of hosting companies and other Internet resources, visit www .cheapmarketingresources.com.

6. *Appoint a webmaster.* Finally, appoint someone to be in charge of maintaining and updating your Web site, and handling any technical problems that arise. You might designate yourself as your own webmaster. Other choices include the hosting service or your Web site designer. The point is that someone has to be responsible for making changes and additions, because as time goes on, you *will* want to make changes and additions to your Web site. Trust me on this.

8 WAYS TO DRIVE TRAFFIC TO YOUR SITE

How do you drive traffic to your Web site without burning through all your available cash in a couple of weeks? Here are 8 cost-effective ways to get hits to your site:

1. *Google.* The world's largest search engine, Google facilitates 250 million Web searches per day for its users. As an advertiser, you can buy preference in Google's search engine, based on keyword, on a cost-per-click basis.

It could cost you as little as a dime a click or more than a dollar a click, depending on the popularity of the keyword you want to buy. If the cost of the keyword is 30 cents per click, and 100 people click on your site that day as a result of a Google search on the keyword you bought, Google charges you $30. Google lets you put a limit on how much you spend per day, so the cost can fit any budget.

2. *Overture.* Another search engine that lets you buy preferential rating on keywords. Overture reaches over 80 percent of

active Internet users by displaying your business in search results on leading sites like Yahoo!, MSN, and Alta Vista.

How do you determine what you can afford to pay? Say your average assignment from Web site leads is $2,000 and out of every 1,000 clicks on your site, you get one project, for a total of $2,000. You can afford to pay $1 per hit if doubling your money on the initial sale is your goal.

3. *Affiliate marketing.* Find Web sites that cater to the same market you do. Arrange for them to feature your products and services on their site and in their e-mails. Online ads, e-mail blurbs, and Web pages talking about your product link to your site where the user can purchase the product or service under discussion. The affiliate receives a percentage of the sale ranging from 15 to 50 percent. To recruit affiliates or make money being an affiliate for other marketers, visit www.affiliatesdirectory.com.

Amazon runs one of the first and largest affiliate programs, enabling you to feature books on your site that are related to your topic and of interest to your audience. When the user clicks on the book page, he is automatically linked to www.amazon.com where he can buy the book online. It's a service for your visitors, and you earn a small commission on each sale.

4. *Co-registration.* In co-registration marketing (Co-regs), the user who visits a Web site is served a pop-up window containing a number of special offers; most frequently these are subscriptions to free e-zines. By arranging to have your e-zine or another offer featured in these co-registration pop-ups, you can capture many new names for your online database at a relatively low cost compared with traditional e-mail marketing.

A number of companies can find such co-registration deals for you. One is VentureDirect Online, www.venturedirect.com; another is E-Tactics, www.e-tactics.com.

5. *Banner ads.* Banner ads have seen a resurgence thanks to the increasing sophistication and popularity of Macromedia Flash. In an attempt to capture the attention of the overloaded Internet user, animation and effects in banners have become more sophisticated and dynamic. Banner ads can work but should be tested conservatively and cautiously. And don't get your hopes of a breakthrough too high. Banner ads usually supplement other traffic generation methods and are only occasionally a primary source of unique visits. Are there exceptions? Of course.

6. *E-mail marketing.* Sending solo promotional e-mails to a rented list of opt-in names is an expensive way to acquire new names. Say you rent a list of 1,000 e-mail names for $200, get a 2 percent click-through, and 10 percent of those sign up for your e-zine (see chapter 10). Your acquisition cost to acquire those two new subscribers is a whopping $100 per name. Business-to-consumer marketers have a better chance of success with careful testing of e-mail marketing, since consumer lists are more reasonably priced than business-to-business names.

7. *Online ads.* While sending a solo e-mail to a company's e-list can run from $100 to $400 per thousand, a less expensive option is to run a small online ad in their e-zine. Cost can be as little as $20 to $40 per thousand. The e-zine publisher specifies the format and length of your ad, which is typically 100 words of text with one URL link. The higher up (earlier) your ad appears in the e-zine, the higher the response.

8. *Viral marketing.* At its simplest, viral marketing entails adding a line to your outgoing e-mail marketing messages that says, "Please feel free to forward this e-mail to your friends so they can enjoy this special offer." To work, the e-mail you want the recipient to forward must contain a special offer, either something free (typically, free content) or a discount on merchandise. According to Bryan Heathman of 24/7 Media, 81

percent of viral e-mail recipients will pass the e-mail on to at least one other person.

SEARCH ENGINE OPTIMIZATION

Because so many Web sites crowd the Internet, you need to make an extra effort to get yours noticed. One way to attract attention is to make your site search engine–friendly—that is, to increase the odds that search engines will find your site.

Two key steps can help you do this. First, submit your site to directories such as Yahoo! and The Open Directory. Second, make your Web site findable by search engines that send out "spiders" and "crawlers" to scour the Web. Some of the information those spiders and crawlers seek can be found in "META tags"—words or phrases embedded within the HTML code used to create Web sites.

Before you create your own tags, it's a good idea to take a look at those of others, especially competitors and colleagues. You can easily open a window and view the META tags of any Web site you visit: From your browser's tool bar, choose the "View" menu. Then click on "Source," and a window will open with HTML text that you can study.

The most important META tags are found near the top of the page in between codes like this: <head> and </head>. If you are creating your own Web site, depending on which software you use, all you have to do to add META tags is type the words you've chosen in the appropriate places.

The key META tags for marketing purposes are Title, Description, and Keywords. These tags control what surfers see when your site is listed in the search engines, which means they'll help people decide whether to visit your site.

"Title" is what your visitors see at the top of their browser windows when they are visiting your site, as well as what they will see in their bookmark lists. So make sure each page has a title that makes sense to visitors, not just to you. Be descriptive; failure to put strategic keywords in the page title is often why Web pages are poorly ranked.

For instance, the title of my Web site www.bly.com is "Bob Bly: Copywriter." Search engines rely on the keywords in the title to help people find your Web site. The person looking for me on the Internet will either search my name or what I do, so my title covers both.

When your Web site comes up in search engine findings, the META tag identified as the "description" is often the opening statement people will use to decide whether to access the link. The description should concisely answer the question "What do you offer?" For example: "XYZ Design provides client-focused, creative and effective graphic design, art direction, and project management for marketing communications."

Keywords are the terms your prospects and visitors will type into the search field when they are looking for talent. So consider the words and phrases they might use to describe your services. Put these keywords in your META tags. You also should include your keywords in the first 25 words of your home page.

Here are some additional tips for selecting keywords:

- Use plurals for your keywords, but avoid excessive repetition.
- Misspell keywords if the misspellings are common. For example, DIRECTV, a digital satellite television service, is frequently referred to as Direct TV. If your name is misspelled regularly, include that spelling in your keywords as well.
- Don't always use obvious keywords. Include phrases that may get fewer searches but higher results.
- Don't let your combined keywords exceed 1,000 characters. The fewer keywords, the greater impact they will have.

Maintaining a high ranking in search engines is a time-consuming process. And even with due diligence, these efforts may not get you into the top 30 listings, particularly if you're competing in a niche with well-established and better-financed competitors.

The best strategy is to register with the major search engines and free directories, and supply your information every time you find a site that offers a free listing. Have a seven-word description ready to copy and paste as well as ten keywords. Devote a certain amount of time each month to maintaining your listings in databases and directories.

I had always thought a good strategy for making your Web site easy to find was choosing a domain name that is clearly descriptive of what you do. For example, www.divorceonline.com if you're a divorce lawyer. But Heather Lloyd-Martin, a copy-writer specializing in search-engine optimization, disagrees.

"This doesn't really work," she says. "Plus, it encourages people to come up with those terrible domains like www .make-money-online-with-internet-marketing.com, which are spammy and are usually downgraded in the engines."

She also downplays the importance of tags. According to Martin, "The search engines key on the content—so that's what's important. The title is also important for positioning and conversion off the search engine results page."

If you want search engines to find you, avoid Macromedia Flash or frame pages. "Search engines can find Flash or frame pages, but it's harder for them," says Heather. "The search engines have indexed Flash for a long time now, but it can be horrid for usability, and it won't gain the best rankings. HTML is truly the best bet."

I recently read an article in a marketing magazine that advised repeating keywords on your site as often as possible and in multiple places, so search engine "spiders" can find them.

But my friend and fellow copywriter Nick Usborne says that this advice is not only wrong, but actually harmful.

"This is the worst possible advice you can give to anyone about optimizing their site for the search engines," says Nick. "It's an element of what is referred to as 'keyword stuffing' and is either ignored by the search engine algorithms or, in bad cases, your page and site will be penalized. Worse still, it results in pages that read very strangely to human visitors.

"Using keywords too often on a page and in the META tags is worse than not using them at all. The frequency or otherwise of keywords on a page has nothing to do with whether a spider will find the page. And if a spider finds the page, it doesn't need a keyword repeated frequently in order to find it."

Since I am not a search engine optimization (SEO) expert, I asked a number of consultants in this area—and others more knowledgeable than I—to comment on the topic of keyword usage on Web sites.

"I think stuffing keywords on a Web page is taking the focus off where it needs to be to be successful in any business," says Sean Woodruff. "That focus should be trained squarely on the customer. Stuffing keywords is a gimmick that is focused on tricking the search engines."

"Yes, search engines are important," says Susan Getgood. "But it is far more important to have a good Web site that sells effectively. We should focus on writing good copy that effectively communicates the offer.

"I expect that keywords appear an appropriate amount in good selling copy versus some artificial stuffing exercise, which doesn't fool the search engines and likely damages your overall communications effort.

"Remember, people do land on your Web site from other sources—advertising, direct mail, and so on—not just from search engines. It is silly to try to optimize for one source, if in doing so, you end up with a suboptimal Web site for all the others."

Apryl Parcher advises, "When writing Web sites, it's more important to put keywords in meta tags and descriptions that are only used by spiders, and not seen by the average person reading your page, and also to give your pages titles in HTML that truly reflect the page's contents.

"While it is true that words are picked up on your home page for the search engine description—unless the text block is made into an image—it's usually the first twenty words or so. So make sure that text is what you want people to see when they pick you up on Google. However, you can go all out in putting appropriate search keywords in your description tags without stuffing your actual copy with them."

"Never stuff a Web page with keywords; it's awful advice," says Paul Woodhouse. "You make sure they're in your title and your meta data. Place them carefully in the beginning, middle, and end of your spiel—and in the H1, H2 tags if necessary.

"Any more than that and you risk being penalized by Google—although you can find many a site getting away with it. Also, it simply reads awful. But don't take my word for it. Go to www.seochat.com for expert advice."

"If you want to attract search engine spiders and repel your human visitors, then by all means, stuff away," says Andrea Harris. "Good Web writing is a balance between satisfying the spiders and the humans. But it's the humans who buy your products and services."

"It's not about 'stuffing' copy with keywords," says Richard Leader. "It's about making sure the keywords are in there. Some years back, I ran an online training company. Our course outlines were quite clearly course outlines to a human reader—but not to a spider. We realized we didn't once use the phrase 'HTML training course,' for example.

"So we added it in a few times—and yeah, it looked a bit

clunky. But with just a couple of mentions—for example, 'In this HTML training course, you will learn . . .'—we increased our search engine traffic, and our conversions. So, my advice is not to stuff but to 'strategically place.'"

"Placing keywords within your site is certainly an important part of getting search engines to notice you," says consultant Joel Heffner. "However, my current favorite way to appeal to search engines is to 'ping' entries that I make to my blogs. Search engines love to see what's been added to a blog. If you create a link to a specific page, the search engine will take note of that page as well."

SHOULD YOU HAVE A BLOG ON YOUR WEB SITE?

Blogs, short for "Web logs," are being heralded by many as the "next big thing" in interactive online communication. "Blogging is a true revolution," raves technology writer Fang Xingdong. "One needs no training and there is no cost."

What exactly is a blog? "A blog is an online journal," explains blogging expert Deb Weil in her *Business Blogging Starter Kit* (www.wordbiz.com). "It's called a journal because every entry is time and date stamped and always presented in reverse chronological order."

According to Deb, a blog is "a platform from which to lobby, network, and influence sales. It's a way to circumvent traditional media and analysts. And blogging can be done instantly, in real time, at a fraction of the cost of using traditional channels."

There are many subcategories of blogs. Political blogs came to national prominence during the Bush-Kerry presidential race; they remain active and popular. Blogs can focus on ideas, industries, technologies, products, companies, or social issues, such as adoption.

Online marketing consultant Rick Bruner says that 20 percent of Internet users—approximately 35 million people—read blogs. The common denominator for a successful blog is a topic that people are (a) interested in reading about online; (b) get enthusiastic or excited about; and (c) want to discuss with others.

If your blog is popular and draws heavy traffic, you may be able to sell advertising on it. Theoretically. But in reality, I don't think many companies are interested in advertising on writers' blogs.

So how can a blog make you, the writer, money? By helping to increase your visibility on the Internet. The hope is that at least some of the people reading your blog will be potential clients—and what they read may impress them sufficiently to convince them to hire you for a writing project.

"I've found my blog 'Contentious' to be a fabulous marketing tool for my editorial, training, and consulting services," says writer and *Writer's Digest* contributor Amy Gahran. "I've seen it work well for independent professionals who seek to establish a relationship with their potential audience."

Many writers have told me that their blogs serve a networking function; they help to build valuable contacts and relationships that can lead to paying gigs. For instance, marketing writer Jennifer Rice won Microsoft as a client because an executive there read her blog. She also got hired to do consulting for a restaurant because of her blog.

"I didn't approach either company," says Jennifer. "I got inbound e-mails from these guys saying they had read my blog and liked how I think. They hired me on the spot."

Another marketing writer, Brian Carroll, told me he landed a book contract with McGraw-Hill largely on the strength of his blog. And writer-consultant Kirsten Osolind reports: "I've scored a column in a national magazine and four clients from my blog."

The bottom line: For the writer, a blog *can* generate a measurable return on investment (ROI). Not directly (readers don't pay to access your blog), but by enhancing your visibility and getting your name around to clients, publishers, and editors.

Blogs are relatively easy to set up. There are a number of blogging software packages—some free, others that you pay for—you can use to start your own blog. Visit their Web sites and follow the instructions. Blogging authority Deb Weil recommends www.typepad.com. My webmaster used WordPress (http://wordpress.org) to create my blog (www.bly.com/blog). I've seen a few others, and the blogs they create all look pretty similar to me.

Be sure to have a link to an "RSS feed" on your blog. By registering with an RSS feed, visitors can actually "subscribe" to your blog—in that the RSS feed automatically notifies them whenever you add a new item or "post" to your site.

One benefit of having a blog is that it can increase both your search-engine rankings and (as a result) the traffic to your Web site.

"The search engines, especially Google, love blogs," says blogger and online marketing consultant Paul Chaney. "You'd be amazed at how many of your posts will end up in the top ten returns. If search engine optimization is a concern to you, blogs are the best way I know to move up the ladder as well as increase your page rank."

Now, here's a warning. If you are a professional writer, the quality of the writing in your blog should be as good as it is in your essays, articles, books, and other conventionally published writings. There is a noticeable tendency among some bloggers to ramble and produce stream-of-consciousness musings for their blogs. Your random thoughts and insights may be of interest to you, but few others care.

What type of content should you post on your blog if you want to attract and interest readers—and be taken seriously by potential clients, editors, and publishers in a position to buy your words? Your blog content should consist of some or all of the following:

- Insightful analysis and carefully considered opinions.
- How-to information—tips, strategies, methods, and ideas.
- Inside information, interviews, and research presenting little-known facts and data.
- Up-to-the-minute links to other blogs and Web sites of interest to your readers.

Your blog should focus on a well-defined area, which of course should be the things you write about in other media: marketing, gardening, distance learning, politics, or what have you.

When writing my blog, I write the entries in Word first, which makes it easy to edit and review each entry. I usually write several blog items at a time, and store them in a Word file called "blog entries."

Keep your posts relatively brief. Messages longer than a few paragraphs or points are best suited to other formats, such as an article, e-book, or special report.

Finally, keep your blog active. Blogger Deb Weil suggests a minimum frequency of at least one new entry every week.

Remember, if you stop posting items to your blog, people will remove it from their RSS feed list—dropping you from the list of blogs they read on a regular basis. You'll be reducing your readership, which goes against the whole point of a blog: to get your ideas and thoughts read by as wide an audience as possible.

10

WRITING AND PUBLISHING YOUR OWN E-ZINE

Do you get any electronic newsletters e-mailed to you on a monthly, weekly, or daily basis? Then you are an "e-zine" subscriber. But have you considered publishing your own e-zine instead of just reading those produced by others?

I publish a free monthly e-zine, and it has been my most successful self-promotion, generating thousands of dollars in extra income every month. Yours can, too.

Next to putting up a Web site, the most effective Internet marketing you can do for your freelance commercial writing services is to write and distribute a free online newsletter, also known as an e-newsletter, or e-zine.

In the previous chapter, we discussed a number of methods you can use to drive traffic to your Web site, including pay-per-click advertising and search engine optimization. When you offer a free e-zine, you give those visitors to your Web site a reason to register. They give you their e-mail address and you in turn provide an e-zine.

Without such an offer, people come and go on your site. Many of them are interested, but don't buy anything or contact you. And you have no way of keeping in touch so you can remind them of your services and publications, or make a sale to them.

Put a registration box on your home page where the visitor can subscribe to a free online newsletter in exchange for giving you her e-mail address. Not only has the visitor shown interest in you, your services, and your products, but by signing up for your online newsletter, she has also given you permission to send her e-mails.

Through your e-zine itself, as well as solo e-mail announcements to your subscriber list, you can generate substantial business and income you might not otherwise have gotten. Instead of "wasting" Web traffic, you convert it to a list of qualified prospects. Figure 10-1 illustrates how this method of online marketing, known as the Agora Model, works.

Internet marketing expert Fred Gleeck estimates that a good list of e-zine subscribers is worth, in extra income to its owner, between 5 cents and a dollar a name per month. If you have a list of 10,000 subscribers and it generates 20 cents per name per month, that's an extra annual income of $24,000 a year.

About five years ago, I started writing and publishing a free monthly e-zine, "The Direct-Response Letter." In it I write about what interests me: direct marketing, copywriting, online marketing, small business, and related topics. My readers—I currently have more than 70,000 subscribers—include corporate marketing types, small business owners, budding entrepreneurs, marketing specialists, writers, and self-employed professionals.

Go to my Web site at www.bly.com and notice the e-zine sign-up box on the home page. You can also click on "Archive" within that box to access an online archive of all past issues of my e-zine and see the design, format, style, length, and content of my e-zine, a sample of which is shown in figure 10-2.

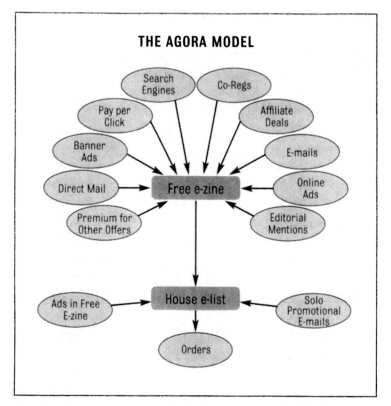

Fig. 10-1. *Having your own e-zine is the fastest way to build a large online list of potential clients.*

Fig. 10-2. *Copywriter's E-zine*

From: Bob Bly

Subject: What's working in online marketing today?

Bob Bly's Direct Response Letter:

Resources, ideas, and tips for improving response to business-to-business, high-tech, industrial, Internet, and direct marketing.   June, 2005

You are getting this e-mail because you subscribed to it on www.bly.com or because you are one of Bob's clients, prospects, seminar attendees, or book buyers. If you would prefer not to receive further e-mails of this type, go to www.bly.com, enter your e-mail address, and hit Unsubscribe.

And feel free to forward this issue to any peers, friends, and associates you think would benefit from its contents. They will thank you. So will I.

Publishing giant reveals the secrets of how to write a best-seller

The president of one of the nation's largest publishing houses recently spent two days answering every question potential authors want to learn. Including:

• What does it take to create a best-selling book?
• How do publishers really decide what books to publish?
• How do you land a literary agent?

A must-have guide for every serious writer—never-before-told information on 10 CDs. I've published five dozen books, and even I learned some new tricks!

For details, click below:

http://bestsellingauthor.com/affiliates/tracker.php?AID=055267&BID=6978

Only 3 companies will sponsor my "Effective Technical Writing" seminar this year

Want to teach your engineers, systems analysts, scientists, techies, and managers to write better and faster? Book me to present my popular "Effective Technical Writing" seminar at your site.

I'm only giving 3 more of these technical writing seminars this year. To schedule a class for your company, call **Fern Dickey** at **201-797-8105.** Or for a free seminar brochure, click below:

[LINK]

[4–5 more articles here]

Now, here's the benefit. Since these 70,000 people read my e-zine every month, they feel they know me. I am someone they trust, no longer a stranger. And so they will buy products and services I either produce myself or recommend.

If I have a new book coming out, mentioning its publication in my e-zine causes a big jump up in the book's sales ranking on Amazon that day: the e-zine helps sell copies.

Or, maybe I want to drum up some corporate writing assignments. By making a special offer, I can quickly get work. In one issue, I offered one-third off my regular rate for writing an e-mail message. Within 24 hours, I had twelve companies that wanted to take me up on the deal.

In another issue, I wanted to generate sales leads so I could get a new client in the software industry. I offered a free audio-cassette, "Selling Your Software with Direct Mail," which was a recording of a teleconference I had given for the Software and Information Industry Association (SIIA).

Within 48 hours after sending out the issue, I had 200 requests for the tape; these inquiries cost me virtually nothing to generate. If I had used a lead-generating sales letter aimed at the software industry, and that letter generated a 1 percent response, I would have had to mail 20,000 letters to get that same 200 inquiries.

You can make these offers within the body of your regular e-zine or in a solo e-mail promotion sent to your e-zine subscriber list. I send out my e-zine once a month, and do approximately two to three solo e-mails each month.

One of the solo e-mails is for one of my books or services; the other is to promote other people's products—typically books, e-books, or courses. For such promotions, I receive an affiliate commission ranging from 30 to 50 percent of the sales generated, as discussed in the next section on affiliate deals.

In fact, you can't really market yourself and your writings effectively online unless you have an e-zine. Here's why:

The Internet is a powerful new channel for marketing both your freelance writing services and your content (e.g., books, tapes, special reports).

On the Internet, renting lists of e-mail addresses, and sending e-mails selling products and services doesn't work, even for big corporations that can afford to do so. The lists are too expensive, and the response rates too low to make them profitable.

Many have tried and failed. The reason marketing to "cold" e-mail lists doesn't work is that people are reluctant to buy online from strangers. And when you send e-mail to a rented list, you are a stranger to them.

Online marketing, on the other hand, is a two-step process. In the first step, you offer a free subscription to your e-zine to everyone who visits your Web site.

While people won't generally buy from a stranger online, they can be induced to request freebies. Offer them a free e-zine in exchange for their e-mail address, and many will take the bait. Tell everyone you meet—publishers, editors, clients, prospects, fans, readers, audiences at your lectures—you will give them a free subscription to your e-zine in exchange for giving you their e-mail address. By actively promoting your newsletter, you can build your subscriber base until your e-zine reaches thousands of readers on a regular basis.

By signing up all these folks as subscribers, you in essence convert them from casual readers and onetime buyers to loyal fans, and eventually to paying customers who buy your writings or writing services when you offer them online.

Many, even most, of the subscribers who sign up for your free e-zine are not potential clients. Sending your newsletter to people who are not potential clients would be a problem if you were printing and mailing a paper newsletter, because you'd be spending a lot of money reaching people who are not prospects. But with an e-zine, the cost of production and distribution is virtually zero, whether you are e-mailing it to 300 or 3,000 or even 30,000 subscribers or more. Therefore, it's not a problem having some "wasted circulation" among non-prospects.

And many of those readers who are not prospects for your writing services *do* need help with marketing. So you may be able to sell them other things, like e-books, books, and information products, whether written by you or other people.

AFFILIATE DEALS

When you publish an e-zine as I do, online marketers will approach and ask you to endorse and recommend their product to your e-mail list on an affiliate basis. You either give the product a nice plug in your e-zine, along with a link to a URL where the reader can order the product, or you send a solo e-mail to your list promoting the product, with a link to the order page URL.

You don't charge the online marketer a penny to promote his product up front. But for every unit sold, you get an affiliate commission. Amazon pays the lowest affiliate commission I get: just 15 percent of the sale price. Most smaller, entrepreneurial online marketers pay affiliate commissions ranging from 30 to 50 percent of the sales price.

The nice thing about affiliate programs is there is virtually no work or effort on your part: Someone else produces the product, writes the promotion, and gives it to you. You can send an e-mail blast to your list at the click of a mouse using one of the services or software packages described later in this chapter.

In return for virtually no work, you can get nice affiliate checks for hundreds or thousands of dollars on each promotion. How many can you do in a month? If you publish a monthly e-zine, I think you can safely do three solo affiliate e-mails in the same month, as well as do a blurb in the e-zine itself on an affiliate product.

That works out to four affiliate promotions a month to your e-zine subscriber list. If each deal brings you a commission check of $500, you will average $24,000 in annual income just from your affiliate promotions.

How do you know when you are doing too many affiliate promotions or sending too many e-mails to your list? They will tell you: You'll get complaints by e-mail, with many subscribers asking to be removed from your list. When that happens, pull back on the frequency until it stops.

When someone asks you to do an affiliate deal or endorsement of their product to your e-list, insist on getting a free review copy of the product. You should never recommend a product to your list that you haven't reviewed and don't think is a great value.

Must you disclose in your e-zine that you are getting paid an affiliate commission on a product you recommend there? Internet marketing expert Deb Weil says, "You don't need to disclose it's an affiliate link. Your reader either doesn't have a clue what an affiliate link is, or notices that it *is* one and is happy to give you the revenue share because of the value of your e-zine."

WRITING AND DESIGNING YOUR E-ZINE

Here are a few tips for creating and profiting from your own e-zine:

1. Use text instead of HTML. It is easier and faster to create, and requires no design work. Set the left margin at 20 and the right at 80, so the column width is approximately 60 characters. Put a hard carriage return after every line; otherwise, when you distribute your e-zine, the lines may break oddly. You can write your e-zine in Word, but save and distribute it as a text file. I separate articles in the e-zine with a horizontal

dashed line, and put the headline of each article between three asterisks on either side.

The major disadvantage rate of text is that you cannot measure the "open rate," which is the percentage of subscribers who actually click and open your e-newsletter to read it. According to Internet marketing expert Deb Weil, open rates for quality e-zines are in the range of 30 to 40 percent.

A relatively new format, "text in an HTML shell," lets you send out an e-zine that looks like text but is actually coded in HTML, so that open rates can be measured. This is a good format to use when you prefer the appearance of a text e-zine, but want the ability to measure open rate.

2. Schedule publication for once a month. To publish more frequently creates too much work; to publish less frequently is missing an opportunity to maintain awareness of you and your writing in the reader's mind.

3. Keep your e-zine brief. Mine has just five or six items per issue, with each article typically just two or three paragraphs. That means you can read any article in less than one minute, and the whole issue in about six minutes, though I doubt anyone reads every article in every issue.

4. In my e-zine, 80 percent of the content is useful how-to tips on my specialty, direct marketing, with the other 20 percent being plugs for products and services. This seems to be the ad ratio most readers will accept; more self-promotion than that, and you risk having people "unsubscribe."

5. Since you're already a writer, you'll have no trouble writing your own e-zine. But what content should be in it? If you're a freelance commercial writer, tips relevant to your writing specialties: online marketing, public relations, speechwriting, direct mail, Web sites, etc.

6. Ask for subscriber feedback; e-zine readers love to be heard. I often tell my subscribers I am working on a new book, name the topic, and ask them to share their knowledge to help

me research my book. They love to do it, and I get free research assistance out of the deal!

7. Make the "from" line of your e-mail consistent, so it will always get through to readers who have put you on their "whitelist" (explained later in this chapter) of e-mails they will accept.

8. Make the subject line of each issue different and interesting to obtain a greater open rate and entice subscribers to read the issue. I find questions work well as subject lines, as long as the question is answered in one of the articles in the e-zine. One of my most effective subject lines was, "Do question headlines work?"

9. After the "From" and Subject lines, put the name of the newsletter and a descriptive tag line that explains the content, theme, and purpose of the newsletter as well as the benefit it offers to the reader. Mine (see figure 10-2) says "Resources, tips, and ideas for improving response." Also put the date of the issue.

10. In every e-mail you send to your list, both your e-zine and solo e-mails, you must include "opt-out" language that shows the reader how to get off your list if he or she does not want to receive any more e-mails from you. Mine says "You are getting this e-mail because you subscribed to it on www.bly.com or because you are one of Bob's clients, prospects, seminar attendees, or book buyers. If you would prefer not to receive further e-mails of this type, go to www.bly.com, enter your e-mail address, and hit Unsubscribe."

11. You can increase your e-zine readership by urging subscribers to pass their issue on to friends and colleagues. I do this with a "viral" marketing message under the masthead and following the opt-out language. It reads: "Feel free to forward this issue to any peers, friends and associates you think would benefit from its contents. They will thank you. So will I."

12. Since you are publishing an e-zine to generate business,

and are not in business just to give away free information, it is acceptable to make a small sales pitch in each issue about your copywriting services, along with your contact information. Here's how I end every single issue of my e-zine, the "Direct Response Letter," without exception:

60-second commercial from Fern Dickey, Project Manager

Bob is available on a limited basis for copywriting of direct mail packages, sales letters, brochures, white papers, ads, e-mail marketing campaigns, PR materials, and Web pages. We recommend you call for a FREE copy of our updated Copywriting Information Kit. Just let us know your industry and the type of copy you're interested in seeing (ads, mailings, etc.), and if Bob is available to take your assignment, we'll tailor a package of recent samples to fit your requirements. Call Fern Dickey at 201-797-8105 or e-mail fern1128@optonline.net.

Bob Bly	22 E. Quackenbush Ave.
Copywriter/consultant	Dumont, NJ 07628
rwbly@bly.com	phone 201-385-1220
www.bly.com	fax 201-385-1138

WHAT TO PUT IN YOUR E-ZINE

By studying my e-zine and other successful e-zines, you can quickly get an idea of the type of content you should feature in yours. The articles should relate to your area of writing specialization of expertise. Therefore, if you are a freelance copywriter specializing in online copy, your articles should relate to search engine optimization, Google adwords, HTML design, domain name selection, online conversion, and other topics related to online marketing.

By far, the most popular, best-read articles for e-zines are short tips: practical how-to information the reader can immediately put to work to improve his marketing, writing, Internet sales, or whatever the topic.

Here's an example of a tip from my e-zine that readers told me via e-mail that they really liked:

Give Your Writing the Breath Test

Short sentences are easier to read than long sentences. But how long is too long for a sentence?

To determine maximum sentence length, use the "breath test." Without taking a gulp of air, and just with the amount of air you ordinarily have in your lungs, read the sentence aloud at a normal conversational speed and volume.

If you run out of breath before you get to the end, the sentence is too long.

Solution: Break it into two sentences at the point where a new idea is introduced.

So when you're writing your e-mail, think in terms of tips and how-to advice. Keep them brief, light, practical, and fun.

What else can you put in your e-zine? Here are a few ideas:

• Letters to the editor—feedback that readers send you via e-mail.
• Announcements of all of your upcoming speaking engagements, seminars, and tele-conferences—your e-zine should be the single source folks can consult to find where they can see you speak.
• Recent projects—brief summary of recent assignments, telling people the clients you worked for and what you wrote for them.

- Recommended vendors—when you've discovered a great vendor, like the guy who came to repair your PC when your hard disk crashed and fixed it in an hour, your readers would like to know about it. Share these resources with them in your e-zine.
- Recommended Web sites—when you come across an interesting Web site that you think your readers would enjoy, let them know about it.
- Book reviews—share your reviews of books on relevant areas such as business, marketing, and writing; include a link to Amazon so your reader can click and instantly order the book online. Join Amazon's affiliate program so you get a commission.
- News—timely and important news events in your field.
- Publications—whenever you're coming out with a new book, or even an article in a major publication, let your subscribers know it.
- Quotations—I enjoy finding and reading pithy quotations, and I share them with my readers in my e-zine.

MAKE SURE YOUR E-ZINE GETS THROUGH TO YOUR SUBSCRIBERS

Everyone seems to agree that e-mail marketing is one of the most effective and powerful forms of Internet marketing today. After all, it is quick to deploy, provides immediate measurable results, and delivers a high return on investment.

But there is a downside. Successful e-mail marketing requires experience, expertise, and knowledge of the constantly changing e-mail filtering, spam-eradicating, firewall-building software industry. It has been said that more than one out of five e-mails have problems with delivery—which significantly erodes response rates and program effectiveness.

It's not enough to build a list of interested customers or

clients, send them an informative, engaging e-newsletter once a month, and market products or services to them in the process. You've got to know how to get the messages *delivered,* and then *read* by the recipient. In other words, creating wonderful e-mail messages is only *part* of the process — the messages are absolutely worthless to you if never received by list members.

As a result of corporate and Internet service provider (ISP) filters, blacklists, and constant e-mail address flux, permission-based marketers face obstacles in their attempt to deliver solicited, confirmed-consent messages to the in-boxes of customers and subscribers with whom they've established relationships.

Deliverability is key. With e-mail, deliverability refers to the ability to complete delivery of a message to a recipient's inbox. So, what can you do to ensure receipt of your messages?

Let's agree on one thing: Delivery *begins* when a recipient grants permission to receive your e-newsletter. If your e-mail marketing strategy is based on this premise, delivery challenges are significantly minimized. With permission, the customer or recipient can provide recourse if an ISP, spam filter, or blacklist blocks your messages.

A number of factors hinder or prevent solicited e-mail delivery:

- *ISP-blocked incoming mail.* The most common version of ISP blocking. Many ISPs, especially large ones, maintain internal blacklists of IP addresses that are denied any incoming connections. Frequent customer complaints about traffic from particular sources are the most common cause of this kind of blocking. ISPs tend to block IP ranges without any notification, as they routinely handle complaints about hundreds of thousands of individual e-mail sources.

- *ISP-blocked outgoing mail.* Your ISP blocks outgoing traffic to another ISP. This is rare, as most ISPs block incoming traffic, but it has been known to happen.
- *Distributed content filters.* Several anti-spam companies help ISPs and enterprise customers cope with the influx of unsolicited e-mail. These blocking systems employ complex content analysis processes that scan message content and create message "signatures" that are disseminated among the filtering company's client base.
- *Public list.* Publicly accessible blacklists and whitelists, maintained by volunteers, are often used by smaller ISPs and companies without dedicated e-mail administrators. Listing criteria can be reliable or nearly arbitrary, depending on the list owner's preferences. Administrators select the lists that most closely match their company's policy.
- *ISP content filters.* Similar to distributed content filters, ISPs often employ content filters created internally or adapted from others. Content filters scan for a variety of red flags. They can even learn new patterns in spam e-mail, such as inserting periods in words that would normally trigger a block.
- *User content filters.* Almost every e-mail client provides junk mail filters. These vary widely in complexity. Microsoft Outlook's filter simply searches for offensive keywords and key phrases, whereas more robust filters can be configured to run from a user's desktop.
- *User lists.* Recent upgrades to e-mail applications, including AOL, MSN, Yahoo!, and Outlook, allow users to compile their own blacklists and whitelists of individual and domain addresses. There are also "challenge/response systems" that extend this process by requiring non-whitelisted senders to respond with a code or other confirmation before their messages are delivered.

• *Message bounces.* A "soft" bounce is a temporary failure in which the e-mail wasn't delivered but may be retried in the future. It could be because the mailbox was full, or the receiving mail server didn't respond to the delivery attempt. A "hard" bounce means the message is permanently undeliverable. Maybe the address is invalid, or a remote server is blocking your server.

Naturally, you want to minimize the number of "hard" bounce-backs, those permanently fatal messages that mean loss of contact and "no sale." There are a number of ways to ensure greater delivery rates. The first requires cooperation from the recipients, as they are the ones who need to add your e-mail address to their "accepted" messages list.

Getting your "From" address added to your recipient's address book or personal *whitelist* — a list of approved sources from which the user will accept e-mail messages — is, more and more, a crucial step in getting your e-mails into the in-box rather than into the spam folder, or worse yet, the trash folder. More and more people, both business and consumer e-mail users, are adopting the use of spam filters, or upgrading their e-mail clients that include some form of spam filtering/whitelist feature.

You need to remind people to take the step of adding your "From" address to their address book/whitelist. Consider adding a single sentence at the top of your e-mail. Here are three examples of effective reminder statements:

To ensure our e-mail is delivered to your inbox, please add the e-mail address delightfulmessages@ourcompany.com to your Address Book or junk filter settings.

To ensure regular delivery of our e-newsletter, please add us (youwanthis@thiscompany.net) to your Address Book. Thank you!

To guarantee delivery of this newsletter, ·please add ournewsletters@mycompany.com to your e-mail Address Book.

You may wish to go so far as to explain to your recipients how to set their junk filter settings in a special section of an e-mail message, or devote an entire mailing to this issue. Review the process for the major e-mail applications and Internet service providers, and write up a step-by-step instructional e-mail message. I've even had a number of clients offer phone customer support assistance to any reader who may need a "walk-through."

The means by which the various ISP and e-mail server programs identify unwanted or inappropriate e-mail messages change fairly often and it is necessary to be aware of new implementations. But, some important essentials can help make sure your e-mails reach their recipients.

To begin with, be careful with terms and characters used in your promotional e-mail campaigns. Microsoft's Outlook junk e-mail filter will send your e-mails straight to the "delete folder" if it finds things such as "for free," "cards accepted," or "order today" in your e-mails. However, the list is under constant revision, and you should regularly update your in-house list of unwelcome words. Visit the URL below to view a current list of words and terms that Outlook will filter: http://office.microsoft.com/assistance/9798.newfilters.aspx.

Among the various filters AOL applies to incoming mail, one in particular (while easily avoided) will *completely block* your AOL message delivery if triggered. This new filter is an HTML validator that scans incoming messages for HTML syntax and formatting errors. If invalid HTML is detected, the message will be rejected.

The error itself does not need to be a glaring omission to trigger this filter. Any syntax inaccuracy may be sufficient. Ending a link tag, for example, with "<a/>" instead of the correct

"</a>" will cause your message to be rejected. This filter was presumably employed to combat a favorite spammer tactic of inserting nonsense HTML code to foil standard content filters.

Establish procedures for proofing e-mail campaigns. Your proofing checklist should include HTML validation. Popular HTML editing software already offers effective validation tools and will highlight any errors on the fly, as your message is being created.

For a complete reference specification of HTML formatting, visit the World Wide Web Consortium documentation pages (http://www.w3.org/MarkUp/). Also, you can use the HTML validator in your e-mail application or a third-party validator such as the W3C Markup Validation Service (http://validator.w3.org/).

10 WAYS TO GET YOUR E-MAILS DELIVERED

Here are 10 ways to help increase the likelihood your e-mail messages will be delivered by the receiving ISP and avoid future deliverability problems.

1. *Create a reverse Domain Name Server (DNS).* Make sure your outgoing mailing IPs have valid RDNS (Reverse DNS) entries set up. This ensures when a receiving e-mail server checks who owns the IP trying to connect to it, you'll come up as the result, passing one of the many basic checks ISPs do to deter spammers.

2. *Set up a Sender Policy Framework (SPF).* An SPF is an additional step to verify an e-mail sender's identity. The protocol is fairly easy to set up; your network administrator should be able to do it in less than five minutes. SPF adds another layer of authentication to your outgoing e-mail and protects against "phishing" attacks on your brand. You should know that some ISPs, such as AOL, *require* SPF to be implemented to be considered for their whitelists.

3. *Make only one connection.* When connecting to an e-mail server, send only one message per connection. Some systems still try to shovel as many messages through one connection as possible, which can be likened to throwing 500 e-mail addresses into the BCC field. ISPs frown on this technique, as spammers who want to get as many messages in before being blocked typically use this approach.

4. *Limit sending rate.* Though the ideal send volume depends on the list's nature, a good rule is to limit your transmission to 100,000 or so messages per hour. Keep in mind you will also need to accept feedback in the form of bounced messages—your outgoing speed shouldn't affect your ability to receive bounces.

5. *Accept bounces.* Some e-mail systems, especially older ones, have a nasty habit of rejecting bounce messages. These "bounced bounces" arrive at the receiving ISP and can raise red flags. Nothing irks an ISP more than sending a response that a recipient doesn't exist, only to have the notification rejected and the mailings continue.

6. *Validate HTML content.* One of the dirtiest tricks in a spammer's arsenal is invalid, broken, and malicious HTML code. If you use HTML in your messages, make sure your code is error-free.

7. *Avoid scripting.* Security risks due to script vulnerabilities in e-mail browsers have increased over the years. The result is that most scripts are stripped out of messages. Some e-mail systems reject messages outright if scripting is detected. For greatest delivery success, avoid using any scripts in messages. Instead, drive your readers to your Web site, where use of dynamic scripting can be fully implemented.

8. *Understand content filtering basics.* Ignorance of filtering approaches is no excuse for not getting messages delivered. Read bounce messages, track which messages had high bounce rates and low open rates, and see if you can reverse-engineer offending content.

the time-consuming process of an initial meeting. Typically, I will send my package, then follow up with a phone call. I tell the prospect I am calling to make sure he or she received the information that was requested and to see if this looks like the type of service he or she needs. I also offer to send additional information or answer any questions. If the prospect responds positively, we might discuss any specific assignments he or she has in mind. I encourage the prospect to send me authorization and background material by postal mail or e-mail, so I can proceed with the work if I am hired.

- *Literature.* Some writers send their packages and do no follow-up. They take on assignments only from prospects who respond to the packages without being prodded in any way. Naturally, any follow-up discussion generated in this manner will be with people who are highly motivated and enthusiastic about your services. However, unless you are so busy that you really don't need more work, you will probably have to do some type of follow-up after you send your letter or samples.
- *Online portfolio.* If you have a Web site, you can, when a prospect calls, ask her, "Are you online right now?" If she says yes, or is willing to go online as you talk, direct her to look at your online portfolio, client list, testimonials, and other key pages of your site that can answer her questions about you and your services.

The advantage of having a Web site is this: When a prospect has an immediate need, she wants to know right away whether you are qualified. The sooner she is assured of your qualifications, the more likely she is to hire you.

When your information kit is only in paper form, there is a 24-hour delay in getting your qualifications into the eager

9. *Monitor delivery and bounce rates by ISP/domain.* After every delivery, run reports by major domain and ISP on your messages. Look for unusual bounce, unsubscribe, spam complaint, and open rates at specific domains.

10. *Monitor spam complaints.* Even the best permission marketers with world-class practices receive spam complaints, particularly if they have a high AOL subscriber base. Monitor the number of spam complaints for each mailing, and establish a benchmark average. Look for mailings with spam complaint percentages that vary from the norm. See if you can determine what may have caused the problem. Was it the subject line? Too many messages, in too short a time? Remember, a high number of spam complaints may result in an ISP blocking current, or even future, messages. Some resources you can use to monitor complaints:

AOL Feedback Loop
http://postmaster.info.aol.com/fbl/index.html

SpamCop
http://www.spamcop.net/fom-serve/cache/94.html

Abuse.net
http://www.abuse.net/addnew.html

Diagnosing the root causes of deliverability problems will help you prevent them. You must monitor your delivery rates *religiously* because the rules around delivery change every day. To reach full delivery, you must:

- *Monitor:* Use a seed list–based monitoring system that tracks your true delivery rates across all major ISPs. Know when a problem occurs, and don't rely on your bounce-backs to give you all the information you need. Some mail just never gets delivered, or is put directly into "junk" folders or trash bins—and you'll never know without such a system in place.

- *Analyze:* When you're at less than 100 percent delivery, it's high time to find out why. You should look closely at the individual e-mail, as well as the e-mail program as a whole. There are lots of reasons for failed delivery, and early detection ensures smooth future deliveries.
- *Resolve:* Create strong relationships with ISP tech-support people to have a valuable resolution resource for troubleshooting.
- *Optimize:* Use information from all sources to solve your e-mail delivery problems. Small changes in copy, list, or server configuration can make a world of difference in your delivery rates.

Make sure you track your deliveries, test for ISP blocking and spam filtering before you distribute a large mailing, and react quickly to problems when they arise. Although complicated, it's imperative in the creation and maintenance of a truly successful e-zine.

E-ZINE DISTRIBUTION

To distribute your e-zine to your e-list, you can either do it yourself using any of a number of software programs designed for that purpose. Or you can hire an outside service to do it for you. Both options are fairly inexpensive.

My e-zine is distributed by an outside service, Person-to-Person; call Peter DeCaro at 866-699-7669. Another e-mail distribution service is Sparklist at www.sparklist.com. For an updated list of e-mail distribution services that can handle e-zines as well as solo e-mails, go to my Web site, www.bly.com, click on "Vendors," and then click on "E-mail Distribution."

11

CLOSING THE SALE

Okay. Let's say you put some of the marketing methods in the previous chapters to work. You then get a telephone call or e-mail from someone who says, "I've gone to your Web site and I'm interested. We need a brochure written. What's the next step?"

The next step is really up to you, and it varies depending on your personal style of selling and the way you want to run your business. Here are some of the follow-up techniques used by writers I know.

- *Meeting.* For many writers, the goal of promotion is to get a meeting with the prospect in his or her office. The purpose is to show your samples and convince the prospect to hire you for the assignment.
- *Mail first, then a meeting.* Other writers prefer to send a letter, resumé, and photocopies of samples through the mail. If the prospect likes the samples, writer and prospect meet to discuss an assignment. If not, the write is saved a wasted trip.
- *Mail first, then call.* Writers who send more complete packages will often try to get assignments by mail, eliminati

prospect's hands when you send it via overnight FedEx; and a longer delay when you send it via the U.S. Postal Service. Having the elements of your information kit posted on a Web site allows the prospect to view these materials instantaneously.

However, even if your prospect reviews your Web site, you should also follow up by sending a paper information kit in the mail. Reason: Once the prospect is done looking at your Web site, she has nothing in hand for file reference.

When you mail a hard copy of your information kit, the prospect has something she can hold in her hands and store in a file folder for future reference. Also, getting your information kit a day or two after visiting your Web site reinforces your sales message and increases your chance of getting the job.

FOLLOWING UP

Everyone agrees that a program of regular follow-up mailings and phone calls to your prospect list is a great way of keeping your name before potential customers and getting more assignments.

However, as a one-person business, you are extremely limited in the time you can devote to follow-up activities. If I were to write a follow-up to every prospect who requested my package this year, I would have no time to complete my assignments.

There are three ways to follow-up leads:

1. The first is with a regular, planned follow-up program. In such a program, you set a regular schedule for follow-up by phone, mail, and e-mail. Frequency is up to you, but the experts say that you can never contact your prospects and customers too often. I agree, as long as your follow-ups are friendly and helpful, not high pressure or pesky.

Actually, the best way to determine the timing of follow-up calls is to ask the prospect, "When would it be appropriate to follow up with you?" If the prospect says, "Give me a call early September," you respond, "Okay, why don't I call you on September 3 at 11 A.M.?" Then schedule that call as an appointment in your calendar or contact management software.

Okay. Now you know *when* to follow up. But *how* do you follow up?

- If you discussed a specific project, call to check on the status of that project.
- If the prospect seemed interested in hiring you but had no project in mind, call to remind her of your existence and see whether there is a project the two of you can work on together now.
- You can pick up the phone and call to say hello every once in a while.
- You can send a friendly keep-in-touch letter or e-mail that keeps the prospect up to date on your recent activities, or simply reminds her that you're available to help.
- You can produce and mail your own promotional newsletter.
- Try sending a postcard several times a year.
- You can send helpful materials such as a new business card, new Rolodex card, change-of-address notice, and so forth.

With a formal follow-up program, you schedule a series of follow-ups and then stick to the schedule. It can be once a month, once every other month, four times a year, at times specified by the prospect, or a combination of these—whatever you prefer. The cumulative effect of all this activity is to place your name foremost in prospects' minds so that when they have a writing assignment, they think of you.

2. If you don't have a regularly scheduled program of follow-up, you can use the second method: an informal program of sending materials to selected prospects, not your entire list, whenever something appropriate comes along.

You can send copies of articles you've written. You can also send tear sheets of other newspaper and magazine articles that would be of interest to your prospects. This method of follow-up is far less time-consuming and works better for writers who are busy.

How does it work? As you're doing your regular business reading and come across an item of interest to a particular client, clip it and mail it to that client. I like to include a short handwritten note that simply says, "Jim, Thought this might interest you. — Bob Bly."

I'll send anything that's relevant to the client's business. This can include article reprints, press releases, even competitors' ads and brochures. Clients and prospects will really appreciate this effort on your part to keep them informed. It will pay off in the long run. A subscription to *Fortune, Forbes, The Week,* or *BusinessWeek* will provide you with a ready supply of fresh, relevant articles to clip and mail out.

The advantage of clipping and mailing articles is that it's highly personalized. The client sees you were thinking specifically of her, and that it's not a mass mailing. The disadvantage is that it's irregular: You can't control what you come up with in your reading, so your mailing of clippings is sporadic and irregular.

.3. When you write and publish your own monthly e-zine (see chapter 10), ask every prospect and client for permission to add their e-mail address to your subscriber list. By doing so, you ensure automatic follow-up with all of your prospects at least once a month through your e-zine.

Here's a common situation: A prospect calls with a supposedly urgent need. You drop everything to do an estimate, you begin to clear your schedule to make room for this new project, you submit your proposal, and then you wait. And you wait.

When you don't hear back, you call to follow up and the prospect says he hasn't had time to look at your proposal yet. You wait some more and, though you dread it, you call again. Or maybe you don't. In any case, you never hear from the prospect again.

This happens all the time — not just to you — and there's little you can do about it, except try to see it from the other side. Here's what it may look like from your prospect's perspective.

On the day the prospect called you, this project was at the top of his list; the next day, something else came along that took priority and kept pushing the project further and further away, until it was on a permanent back burner. They never bothered to let you know, probably because they got caught up in their own world. It happens to all of us.

So here's a little reality check for difficult follow-up moments:

What they say:	I have a project. Could you send your information?
What you hear:	They want me.
What they mean:	They're gathering information.
What to do:	Send your info. Follow up in a week.
What they say:	Your info is here somewhere but I haven't looked at it yet.
What you hear:	They chose someone else.
What they mean:	Other things have come up and the project isn't quite as urgent.

What to do:	Ask when to call back. Keep in touch.
What they say:	Your materials look interesting, but we haven't decided what direction to take. We'll be in touch.
What you hear:	They chose someone else.
What they mean:	Things have changed. The project is not a priority.
What to do:	Keep in touch quarterly for other possible projects.
What they say:	Nothing. No callback.
What you hear:	They chose someone else.
What they mean:	They're busy with other things or maybe they did choose someone else. It's not the end of the world.
What to do:	Keep in touch every few months by e-mail, mail, and phone.

Follow-up is essential, but exactly how to follow up is the real work of marketing. When pursuing a prospect, you may wonder just how hard to push. You don't want to be perceived as a pest, but when you get no response, it's easy to go crazy imagining all kinds of things. So how do you know what to do?

There are no rules, of course, but when in doubt, err on the side of too much contact, rather than too little, or else you'll never know what opportunities you missed. Go with your gut, not your paranoia. And use these follow-up guidelines:

1. Ask if it's a good time to talk, always. If the prospect says no, respect that. Don't try to give a shortened spiel.
2. Tell prospects how you found them. People will become instantly more receptive if, in a letter, e-mail, or on the phone, you begin by saying, "I got your name from . . ."

3. Ask if they want you to call back and, if so, find out when is the best time to talk. If you sense they're just saying "yes" to get off the phone, ask if it's really worth your time and theirs to pursue the relationship.
4. Wait until they're ready to listen to you. Otherwise you'll waste your breath.
5. Listen to their response. That's the key. Just because you place the call doesn't mean you have to do all the talking.
6. Know when "no" means NO, and let it go.

MEETING WITH POTENTIAL CLIENTS

From your perspective, the purpose of a meeting is to get the prospect to give you an assignment, at the price you want to charge. But the prospect has a different point of view. He or she doesn't care if you need the work to pay your rent. The prospect's only concern is finding the best solution to his or her business problem. Your goal, then, is to help your prospect solve that problem by hiring you—and then make him or her feel comfortable that the right decision has been made.

There are two approaches to handling the business meeting: the conventional way, which centers on the writer's portfolio, and a different approach, "consultative selling." Let me describe them both and show why the consultative approach is better.

The typical writer walks into the client's office lugging an oversized portfolio. By its sheer size, the portfolio—not the writer, the client, or the assignment—becomes the center of attention. Thus the focus is shifted from the client and the client's problem (his or her main concern) to your portfolio.

The portfolio is shoved onto the client's desk, forcing the client to look at the samples. The client turns the pages while the writer drones on about the background to each and every piece of writing, as if the client cared. If the client looks interested in something, the writer boasts more. If the client has a sour look, the writer quickly explains how that particular sample was much better before the ad agency mucked with it. If the client's eyes glaze over, the writer helps turn the pages faster.

At the meeting's end, the client is so bored and the writer so insecure that neither wants to discuss business. The meeting ends rapidly. Perhaps there will be a callback for work. More likely, not.

Consultative selling, on the other hand, focuses on solving the prospect's needs, not on displaying your portfolio as if you were showing rug samples or clothing swatches.

The writer walks into the office, holding not a portfolio but a briefcase (with samples tucked in a folder or notebook hidden safely away inside it). Instead of showing work, or reciting his or her resumé, the writer says to the client, "Tell me about your marketing problems." The writer takes on the role of marketing consultant, helping the prospect to explore, discuss, and analyze marketing needs.

Once these needs are clearly defined and brought to the surface, the writer begins to show how his or her services can contribute to a solution. In a sense, the writer is saying, "Here is your problem and here is what you need. Would you like me to go ahead and create it for you?" Once you reach this stage your chances of getting the assignment are excellent.

Most writers—indeed, most service sellers—are too eager to attend meetings without qualifying whether the company is a good prospect and without setting an agenda or objective for the discussion. As a result, they waste a lot of time in meetings that are unproductive and unnecessary and could easily have been avoided.

After many years in this business, I think I've finally discovered the secret of successful meetings with clients and prospects. It is this: *Act like a consultant, not a writer.*

Let me explain. Too many writers act like writers, not

business professionals, and this doesn't impress clients. Symptoms of this behavior? Always forcing the client to look at your latest samples. Always trying to "sell" the client or push for more work. Always bringing the subject around to your "real writing" (e.g., your Great American Novel or Great American Screenplay) and reminding the client you do other things besides "commercial work."

But clients are not interested in writing per se. Nor are they really concerned with your personal dreams, hopes, and ambitions, though they may have such dreams themselves. Rather, their main agenda is "Can you help me solve business problems and improve my profits with your words?"

The successful writer concentrates on demonstrating a satisfactory answer to this question. In a face-to-face meeting, you will get your best results with a client by acting like a listener, counselor, problem solver, and business consultant, not an *artiste*.

Instead of shoving samples in front of the client's nose, the successful writer says to the client, "Tell me what you've done recently." Instead of trying to push the client into increasing the size of the assignment, the successful writer listens closely to the client's needs. Instead of distancing himself from the client, the smart writer becomes part of the client's business team.

It is a mistake to place your self-interest above the client's. Yes, you want more work. But the client isn't interested in your financial needs. His interest is in getting good copy at a reasonable price. No client wants to hire a writer to produce copy they really do not need.

To sum up: In meetings, be a good listener. Offer helpful advice. Try to help clients solve their marketing problems, or at least organize their thoughts enough to see clearly what the next step is (and that may be hiring you!).

Be happy and enthusiastic about an assignment when it is offered to you. Never pressure a client into giving you work he really doesn't want to assign. The client will be happier. And you will profit in the long run.

"Good writers come in all sizes, shapes, and ages," said the late Jay Chiat, founder of the California-based ad agency Chiat/Day. "What they all seem to have in common is the ability to hear, to listen, to understand."

THE INITIAL MEETING: FEE OR FREE?

One question that arises is whether to meet with potential clients at all, meet with them at no cost, or ask a fee for the initial meeting. Another issue: If you do free meetings with clients, how many free meetings can the client expect before you begin charging for your time?

I like the policy set forth by the newsletter "Creative Business," in its Professional Standards of Practice statement: "Except in unusual circumstances, a creative firm should make one free, introductory visit to a prospective client. Subsequent calls should be part of a billable assignment, unless both parties agree otherwise."

This makes sense for clients within driving distance. For out-of-town clients, you should definitely have your expenses paid and probably be paid your day rate for the meeting.

If an out-of-town client won't pay your day rate or travel expenses, are you willing to invest so much of your time and money with no promise of an assignment? And is the assignment that big, or the account so lucrative, that you should be making this investment? You must decide for yourself.

Another option is to tell the client that you charge a fee if you come to their office, but you will waive the fee if they come to you instead.

WHAT TO WEAR

At sales meetings with prospects and working meetings with clients, always wear business attire. When in doubt, opt for formal and conservative rather than informal or colorful.

"The woman who interviewed me gave me an instant up-and-down look that made it quite clear I did not understand how they did things—and of course, they were right," says one woman freelance writer who showed up for a sales meeting in leisure clothes. "They had an image to uphold, in everything from their clothes to their public relations and speechwriting, and a lucrative freelance account that they were naturally hesitant about handing over to someone who couldn't dress the part.

"They did hand it over, and we get along smoothly. But for client meetings, I've dressed the part ever since. I no longer think it's about giving up my personal style or my autonomy; it's more about sending the message: 'I understand your corporate image all the way down to my polished black pumps.'"

Opinions of professional salespeople on how to dress for a sales meeting vary. Jill Silver, a trainer and consultant with Ergo Training, Inc., in New York, dresses down if the client is dressed down. Matthew E. Kirschner, a sales-training manager at Reuben H. Donnelley in New York, disagrees. "I feel you have to maintain a certain level of professionalism," said Kirschner in an interview with *Selling* magazine. "If you're dressed at or below the level of the client, they won't have the proper respect for you."

Use your own judgment. But keep this in mind. You risk turning some prospects off by dressing too casually. But you are always dressed acceptably for any meeting when in formal business attire.

Many freelance writers consider the ability to wear comfortable clothes at work a major plus of the freelance life. "The

worst day of freelancing is better than any day in pantyhose,"
says advertising copywriter Dianna Thorington in an article in
"The Paladin Report." By all means, dress comfortably at
home. But dress up when going to client meetings, especially
on their premises.

WORKING UP A COST ESTIMATE

Once the client decides she wants to hire you, the only obstacle
is coming up with a price that is agreeable to both of you.

Since, as discussed in chapter 5, I provide clients with a
printed fee schedule, with most assignments it is a simple matter to quote my fee. I just point out the type of assignment and
read off the fee from the schedule. This way, clients understand how I determine the fee for a project, and they are also
assured of honest dealings, since my prices are published for
everyone to see.

On most projects I can quote a price immediately, based on
my fee schedule. If the project is unusually complex, I may
want to think about it and work out an estimate before quoting a fee.

In such a case, I usually ask the client what the budget is for
the project. If the budget is too small for the job at hand, it
saves me the time of making an estimate. I simply tell the
client that my fee would be much more than the firm has bud-
geted for. If the client indicates that more money is available, I
go back and work up the estimate.

However, I am not totally inflexible. Occasionally, if a regular client requests it, I will do a project for a slightly lower
fee as a favor. My philosophy is that good clients are valuable
and they have the right to ask you for something special now
and then.

Don't feel that you must come up with a fixed-price quotation the instant the client asks for it during the initial meeting

or telephone conversation. If you can give the client a rough range or an exact price right then and there, fine.

But if you can't, it is perfectly acceptable to say, "I'll need some time to prepare a price quotation. Let me review my notes from this meeting and the background material you are giving me. Then I'll get back to you with my understanding of what you want and what I would charge to do the job. Fair enough?"

No intelligent client will find this unreasonable; indeed, most will expect you to go through this process. Do not let an in-a-hurry prospect force you into quoting a casual, off-the-cuff "guesstimate" and then have the client hold you to it later as an iron-clad quotation.

GET IT IN WRITING

Once you agree to a fee and a deadline, put the terms of your agreement in writing. Ask the client for a purchase order or letter of authorization. Or send a contract or letter of agreement (see samples in appendix F) and require the client to sign it.

Without a piece of paper confirming your agreement, you are asking for trouble. There are some unscrupulous people who, for whatever reason, might refuse to pay you after you've written copy for them. Without a signed contract, you have no proof that they hired you and will have difficulty collecting the money owed you.

Also, a signed agreement helps clarify the terms and conditions of the assignment and reduces the potential for misunderstandings later on.

Once the purchase order, contract, or signed letter of agreement is in hand, the next step is to complete the assignment in such a way that the client is satisfied. You may think your ad is brilliant. But if the client doesn't like it, you won't get more business from them. Chapters 13 through 15 show you how to complete assignments, deal with clients, and handle other details of running your freelance writing business on a day-to-day basis.

One other suggestion: When putting a deadline in a client contract or letter agreement, specify the time and method of delivery as well as the date; for example, "You will receive your copy by e-mail by three P.M. or earlier on Tuesday, July 29, 2005." If you expect to finish the job by the end of that day but don't specify a time, many clients will call you in a panic at eight that morning and ask, "Where is it?" Always specify date and time in your deadline.

WHAT TO DO IF THE CLIENT SAYS "YOUR PRICE IS TOO HIGH"

Do not be too quick to lower your rate the minute the client balks, hesitates, or complains that your price is too high. If you reduce your price to what the client wants, the client will be led to think that your original price was inflated to begin with and will automatically challenge you on every price you quote.

A better way to overcome resistance is to find out what the client wants to spend, then offer a reduced level of service within that budget.

Example: A client calls me and wants a direct-mail package to sell a piece of software by mail. My fee is $6,000, which the client says is way too high. I ask why it is too high. He says, "Because I am only planning to mail initially to my current customer list of six thousand names. If the mailing is successful, then I would use outside mailing lists and mail to twenty-five thousand names as a test."

My reply is "You need the full-blown mailing package to sell the product to strangers who don't know your company. But often a less elaborate piece can be effective when you are mailing to your customer list, especially if you personalize the letter. I can write a strong two-page sales letter to be mailed to your customer list. I will charge $3,500. When the letter is successful, and you have made some money, come back to me and I will give you the complete package for the fee we originally discussed."

In this way, I am lowering the fee by quoting a smaller fee for a smaller project, not by backing down and quoting a smaller fee for the same project, which in my opinion would be a big mistake.

In some cases, of course, the client will still feel your fee is too high. If you are in need of the work, for either financial or psychological reasons, you are certainly free at that point to "give in" and agree to do the job for the price the client offers. Lord knows, I've certainly estimated low and reduced my fee many times to make sure I could pay my mortgage and feed my family. But I dislike doing it.

Now that I'm in a position of having much more work than I can possibly handle, I simply tell people, "This is my fee. If you cannot afford it right now, I certainly understand. There are others who charge less than I do; I'm sure one of them can handle this job for you, and I wish you the best of luck." For long-term clients who come to me on a regular basis, I'll make an occasional exception and do a job within a preset limited budget that is below my normal rate.

Many of the prospects you turn away because your price is too high will in fact never hire you. But you would be amazed at the number of people who do come back to retain your services. Some prospects expect writers to be frightened and bend to their every whim, and are impressed when you do not.

The lesson is that if you give a fair price for a fair day's work, stick by your guns. You are entitled to your fee and should not work for less than what is fair. You are trying to offer a professional service and get paid a professional fee for it. Don't let fear get in the way.

Before you begin any job, even if the client wants you to start now, make sure the two of you have discussed and agreed upon the fee and the deadline—verbally and in writing. If it's a large project and there will be intermediate deadlines between contract signing and delivery of the finished manuscript, put these dates in your agreement.

12

RUNNING YOUR FREELANCE WRITING BUSINESS

Although it is fun, sometimes even exciting and romantic, to be a writer, never forget that you are in business. A freelance writer is a self-employed professional running a small service business specializing in writing, usually but not always from home.

As a business owner, to ensure profitability you must run your business just as any other businesspeople must manage theirs. In this chapter I give some advice on running specific aspects of your freelance writing business.

SCHEDULING AND COMPLETING WORK

After "How much will it cost?" the most common question clients ask is "How long will it take?"

The answer depends to a large extent on how fast you write. And speed varies greatly. Some writers can do in literally an hour work that might take another writer two days to complete.

A good question to ask yourself when calculating your schedule is "Is there any outside factor that could prevent me from completing this project on time?" For example, if you don't have all the information you need to write a brochure, you'll be delayed until you get the information. Or perhaps you need to interview someone and that person is unavailable. These outside factors should be considered when setting deadlines.

Let's say the client provides you with complete information, and interviews are no problem. How long should it take you to complete the copy?

An overwhelming majority of my freelance friends tell clients that two weeks is their normal turnaround time on a single project. Two weeks gives you enough time to do a thorough job, and most clients can live with it.

Of course, the deadline might vary with the size of the project. Here is a rough guideline:

Project	Time Required for Completion
Ad, sales letter, press release, teaser e-mail, online ad, or other short piece of copy	1 week
Direct-mail package, booklet, sales brochure, short newsletter, feature article, speech, slide presentation, film script, landing page, or other medium-length assignment	2 weeks
Catalog, long brochure or newsletter, series of booklets, ad campaign (3 or 4 ads), single complex direct-mail package, 2–3 simpler direct-mail packages, or other major project	3–4 weeks
Seminar, annual report, lengthy catalog, manual, or other large project involving extensive research, editing, or rewrites	4–6 weeks

Add a few extra days to the schedule if the client wants you to produce an outline before writing the copy. If the assignment is unusually complex or technical, or if it deals with an area that is new to you, add an extra week. You'll also need more time if you are already busy with other projects when the client calls with a new assignment.

Although it is probably better to have too much work than too little, do not take on more work than you can handle. The quickest way to lose a client and gain a bad reputation is to miss a deadline.

Some book and magazine publishers may tolerate late manuscripts. Most commercial clients do not. If you miss the deadline, the client certainly won't trust you a second time and may decide to cancel your contract and not accept (or pay for) the work you've already done.

So don't miss a deadline. Don't schedule work unless you're sure you can meet your obligations.

HANDLING RUSH REQUESTS

Frequently clients will ask you to handle jobs on deadlines shorter than you're comfortable with. For example, although your policy is to take two weeks to do an ad, the client calls and wants it tomorrow. What do you do?

Again, it depends on the type of writer you are. Specifically, do you enjoy rush jobs and work well under pressure? Or does pressure hamper you, putting you under unnecessary stress and preventing you from doing your best?

My philosophy on rush jobs is to try to accommodate my regular clients when possible, without compromising quality. I will promise an ad in one week instead of two, if I have time, because I know I can do it.

But I won't do the ad overnight, even if I have time. I find I need at least several days to soak up the facts, try different ideas, and write and rewrite until I have the best possible ad. I need to put my copy in a desk drawer, sleep on it, and look at it fresh the next day. And I may repeat that process several times. That's why I can't take on overnight work.

Never start a relationship with a new client on a rush job. Otherwise, the client will treat rush deadlines as the norm and complain, "But you did the last job in a day!" Whenever you take on a rush assignment, make it clear that the job is indeed a rush—not the norm—and you are making a special effort on the client's behalf.

Rush assignments should be accepted when unavoidable, to provide your clients with good service. But they should not become a normal way of life.

MEETING YOUR DEADLINES

Here are some suggestions that can help you meet your deadlines:

1. Never take on more work than you can handle.
2. Never load your schedule to its maximum capacity. Always leave some extra time open so you can handle clients who call at the last minute with additional assignments, rush work, or revisions on current projects.
3. Keep a list of your current projects and their due dates posted on the wall near your desk or some other location where you will be sure to see it every day.
4. Jot down all project deadlines in your appointment book, electronic scheduler, or any other calendar you consult on a daily basis.
5. Try to schedule deadline dates so they fall on a Monday or Tuesday. This gives you the weekend to work on the project if you fall behind.
6. Use e-mail for instantaneous delivery of your copy to clients. If the client insists on a hard copy, use one-day

delivery services (Federal Express, Express Mail) or messengers to deliver your copy to the client.

7. Plan for the unexpected. What happens if you get the flu and have to miss a day or two of work?

8. Make arrangements with a colleague you know and trust for the two of you to be each other's "covering writers," similar to the way physicians have covering doctors to handle patients and calls when they are not at work. This arrangement should be established now, not at the last minute when you desperately need it.

HOW TO PREPARE COPY FOR THE CLIENT

For the rare client who wants hard copy, your manuscript should be printed out on good-quality white paper. I recommend you use a black and white laser or ink-jet printer. I'm happy with my Hewlett Packard LaserJet 4si. It is very reliable and prints 19 pages a minute. Also, it can be loaded with 1,000 sheets of paper, so it requires infrequent paper changes.

Copy should be perfectly typed, with no spelling errors. This is easily accomplished if you have a spell checker on your word-processing software and are a careful proofreader. Use generous margins so that your manuscript doesn't have a crowded appearance.

Use standard typefaces. I use 11-point New Courier or 11-point Prestige Elite for sales letters; 12-point Times New Roman for brochure or ad body copy, 12-point Arial Black or Impact for subheads, and 14-point or larger Arial Black or Impact for headlines.

Print out and proofread every piece of copy before you submit it. Have another person proofread it, too, if possible. Make every effort to catch mistakes. Other than that, there is no right or standard format for manuscripts. The important thing is that it looks neat and clean.

When you e-mail copy, make sure you have the client's correct e-mail address. Send the copy as an attached file. Ask the company what file formats they can work with, and e-mail your file in one of these formats. Most clients can open and read PC files in Word, WordPerfect, ASCII, RTF, or text, and the major word-processing programs let you convert between these formats.

If you send hard copy instead of e-mail, the copy should be mailed flat in a 9- by 12-inch envelope. I put a piece of stiff cardboard in the envelope so that the pages of my manuscript aren't folded or wrinkled in handling. I put a blank sheet of paper on top of the manuscript to protect the first page and use a paper clip to affix the sheets to the cardboard.

There is no need to include a cover letter with your copy, because the client is expecting the copy and knows what it is. But if you feel more comfortable writing a short cover letter, by all means do so.

With a client who prefers not to receive e-mail (rare), I usually mail copy using either Express Mail or Federal Express to guarantee next-day delivery. Do not send copy through regular first-class mail because delivery is unpredictable and your copy may not arrive on the client's desk in time.

Federal Express and other next-day delivery services ensure that your copy arrives by the due date. If the deadline is not tomorrow, your clients will not complain if they get the copy a day or two earlier than expected.

REVISIONS

On some of the assignments I handle, I am not asked to make revisions, for one of two reasons:

1. The client approves the copy, has no changes to make, and will run my ad exactly as I have written it.

2. There are some changes, but the client finds it easier to make these changes himself rather than have me do it. For instance, if the client wants to delete a paragraph or change a *the* to an *a*, he certainly doesn't need my help to make such changes. This is easy for clients to do if they get your copy as a computer file via disk or e-mail.

However, on most jobs, clients will come back to you and request some rewrites. This doesn't mean they are dissatisfied; it just means they want to make changes, and that they need your help to make them.

I tell clients that a minor rewrite on a small job (ad, letter, press release) can be completed in a day or so, while an extensive rewrite on a larger project (brochure, article, catalog) may take two or three days. And I state these turnaround times in my standard client agreements to make sure the client has a realistic expectation on the speed of turnaround. Of course, the more extensive the changes, the more time it takes to make them. You really can't tell what is involved in doing a rewrite until the client explains to you what kind of changes he wants.

Reviewing copy requires some work on the part of the client, and clients must be made to understand this. The writer cannot produce a satisfactory rewrite unless the client explains, in detail, what is wrong with the copy and what changes are desired.

The best way to communicate this is for the client to go through the copy line by line, and provide detailed comments on every section requiring changes. These comments can be made directly on the electronic file using the Word tracking feature; marked in blue pencil on the original manuscript; or detailed in a separate memo to the writer. Make sure your client understands that you are not asking her to do the rewriting; you are asking for specific changes and clear direction so you can produce a satisfactory second draft.

Once you receive the marked-up copy, go over it. If anything is unclear, call the client for clarification. Do not accept comments that are vague or ambiguous. Ask the client to give specific criticism. Resolve any contradictions in the comments (e.g., saying one thing on page 3 and the exact opposite on page 5). After having this discussion with the client, you should feel confident about your ability to rewrite the piece to the client's satisfaction.

If you disagree with a client's comments, tell him politely— once. If the client agrees with you, fine. Otherwise, make the change as outlined.

After rewriting the manuscript, key in the changes and print out a clean copy. Put it aside for a day, then proofread. Make any final corrections or changes, key them in, and e-mail, mail, or fax the revised copy to the client. At this point, the copy should be acceptable to the client as is or with very minor revisions.

BUILDING THE WRITER-CLIENT RELATIONSHIP

Your goal should be to win clients, not assignments. Although it's always good to get an assignment, your income will grow larger when you build a stable of regular clients who keep coming back to you again and again.

Here are some things you can do to encourage this type of ongoing relationship:

- Seek out clients who can provide a steady flow of assignments rather than just an occasional project.
- Go out of your way to please these clients and do a good job for them.
- Build a personal relationship. Visit with the client now and then. An occasional cup of coffee or lunch out wouldn't hurt.

- Send an occasional gift on special occasions or as a thank you for help, such as a client referring a colleague to you.
- Participate in client activities. Accept any invitations you receive to attend holiday parties or similar events. Make sure you say hello to the client at conferences and other industry events. Drop by the client's booth if the client is exhibiting at a local trade show.
- Send the client copies of pertinent articles, news clippings, and competitors' ads. Keep in touch by e-mail. Send an occasional letter or card.
- Pick up the phone and say hello every now and then. Just say hello. Don't beg for new business.
- Cultivate relationships with as many people in the client organization as you can. Even people you think are unimportant can have a major say over whether you get hired.
- Be especially considerate of secretaries, assistants, and receptionists. They wield a lot of influence over who gets through to the boss and who doesn't. And one day they might be promoted and become your clients. Get to know them on a first-name basis.
- Never be rude or lose your temper. Always be patient, courteous, and friendly.
- Remember that clients have all the power. The client can choose not to continue working with you at any time, for any reason—or for no reason. The client always has a choice. You would not be in business without your clients.

TIME MANAGEMENT

Time is precious to the freelancer, for it is really the only thing you sell, and your supply is sharply limited by the number of hours in a day. So it pays to make every hour count.

There are many excellent books and articles published on time management, and I suggest you read a few. In particular,

I recommend *The Complete Idiot's Guide to Time Management*, written by my colleague Jeff Davidson. In the meantime, here are some time-management tips specifically geared to the freelance writer.

- Organize your office so that everything you need—computer, disks, stamps, files, paper, telephone, paper clips, rubber bands, envelopes—is within easy reach.
- Keep files for current projects in a separate file holder on your desk.
- Consider getting part-time administrative help a few days a week to relieve you of some of your paperwork burden.
- Use outside services: messengers, typists, tax preparers, bookkeepers, proofreaders, Internet researchers, Web designers.
- Keep in mind that the only time you make money is writing, thinking, or researching a client project. Always look for ways to turn nonproductive hours into billable time.
- Try to group errands together so you leave your office only once a day.
- Use modern tools—computers, software, online databases, e-mail—that can increase your productivity. For example, I purchased a program that allows me to create an index for any book I'm writing in one-third the time it normally takes.
- Experiment until you find the working schedule and routine that's best for you. Some writers, for example, need to write without interruption, while others break up writing with other activities, such as phone calls or reading.
- Be careful about accepting too many social or business engagements outside the office. Value and protect your time. If you live in the suburbs, going to a lunchtime meeting of a business club in the city can take the better part of your day. I eat lunch at my desk or at a coffee shop

around the corner and rarely take more than 20 minutes to do so. I value my time like it's gold in Fort Knox.

- Try to do most of your business by mail, phone, e-mail, and fax. Remember, if you're out of the office traveling, you're not at your desk making money. One way around this is to charge a fee for any out-of-office visits to clients' premises.
- Set priorities. Don't waste time on trivial or unnecessary tasks when you have important assignments waiting to be completed. It's human nature to dawdle over a letter to a friend or linger over coffee at lunch, but don't give in. Set priorities, and do important tasks first.
- When you feel your energy ebbing, take short breaks to rejuvenate yourself. A walk around the block is a pleasant diversion. But limit your breaks to 5 to 15 minutes. Don't use them as an excuse to procrastinate.
- Label your copy with the document's file name at the top of page 1 of each document. This will make it easier to find the right computer file later simply by glancing at the hard copy in your Pendaflex file.
- Get sufficient rest. Eventually lack of sleep, rest, and relaxation catches up with you; the human body has limits. Don't schedule work so tightly that you are taxing your capacity five or six days a week, 52 weeks a year.
- Allow for a personal life. Realize that taking your kids to the dentist can eat up almost half a day of billable time, but sometimes you have to be the one to do it.

OVERCOMING WRITER'S BLOCK

What happens if you get stuck on a project and are unable to continue? Fortunately, there are a number of proven ways to avoid or overcome writer's block.

One way to eliminate the problem is to work on multiple

projects at the same time. The late Isaac Asimov once said, "I am so prolific, I always have four or five projects brewing at any one time. That's my secret for avoiding writer's block. Whenever I get tired of one project, I turn to another until the well of inspiration fills up again. It also enhances the cross pollination of ideas."

I have had great success with this method. At any one time I am working on one or two books, one or two magazine articles, plus half a dozen or more copywriting assignments. If I wake up and don't feel in the mood to do copywriting, I work on my book that day.

On the other hand, if I feel burned out from three solid days of book writing, I welcome the chance to write a sales letter or ad. It's especially nice to have a mix of short- and long-term projects. The long-term projects give you stability, the short-term add variety.

One cause of writer's block is the fear that a project is too big or too difficult to tackle. In this case, I recommend that you break the job into several small portions and do one portion every day, or every other day.

For example, I was faced with having to write a six-page technical brochure in a week's time. The job seemed overwhelming, especially with all the background material I had to read. Instead of panicking, I wrote out a schedule:

Monday	Start reading background material.
Tuesday	Finish reading background; start typing up notes.
Wednesday	Finish typing notes; begin rough outline.
Thursday	Complete outline.
Friday	Write pages 1, 2, and 3.
Saturday morning	Write pages 4, 5, and 6.
Saturday afternoon	Edit first draft of brochure and print clean copy.

Sunday morning	Edit copy again and print out clean manuscript.
Sunday evening	Proofread and correct draft.
Monday morning	Final proofreading; print clean copy.
Monday, noon	E-mail copy to client so they receive by 3 P.M.

Following this schedule, I was able to meet my deadline easily and without great stress.

Writers often get blocked when faced with an unfamiliar assignment; for example, a writer used to writing technical manuals may feel he is on uncertain ground when asked to write a direct-mail package.

This is where networking pays off. If you have to write something and you don't know how to proceed, call a writer you know—a friend, a casual acquaintance, or even a friend of a friend—and ask for advice. Most writers will be more than happy to share their know-how, especially with a fellow writer. They can answer your questions and help you get started.

The most intimidating assignments are types of projects we haven't done before. But most of the things you think you can't write, you can.

When asked to write a type of project you are not familiar with, get examples of past projects from the client, and supplement these by collecting some more on your own, if you can find them. Study them carefully. Analyze them as carefully as a cardiologist looking at an EKG. Break them into their component parts. Take notes on the structure, length, tone, and flow.

If you find something very similar to what you have to produce, you can scan it into your PC to use as a template. You don't copy the text, of course, because (a) it's plagiarism; and (b) you are not writing about the same company or product. But a template can help with structure and organization of the piece. This will give you a good feel for how to put that particular type of piece together.

BILLING CLIENTS FOR SERVICES RENDERED

Unlike magazine and book publishers, commercial clients need an invoice from you in order to process your payment check.

Some writers buy preprinted invoice forms from stationery stores or office supply catalogs. I find it simpler to type out my own invoices, using the format shown in appendix F.

The invoice should be dated and addressed to the client by company and name. It should include the name of the project, a brief description of the project, the dollar amount owed you, and the payment terms (net 30 days is typical).

Invoices should be sent promptly; I usually send an invoice within a week of completing the assignment. Before mailing your invoice, read the client's purchase order carefully, especially the fine print on the back. Some clients have special instructions for how an invoice should be sent; for example, two of my clients require the invoice to be sent in triplicate.

It is in your best interest to send an invoice with complete information and in the format requested by the client. Improperly submitted invoices, or invoices that are incorrect or lack complete information, often get routed from office to office or sit on someone's desk awaiting attention, which in turn can delay payment.

Every invoice should include your address and phone number in case the accounting department needs to contact you. Invoices should also refer to purchase orders, contracts, or other authorization provided by the client. Also include, for tax purposes, your federal tax ID number or social security number.

COLLECTING UNPAID BILLS

Although you may request payment within 30 days, some clients take longer. Large corporations may routinely pay in 60 days or even 90 days, while some small firms play games with suppliers, delaying payment or pretending to lose bills.

In most cases, you will have no trouble collecting payment. But occasionally, a client will not pay a bill on time, even when reminded to do so. As a rule of thumb, expect 2 percent of your accounts receivable to be bad debt.

Here is what you should do to minimize bad debt and collect more of the money clients owe you:

1. Send a polite letter requesting payment. Your letter should not accuse the client of any wrongdoing, but should simply remind him that a bill is outstanding and payment is now due. Do not threaten or sound angry. Assume the client forgot and did not intend to cheat you.

2. If you don't hear anything within two weeks, send another letter. Again, be polite. But this time be a little firmer. Remind the client that the invoice is now past due and that you would appreciate prompt payment (see sample collection letters in appendix F). If you have a contract, purchase order, or other authorization signed by the client, enclose a copy with your letter. Also enclose a reply envelope. Send the letter certified, return receipt requested. This provides legal proof that you sent a letter and that the other person received it.

3. If you don't get paid within two weeks after the second letter, try a phone call. Keep a record of your calls and what was said. Don't threaten. Instead, ask if there is any reason why your bill is not being paid. Acknowledge the reason, but remind the client that you have an agreement, you completed the work, and payment is now due. If the

client pleads financial difficulty, be understanding but firm. If the client can't afford to pay the whole bill at once, suggest a schedule of partial payments.

5. Immediately after your conversation, send a certified letter (return receipt requested) repeating the points made in the conversation and noting the client's promise to pay your bill. From this point on, use a series of certified letters and phone calls, spaced about two weeks apart. Do not let up. Constant calls and letters tell the client, "I am not about to forget about this bill, and I expect you to pay it."

6. If you are still unsuccessful, write a final letter saying that unless payment is received, you will have to take immediate action.

At this point you have two choices. You can turn the bill over to an attorney or collection agency, who, for a percentage (30 to 40 percent) of the money owed you will use every device at their disposal to collect the money. You don't pay them until the money is collected.

Or you can take the client to small claims court if the amount owed is below the limit allowed in small claims court. This amount varies by state, and is typically around $2,000 or so.

TAXES

My tax advice is simple and straightforward: Do not do your own tax returns. Hire a certified public accountant (CPA) to do your taxes for you. The tax returns of a self-employed person are many times more complicated than the tax returns of the average salaried worker. You won't do as good a job as a CPA, and you will waste a lot of billable time sweating over the calculations and paperwork.

As a freelancer, you pay estimated quarterly tax payments,

based on the amount of money you earned in your freelance business last year and what you are earning or expect to earn this year. Your accountant can figure your quarterly estimated payments and provide you with the forms.

In an issue of his newsletter, *Tax Planning Letter*, Wayne Kolb, my accountant, provides the following tax ideas for small businesses; be sure to check with your own accountant:

• *Take a write-off for business equipment.* Most business equipment is depreciated over five to seven years. However, small businesses can take an immediate depreciation write-off for up to $17,500 as specified in the Section 179 deduction. Even equipment purchased at the end of the year is eligible, but it must be used more than 50 percent for your business, and only the business percentage can be written off. You should keep records to prove business usage for equipment — cellular phones, photocopiers, computers — that can also be used for personal purposes.

• *Hire your children.* If your child is under 18 years old and your business is not incorporated, you are not required to withhold FICA (social security) tax. Your child can earn up to $3,900 before any income tax is due. You can pay your child the $3,900 and deposit an additional $4,500 into an IRA account in his or her name. Your child will pay no income tax. The wages earned must be reasonable for the job done.

• *Set up a SEP plan and deduct contributions to it.* A SEP, or simplified employee pension, is the easiest pension plan for a self-employed writer to set up and maintain. Contributions, which are tax-deductible, are based on a percentage of your earnings and can be far in excess of the $4,500 annual limit to which an IRA is subject.

• *Don't overlook miscellaneous expenses.* Although keeping track of every little miscellaneous business expense can be a pain in the neck, it pays to do it anyway. Remember, for every

$1 in legitimate business expenses you incur, that's another dollar you don't pay income tax on. Save your receipts and regularly enter your business expenses into a paper or PC-based expense ledger. Your accountant can set this up for you.

• *Deduct self-employed health insurance premiums.* Freelancers can generally deduct a portion of their health insurance premiums in any given year on Schedule C of their income tax returns. Be sure to show your accountant all health care insurance premiums and other medical expenditures.

13

HOW TO ENSURE THE CLIENT'S
SATISFACTION WITH YOUR COPY

To be a successful freelance writer, you must produce copy that satisfies most of your clients most of the time. In this chapter, we look at how to write copy that makes your clients so happy, they give you lots of repeat business and referrals.

RESEARCH

The first step in writing copy that pleases your client is to collect all published background material on your product, your industry, and your market. This material will provide you with the facts you need to write strong, specific selling copy.

John Forde of Agora Publishing says the willingness to do research is a key trait that distinguishes good copywriters from mediocre ones. "The copywriter needs to know what to look for and where to look. And he can't be the type that's afraid to ask for direction."

Here is a checklist of things you should collect from the client and then study before writing your copy. Obviously not every client will be able to provide all of this. But ask for it anyway, and take whatever you can get:

- ❏ Web site containing product information
- ❏ Tear sheets or reprints of any previous ads
- ❏ Examples of competitors' ads and sales literature
- ❏ Product brochures, data sheets, catalog pages, and any other sales literature describing the product
- ❏ Reprints of articles or papers relevant to the topic
- ❏ Copies of speeches
- ❏ Scripts from slide presentations, videotapes, and films
- ❏ Press releases and press kits
- ❏ Operator, user, or instruction manuals
- ❏ Package copy (labels, boxes, containers, etc.)
- ❏ Letters of testimonial from satisfied customers
- ❏ Complaint letters
- ❏ Evaluation forms for seminars, training programs, and consulting services
- ❏ Product reviews
- ❏ Marketing plans
- ❏ Advertising plans
- ❏ Business plans
- ❏ Press clippings
- ❏ Direct-mail packages and sales letters
- ❏ Company memos and other internal documents describing the product
- ❏ Product specifications
- ❏ Proposals
- ❏ Engineer's drawings
- ❏ Market research studies
- ❏ Focus group transcripts
- ❏ Annual report or company capabilities brochure (for general company background)
- ❏ Back issues of company newsletters
- ❏ List of customers, clients, or users
- ❏ Sales figures for past five years (dollar amounts, units sold)
- ❏ Samples of the product

❑ Names and phone numbers of several people in the company the writer can call for further information on sales and technical aspects of the product

❑ Names and phone numbers of several customers the writer can call to get the customer's point of view

ASK QUESTIONS

Study the source materials the client sends you. As you read, highlight useful information with a yellow marker. When you are done highlighting, type all the highlighted sections into your PC as a computer file. Single-space this file, then print it out. You now have condensed a big pile of miscellaneous documents into one concise, tight source document, which makes the writing much easier.

After reviewing the source material, you will have questions. Arrange with the client to get you the answers. These answers may be found in additional source documents you don't have. Or it may require you to interview a subject matter expert (SME) at the client company to get the facts you need. Interviewing can be done in person, over the phone, or even via fax or e-mail.

Here are some of the questions you should ask your client about the product and the potential buyers to whom you are writing. The client may not have all the answers or even the time to answer so many questions. Do as much research as you can within the limitations of their resources.

- What are the product's features and benefits? Make a detailed list.
- Which benefit is the most important?
- How does the product differ from the competition's? (Which features are exclusive? Which are better than the competition's?)

- If the product isn't different, what attributes can be stressed that haven't been stressed by the competition?
- What technologies does the product compete against?
- What are the applications of the product?
- What industries can use the product?
- What problems does the product solve in the marketplace?
- How is the product positioned in the marketplace?
- How does the product work?
- How reliable is the product?
- How efficient?
- How economical?
- Who has bought the product and what do they say about it?
- What materials, sizes, and models is it available in?
- How quickly does the manufacturer deliver the product?
- What service and support does the manufacturer offer?
- Is the product guaranteed?
- Who will buy the product? (What markets is it sold to?)
- What is the customer's main concern (price, delivery, performance, reliability, service, maintenance, quality, efficiency)?
- What is the character of the buyer?
- What motivates the buyer?
- How many different buying influences must the copy appeal to? If you are writing an ad, read issues of the magazine in which the ad will appear. If you are writing direct mail, find out what mailing lists will be used and study the data cards, which are written descriptions of each list.
- What is the objective or purpose of the copy you are writing? This objective may be one or more of the following: to generate inquiries, produce orders, answer inquiries, qualify prospects, transmit product information, build brand recognition and preference, enhance company

image, or instruct the buyer on product usage, applications, or care.

Before you write copy, study the product: its features, benefits, past performance, applications, and markets. Digging for the facts will pay off, because in advertising, specifics sell.

When you have a file full of facts at your fingertips, writing good copy is easy. You simply select the most relevant facts and describe them in a clear, concise, direct fashion.

But when copywriters don't bother to dig for facts, they fall back on fancy phrases and puffed-up expressions to fill the empty space on the page. The words sound nice, but they don't sell because the copy doesn't inform.

SHOULD YOU SUBMIT A COPY PLATFORM?

A "copy platform" is a document that is a sort of outline of the copy you plan to write for the client, as you envision it. There is no standard format for writing a copy platform, and everyone does it differently. But a typical copy platform has the following sections:

1. *Headline*—the proposed headline for the piece. You may submit a single headline, or give the client a few different headlines to choose from. If you offer a choice, don't send too many; three to five is about right.
2. *Overview*—a one- or two-paragraph description of the approach you plan to take in your copy with a rationale or justification for it; i.e., tell the client the reasons why you think your copy approach will be successful.
3. *Outline*—a numbered or bullet-point outline showing the major points to be covered in the copy, in the order in which they will be presented.

4. *Offer*—describe in a paragraph your call to action: the price, terms, conditions, premiums, guarantees, method of payment, and response vehicle (Web, phone, mail, fax).

5. *Target market*—describe in a paragraph the audience. For a business audience, list industry, size of company, job title, and function. For a consumer audience, describe demographics, psychographics, affinities (e.g., coin collectors), and buying history (e.g., spent $100 buying something through the mail within the last 12 months).

An alternative to the copy platform, and one I find works very well, is to write just the first page of the promotion (assuming it is a long-copy sales letter or landing page) and submit that to the client.

The headline and lead are the most important part of the promotion, and set the tone for the rest of the piece. Well, your first page contains both those elements, the headline and the lead. So if the client likes that first page, you can proceed with confidence finishing the rest of the letter or landing page.

Without first submitting a headline, lead, or copy platform, you risk surprising the client when you hand in your first draft. The client may say, "I don't like this approach; why didn't you run it by me first?" And then you are faced with the unpleasant task of rewriting the entire promotion in a compressed time frame with an impatient and unhappy client looking over your shoulder.

On the other hand, when you let the client see some headlines, a lead, and a copy platform before you proceed to writing a full draft, the client can "buy into" your creative concept early. This way, there are no surprises when he gets your first draft. And the fewer surprises there are, the happier your clients will be.

WHEN BREAKING COPYWRITING RULES REAPS REWARDS

"Be concise."

"Use short sentences."

"Put a benefit in the headline."

"Use colloquial language."

"Avoid jargon."

If you take a class, attend a lecture, or read a book or article on copywriting, you'll hear these and other copywriting "rules" repeated again and again. Following the rules makes you a better advertising writer, because the rules work 90 percent of the time.

But the top copywriters succeed because they know when to break the rules. They know that short sentences usually work best—but not always. They know that technical jargon turns most readers off—but some audiences like it. They know that putting a benefit in the headline is usually the best way to get your message across, but that sometimes another technique can increase ad readership.

When do you stick with the rules and when do you break them? There's no easy answer. I can't give you a laundry list of dos and don'ts or 10 easy tips or 5 simple steps. Using and breaking rules effectively requires a writer's ear, a firm command of language, and years of practice; it is the essence of the copywriter's craft.

Knowing that rules can and occasionally should be broken will improve your writing immensely. Too many of us take copywriting's rules, such as those of Ogilvy, Caples, Hopkins, and *BtoB* magazine's Copy Chasers, as commandments. In reality, they are tools designed to help writers produce more effective copy. If breaking the rule improves the copy, then the rule should be broken.

I can help you feel more comfortable with this idea by

showing you some samples. Here are a few of copywriting's "sacred cows," along with examples of when they should be put out to pasture.

Sacred Cow No. 1: Be Concise

This is a favorite rule among not only copywriters but all writers (except experimental novelists and counterculture journalists). "Omit needless words!" writing instructors exclaim, urging us to cut copy to the bone. But I can think of at least three situations in which conciseness is not a virtue, and extra words can make the writing better.

The first situation is when you need to explain something that may be clear to some readers but not to others. Let's say you're writing a computer catalog and you want to describe a computer. The most concise description would read "2 GB RAM." Do most people today know what RAM is? My wife does, but my mother doesn't. So, to make it clear to both I add words: "2 GB of internal memory."

But is 2 GB a number people can visualize? Does it mean anything to them? If not, you may need to add even more words to make the benefit clear: "Features 2 GB of internal memory — enough to run the most sophisticated business software and store as many as 20,000 full-length books!"

The second reason to use extra words is to add emphasis, to ensure that the reader understands you. For example, mail-order copywriters are fond of emphasizing the "free gift" you'll receive when you join a record club or subscribe to a magazine.

Any English teacher can tell you that "free gift" is a redundancy, because a gift by definition is free. But the copywriter's job is to sell, not to write compositions for an English class. And as a copywriter, you realize that the consumer's natural reaction is to think that the gift comes with strings attached. So you add the word "free" to emphasize that there are no strings attached — the gift is indeed just that, a gift.

The third situation where more words work better than less is in highly personal copy: copy that speaks to the reader's needs as an individual, not a businessperson. An engineer is probably dispassionate when it comes to pump selection, but shopping for a life insurance policy is an emotional purchase as well as a rational one.

The most concise approach to writing an ad for life insurance would be to list the monthly payments, amount of insurance, and criteria for acceptance. But the successful ad will talk about the emotional issues: caring for one's family, planning for the future on a person-to-person level. That takes extra words, but the words are well spent.

Sacred Cow No. 2: Avoid Jargon

Jargon is language more complex than the ideas it serves to communicate. Every business writing text warns us to avoid jargon and write in plain, simple terms. But jargon, if properly applied, can make copy more effective.

The most common exception to the "avoid jargon" rule is in copy aimed at special audiences: farmers, chemists, architects, warehouse managers. Jargon can strengthen your link to these specialists because it shows them that you are "in the know," that you understand their business and empathize with their problems. If you don't speak their language, or if your copy defines terms that they already know, readers suspect that you lack expertise in their business.

Jargon is also useful for introducing an unfamiliar concept. The technique is to use the term in quotation marks first, then define it, as shown in this example: "The heart of Syscom II is its unique Sys-II 'operating system'—built-in software that controls system operation and allows Syscom II to run thousands of popular business applications."

Finally, jargon sometimes can make a product seem more impressive or more valuable. Listerine, we are told, is the only mouthwash that kills "halitosis." Sounds impressive, until you realize that halitosis is a scientific term popularized by the Listerine people to sell more mouthwash.

Sacred Cow No. 3: Put a Benefit in the Headline

If you believe David Ogilvy when he says that 80 percent of your audience skips the body copy and reads the headline only, this rule makes sense. And this is true, most of the time.

One exception is ads aimed at readers who already want what you're selling. For example, the Institute of Children's Literature has had great success with an ad selling a home correspondence course in how to write children's books and stories. The ad's headline, "We're looking for people to write children's books," does not contain a benefit. Nor does it promise a reward. Instead, it addresses a specific audience: people who want to write and publish children's books.

These people want to be authors. Their dream is to publish a book. So there's no need to sell them on the benefits of writing. Instead, the ad breaks the rule by grabbing the attention of a select, highly motivated audience and then building their interest in the course.

Sacred Cow No. 4: Use Simple Words

Simple words are the easiest to understand. And because copy is written to communicate, short words are best — usually. An exception to the rule is when you want to use a big word to make your subject seem more important or impressive. For example, let's say you're selling expensive, top-quality reproductions of antique pistols. The simplest description of the product is "guns." But "firearms," though a bigger word, sounds more distinctive. And that's why it works better: The reader might pay $295 for a firearm but not for a mere "gun."

Same thing with Mont Blanc. If I told you I wanted to sell you a pen for $100, you might not be interested. But if I call it a "writing instrument," the price seems more palatable, since you have no preconceived notion of what a "writing instrument" should cost.

Sometimes, giving a product a more impressive title can convey an image of added value. Recently I received a brochure promoting a "selling system." The system turned out to be an in-plant seminar. But somehow the term "selling system" sounds more impressive than calling it a course, seminar, or training session.

Sacred Cow No. 5: Use Short Sentences

Advertising copywriters are crazy about short sentences. And that's okay, because short sentences are usually the best sentences. But not always.

Sometimes you want to express complex ideas or thoughts that are interconnected. Putting them in one sentence makes the connection clear. Breaking them up into many short sentences clouds the message by cutting the connection. Here's an example:

> We back you up with the support you need — from engineering assistance to training and worldwide field service — to ensure ongoing network performance.

Written in the copy style of the modern Madison Avenue agency, this would read:

> We back you up. With total support. From engineering assistance. To training. And worldwide field service. All to ensure ongoing network performance.

As you can see, too many short sentences, sentence fragments, and sentences beginning with conjunctions sound unnatural and stilted — not at all the conversational tone the writer thinks he's achieving. Rudolph Flesch, author of *The Art of Readable Writing,* calls this type of clipped copy "machine-gun style" and warns us to avoid it.

Sacred Cow No. 6: Avoid Negatives

The logic behind this rule is: People have imperfect memories. If your headline reads, "New cherry fizz contains no salt," they're likely to remember it as "Cherry fizz contains salt." But some situations call for a negative.

Years ago, Kentucky Fried Chicken began selling chicken nuggets. One logical argument for buying Kentucky Fried's nuggets instead of McDonald's Chicken McNuggets is that Colonel Sanders already is an expert at chicken, which McDonald's isn't. The television commercial began with a negative concept: You wouldn't buy a taco from a Chinese restaurant, or an egg roll from an Italian restaurant, so why buy chicken nuggets at a burger joint when you can get them from a chicken professional, Kentucky Fried Chicken?

A radio commercial for a New York furniture store begins with this harsh warning: "Don't buy furniture today!" That makes you stop and listen, because it's unusual to hear an advertiser tell you not to buy. The commercial goes on to say that you can save hundreds of dollars if you hold off until the big furniture sale this coming Saturday.

Sacred Cow No. 7: Don't Knock the Competition

I learned this rule in Advertising 101: Don't mention the competition in your advertising because it gives them free exposure. Goodrich commercials used to say, "We're Goodrich, not Goodyear." Everybody remembered Goodyear and forgot Goodrich. This rule makes sense when there's no clear leader, no number-one brand. Everybody's competing against everybody else, so you can win customers by selling the advantages of your product over all the others.

But in markets where there's clearly a leader in the field, you've got to convince people to switch from the comfortable favorite to you, the up-and-comer. And often, the reason is that you're similar to the leader but you do one thing better. To get that message across, you can't avoid talking about—and comparing yourself with—No. 1.

Examples abound: Express Mail ads are explicit about the cost savings of Express Mail versus overnight-delivery leader Federal Express. MCI commercials stress MCI's 30 to 50 percent lower long-distance phone bills than AT&T's. The C&C Cola people know they can't outdo Coke and Pepsi in the image department, so they advertise good taste at half the price.

Sacred Cow No. 8: Go Straight to the Point

The question then becomes: What is the point? In a product ad, should you spend a paragraph describing the reader's problem before you get to the product and how it solves the problem? Or should you go straight to the product pitch?

Normally, it's best to get right to the meat of the ad; otherwise you'll lose your reader. But the reader may not be aware of the problem the product solves, or may not think of it too often. Here's the lead paragraph of an ad that "warms up" before getting to the point:

> Sugar entrained in evaporators and pans means sugar lost in condenser discharge streams. And if it isn't bad enough that wasting sugar costs you money, the sugar you dispose of in your refinery or factory wastewater decomposes. This results in biological oxygen demand, a depletion of oxygen in the water that's a major source of pollution.

A waste of space? No, because many of the people running sugar refineries don't realize that entrainment is this serious.

The copy has to point to the problem and highlight its adverse effects before the ad can begin to sell the solution.

On the other hand, an ad stressing a product's energy efficiency should begin with a talk about energy savings. Copy that explained the negative consequences of wasting energy would be wasting words, because buyers already know how precious and costly energy is.

ADDITIONAL WRITING TIPS

Here are some additional tips that can greatly increase the effectiveness and quality of the copy you produce for your clients.

1. The most effective sales materials are tightly targeted to specific audiences. Thus, "accounting services for ad agencies" will do better than "accounting services."
2. Always have an offer, a next step to take, and tell the reader about it: "Call us now for a free no-obligation analysis of your current payroll processing procedures."
3. Use statistics and facts that demonstrate that the client is reliable, skilled, and usually pleases its customers: "Every locksmith who works in our shop is certified as a security specialist by the prestigious Master Craftsman Guild."
4. Use actual testimonials from satisfied customers, with attribution, in your copy.
5. Toss in a few facts, statistics, or buzzwords that show prospects the advertiser understands their industry and their needs: "It's true: Half the people in the U.S.A. don't even see a dentist. And they represent a prime prospect for your dental practice."
6. Put your headline or some of your subheads in the form of a question to engage reader interest: "Every car-wash

owner should know these 7 business success secrets. Do
you?" Or: "Why haven't satellite dish owners been told
these facts?"

7. Write from the customer's point of view: not "Introducing our Guarda-Health Employee Benefit Program" but
"At last you can combat the huge health insurance premiums threatening to put your small business out of
business."

8. Whenever possible, put in a time reference to add im-
mediacy. Instead of "How to reduce your building maintenance costs 40 percent" write "How to reduce your
building maintenance costs 40 percent this year."

9. Ensure the buyer's satisfaction. Emphasize the advertiser's guarantee in the copy. If the advertiser does not
explicitly guarantee its product or service, give examples of how they will go out of their way to please the
customer.

10. Turn a negative into a positive. If your client is a new
company and hasn't sold a lot of its product, you can
phrase this as "Not one widget buyer in a thousand has
ever experienced the advantages of the new XYZ widget
design."

BOOSTING YOUR WRITING PRODUCTIVITY

The faster you can write, and the more work you can turn out
at an acceptable level of quality, the more money you will
make. Also, being a fast writer makes it easier for you to meet
tight client deadlines, which seem to be growing tighter with
every year: Everyone is in a hurry today, and everyone wants it
yesterday. If you can accommodate tight turnaround times,
you can please that substantial portion of the market that val-
ues promptness over quality.

Here are a few tips for increasing your writing speed and productivity:

• Write during the hours you have peak energy. For some writers, this is early in the morning. Others do their best work late at night. Most writers say their lowest energy period is in the afternoon, after lunch. This is a good time to do non-writing tasks such as paying bills and making phone calls.

Home Office Computing quizzed its readers, who are home-based entrepreneurs, about work habits, and found that 80 percent begin their work day at nine A.M. or earlier. Only 15 percent regularly burn the midnight oil.

• Many writers are most productive when they have long, uninterrupted blocks of time in which to write. To create these blocks of time, you can start early, working in the morning before clients get in and the phone starts ringing. Or you can work at night, after regular business hours.

If you have caller ID on your phone, which identifies on a display who the caller is, you can let your voice mail or answering machine pick up nonessential calls and return to them later in the day, after you're through with your intense writing for the morning or afternoon.

• Outline—the more detailed you make your outline up front, the easier it will be to write your copy when it's time to write, and the faster you'll get the job done. Make outlines more detailed and comprehensive rather than less so, and submit the outline to the client for approval.

In addition to making your life easier, detailed outlines are appreciated by clients, because the outline lets them know what to expect. It also gives them input at the early stages when making changes is not difficult or time-consuming. And, if the client questions your copy, you can show how it matches the detailed outline they approved.

• Before you do any job, set up a file on the computer. Put in the headers and footers, page numbers, heads and subheads from your outline, and any boilerplate or mandatory sections of copy, such as the client's address, warranty information, or a copyright line. Get these mechanical details out of the way early so you can concentrate on the writing later on. When you set up computer files first, writing becomes a matter of filling in the blanks within the file, which makes the whole process easier and less intimidating.

• Some sections of your copy may be deliberately lifted from previous client documents, either as is or with some minor editing. Get a scanner so you can scan these documents and import them into your project file. Better yet, ask the client to e-mail background materials to you as electronic documents, from which you can cut and paste sections directly into your copy. This saves time and effort by eliminating the need to re-key the source documents manually. For one client, every product brochure may contain the same two-paragraph boilerplate corporate bio. Why re-key this every time?

• Do the easy sections first. In every assignment, some sections are easier, almost rote. Do these first and put them into your document file for the job. Doing the easy parts first helps you make significant progress in a short time, which can buoy your spirit and motivate you to press on.

• Save on your hard disk files of copy you've created for your various clients. Again, you can save an enormous amount of time by cutting a section of an old document and pasting it into the place in a new assignment for that same client where it fits perfectly.

• Also, copy done for one client can be imported into a new document for a new client and modified to fit the new assignment. For example, most direct-mail reply cards are pretty similar in nature. Instead of writing the reply card from scratch each time, model your new reply card on previous reply cards, importing those files and modifying them for the new copy. This saves time and effort and helps you make rapid progress.

REVISIONS

Recently the head of a large public relations agency said to me, "Boy, I don't envy you being a freelance copywriter. That's got to be a tough job, writing copy and then having clients make all those changes and revisions."

To a degree, he's right. H. G. Wells once observed there is no greater human urge than the desire to rewrite someone else's copy. And certainly, if you've been a writer for any length of time, you know that for many writing projects the most tedious part is routing the drafts, making changes, generating revisions, and getting approvals.

Why is there so much revising and rewriting of copy by clients and editors? Aside from the possibility that the copy being submitted is simply bad copy, I think there are two major reasons.

The first is that writing is one of the few activities in the business world where there is no RFP (request for proposal), no predefined and agreed-upon specification to which the work must conform.

If I order a computer system, part of the vendor's selling process is to precisely define my needs and requirements. In their proposal to me, the vendor will spell out exactly what is to be delivered—down to the dimensions of the computer screen, the size of the hard drive, even the brand and type of modem. As a result, it's rather simple to determine whether the vendor has fulfilled my requirements.

But in the writing business, it's different. It would be absurd for the client to request, in advance, an article with so many subheads, so many commas, so many sentences beginning with the words *and* or *the*, so many paragraphs of such and such length.

And here's the root of the problem: If we cannot define a specification or requirement for the work before it is ordered, how can the professional writer be absolutely sure he or she is precisely meeting the client's preferences and expectations? We can't, of course—hence, the tendency to edit and rewrite any piece of submitted copy.

The second reason why copy is rewritten is best summed up by an ad agency executive from the television show *Thirtysomething* who, when asked to defend a campaign, replied, "Nobody knows anything."

To some degree, he is right. There is no formula that guarantees a successful ad or bestselling novel. All creative efforts are educated guesses; all published materials are tests which determine the validity of our approach to the market.

A roofer can guarantee that the roof he installs for you won't leak. In fact, roofers have to make such guarantees, or they won't get hired. But an unknown novelist cannot guarantee that her first book will be a bestseller, any more than a copywriter can guarantee that the direct-mail package he writes for a client will sell a certain number of insurance policies or book club memberships. Because writing is an art or a craft, and not an exact science, the professional writer's opinion is always subject to question and debate, in part because she cannot with certainty say she is right. .

Few people constantly and boldly challenge the opinions of their neurosurgeons, accountants, attorneys, mechanics, or electricians, because these professions are viewed as scientific, and the practitioners are seen as technical experts with arcane knowledge beyond the understanding of ordinary mortals. But, in fields where decisions are more subjective—copywriting, graphic design, interior decorating, landscape architecture— clients frequently question the practitioner, because the client believes his opinion to be equally valid.

As writer Hugo Williams observes, "The tricky thing about

the writing industry is the more or less accepted notion that everyone's opinion, even on matters of grammar, carries equal weight." Even if the client gives the professional carte blanche at the beginning of the project, the instant he sees something that is not exactly the way he would have done it, a revision or change is demanded.

Can anything be done to correct this situation and enable professional writers to make their clients happier faster?

1. Writers and their clients may want to establish a set of specifications or guidelines for certain projects. Should product sheets be promotional or technical? Benefit or feature oriented? Deciding in advance can prevent disagreements later on.

2. Think about presenting your ideas in memo or outline form before you go to first draft. This is the copy platform we discussed earlier. Get your client to comment on and approve the proposed direction before proceeding.

3. Writers should pay close attention to the tone, style, and length of the client's existing published materials. If your style and theirs mesh, fine. If not, ask if they're looking to create more of the same, or if they want new materials done with your special flair and touch.

For instance, if I observe that all the sample pieces a new copywriting client has sent me are done in a certain style, I may ask, "Are you open to a different approach, or do you basically want another ad along these lines?"

And what if they're inflexible? If I don't like their approach or cannot duplicate it, I walk away from the job.

14

KEEPING CLIENTS SATISFIED

There are basically three things you can do to keep your clients satisfied:

1. Do the best job you can on every piece of copy you write.
2. Never miss a deadline.
3. Give clients more than they expect.

These three rules are really very simple to follow.

1. DO THE BEST JOB YOU CAN

As I have pointed out elsewhere in this book, if you charge by the project, the faster you write, the more profit you make per hour. However, you should never rush a job or spend less time on it than is needed to increase your profit on that job. If you do, you will be the loser in the long run.

If a job is taking many more hours than originally anticipated, my advice is to keep on working and spend as much time as it takes to write the best piece of copy you can. Don't worry about your profit. The client is concerned with the quality of your work, not your profit or loss.

Never submit work that is less than your best. You cannot defend such work if the client doesn't like it. You have a professional obligation to give every client your best effort even if you could get away with less. Doing second-rate work is the fastest way to lose your current client and get a poor reputation in the business. So always do your best.

On occasion I have agreed to a super-rush deadline, thinking I was doing the client a favor by turning around a job that normally requires two weeks in a couple of days. The client then complained, "This seems like it was done in a rush and is not as in-depth or detailed as I would have liked." I felt like answering, "Of course it reads like it was done in a hurry— because it was, at your request." Instead I revised the job quickly to the client's satisfaction. Now I either negotiate a compromise deadline, turn the job away, or, if the client absolutely needs something in a rush mode, do it with the warning that satisfaction is not guaranteed and I can only deliver a "best effort" within the allotted time frame.

Freelance direct-mail writer John Clausen tells a similar story: "I accepted a three-project job, even though there was a serious illness in my family and my attention, not to mention my time, was being directed away from the writing. The next morning I read the copy and recognized it for the gibberish it was. Too late."

Sometimes, as Clausen points out, the client will not give you a chance to revise the piece, and you can lose that project or the entire account. "I offered all manner of restitution, but the damage had been done," says Clausen, who never did another job for that valued client.

2. NEVER MISS A DEADLINE

Next to price and the quality of your work, your reliability when it comes to deadlines is what clients are most concerned with.

In commercial writing, deadlines are critical. The client who needs your sales letter on January 3 will miss a critical mailing date if you are late. The client who gives you a November 14 deadline for brochure copy may have no literature to hand out at an important trade show if you submit your copy on November 21. The same goes for ads, speeches, and other copy.

Here are some tips for not missing deadlines:

- Don't take on a project if you can't meet the deadline. It is better to refuse the assignment and explain why than take on the assignment and miss the deadline.
- Don't take on more projects than you can comfortably handle. Never risk a missed deadline or do a second-rate job because you wanted to book more work.
- Negotiate with the client if proposed deadlines are too short. In some cases the client can and will give you more time. Take it!
- If there is research involved, start collecting your research materials as soon as you get the assignment. Failure to acquire key research materials early could hold you up later on.
- If you have to interview people at the client company for information relevant to the project, call them to arrange these interviews as soon as possible. You can do the interviews at a mutually convenient date, but get their commitment now. If you call them for the first time at the last minute, they may not be available to you.
- Work evenings and weekends if you have to.
- Hire someone to do some of the routine work such as typing drafts, proofreading, collecting research materials, or checking facts.

3. GIVE CLIENTS MORE THAN THEY EXPECT

"Don't cheat or take advantage of your client; you'll be the loser," advises publisher and author Russ von Hoelscher. "Instead, win success by giving your clients their money's worth. And if you really want great success, give your clients more than their money's worth."

This doesn't mean you should give away your ideas and words for free. Far from it. But giving a little extra shows clients that you genuinely care about their business success and want to help them.

For example, I was asked to write a brochure on a software product so new that it had not been named yet. Although the client didn't ask for it, I submitted a list of names along with my manuscript. They didn't use my names. But they were appreciative, and the next assignment was even bigger. And I knew I had earned a lot of goodwill, not a bad investment for twenty minutes spent writing a few suggestions on a sheet of paper.

In another situation I met with a consulting firm that was considering producing a brochure. By asking questions, I learned that the firm planned to mail the brochure to people who were called cold over the phone. By suggesting that a sales letter would be a better way of generating interest in the firm's consulting services, I won a $2,500 brochure assignment plus an additional $1,000 assignment to write the sales letter. I was successful with this client because the firm viewed me as a marketing consultant, not just as a writer.

"Be everywhere, do everything, and never fail to astonish the client," says Margaret Getchell of Macy's. Good advice.

BE DILIGENT ABOUT OFFERING SUPERIOR CLIENT SERVICE

If you've already put these principles to work and are getting good results, you may think, "Things are pretty okay with my clients at this point; now I can relax." Not so. One of the key secrets of ensuring client satisfaction is diligence: keeping at it week after week, month after month, for as long as you're in business.

Client satisfaction is not something you practice one month, then coast on when things are going smoothly. It is an attitude, a way of doing business, that must be diligently applied every waking moment, every minute of the business day.

It takes months, even years, of excellent client service to form solid, lasting relationships with the most profitable, lucrative clients. And all that can be destroyed with one slip, one mistake, one lapse, one error that gets the client ticked off at you enough to make them walk. Therefore, you can't "relax" when it comes to applying the principles of maximum client satisfaction expressed in this chapter. You have to do it every week, every day, every hour, every minute. Tiring? Possibly. Doable? Yes. Rewarding? I guarantee it.

Another reason why diligently practicing maximum client satisfaction and never letting your guard down is important is that, in this "age of the client," only those firms that create maximum client satisfaction will survive and prosper.

"Let's make sure that our clients are satisfied," suggests Lois Geller, president of Lois Geller Direct in an article in *Target Marketing*. "Lack of client service can break all of our efforts. If we are to cement buyer loyalty, client satisfaction must be a key objective."

Low levels of client satisfaction can cost your business a lot of money. According to investment consultant and author John M. Cali, Jr., 91 percent of unhappy clients who have been treated discourteously will not buy from the offending business again unless deliberate steps are taken to get them back. Just as bad, says Cali, is that the average unhappy client will complain about the poor treatment he or she received from

you to nine or ten other people, and 13 percent of these unhappy clients will tell more than twenty other people!

According to the American Productivity and Quality Center:

- Sixty-eight percent of clients stop doing business if they
  receive poor service.
- Clients are five times more likely to leave because of poor
  service than product quality or cost.
- Clients who receive poor service tell nine to twenty other
  people.
- Losing a client costs five times the annual value of the
  client account.
- The average happy client tells five other people.
- Fifty to 75 percent of clients who have their complaints
  solved quickly return and buy again.

DIFFERENTIATE YOURSELF FROM THE COMPETITION

Many business authorities say the only way to succeed is by
being great at everything you do. The book *In Search of Excellence*, coauthored by Tom Peters and Robert Waterman, in-
spired a new breed of business authors, speakers, and seminar
leaders proclaiming that only "excellence" will win clients and
profits in the 1990s.

While striving for excellence is a laudable goal, there are
two problems I have with experts saying you have to be great
or excellent to stay in business. First, it puts tremendous pressure on you. It's hard enough today to juggle all your client responsibilities and still get all your work done on time. To have
to be great in everything you do as well? It's too much!

Second, it's not true. You see, to stand head and shoul-
ders above your competition, you don't have to be "great" or
"excellent," you just have to be significantly better than the
competition.

And in giving excellent client service, that's fairly easy, because, despite all we read in the business press about the importance of client service, most businesses are not all that great when it comes to client service. So you don't have to be great; you just have to be better than they are. And because they're so mediocre, it's easy for you to beat them.

"You beat 50 percent of the people in America by working hard," says A. L. Williams, the self-made millionaire life insurance salesman, in his book *All You Can Do Is All You Can Do*. "You beat another 40 percent by being a person of honesty and integrity and by standing for something. The last 10 percent is a dogfight in the free enterprise system."

LISTEN TO YOUR CLIENTS

Failure to listen is usually caused by eagerness to speak. When you find yourself cutting off the other person's sentences, or not listening but instead sitting there waiting for the client to finish so you can talk, you're not really listening. And that's bad for two reasons.

First, if you don't listen, you don't know what the clients really want you to do; therefore, you can't do it. And if you don't do what the clients want, you don't have satisfied clients.

Second, it annoys clients. If they see you are not listening, they will feel you are not interested in them and their problems. Equally as important as listening is to let the clients know you are listening.

This can be accomplished with brief verbal responses that show you are paying attention ("I understand," "That's interesting," "Really?" "Uh-huh," "Tell me more," etc.). Another useful technique is to pause for a full second or two after a client has finished speaking before you begin your reply.

If you jump in too soon, a client may get the false impression that you weren't really listening and were just waiting for your turn to speak. By pausing for a second or two, you convey the impression that you have listened carefully and are still formulating your response.

Do not put a client on hold or have call waiting, which can cause an annoying, interruptive tone. Give your clients your full attention and all the time they need. Be efficient, but don't let them feel they are being rushed. Have incoming calls routed to voice mail or a secretary so your conversations with clients aren't interrupted.

Clients today perceive they are in a buyer's market. They know they can switch vendors, and it takes little aggravation or unhappiness to prompt them to look into doing so.

Selling wins the first order, but service is just as important as selling — perhaps even more so — in securing repeat orders, year after year. And that's the best way to build a profitable business in today's client-focused marketplace.

GIVE CLIENTS WHAT THEY WANT

"Find out what the client really wants," advises Ford R. Myers of Ford Myers & Company, a marketing communications firm. "Ask what the client expects. Get over the fear of hearing things you might not want to hear. These may be precisely the things you need to know to establish a good relationship."

Ford's tips for good client service include the following:

- Understand the business objectives of the client and the project.
- Listen to what the client says.
- Don't create problems, solve them.
- Be sensitive to the client's corporate culture, demands, and internal politics.
- Write superior copy.

- Be available to participate in meetings and telephone conferences.
- Become known as an expert in your field.
- Express your opinion, but remain diplomatic and defer to the client when appropriate.
- Use up-to-date computer systems and software that are compatible with the client's systems.
- Adapt to innovations.

In addition to asking clients what they want up front when you start, talk to them to get periodic assessments of your progress and whether you are meeting their needs. "Always ask for early-on assessment of the direction and content of the work you are doing," writes Jean Ban in "Paladin Network." "Clarifying and confirming direction early keeps projects on track."

DON'T BE A PRIMA DONNA

"The one thing I have learned over the years is not to be a 'prima donna' writer," says Dianna Huff, a successful freelance copywriter. "I sweat over my copy all the time but have come to realize that a client knows his company best and if he wants to make changes, so be it.

"I get feedback all the time from potential clients who say that the writer they are working with gets annoyed when they want to make revisions. My best client for two years called me initially because she said she was tired of her current writer yelling at her every time she changed one word."

Cameron Foote says, "Your first draft is your recommendation. After that, if the client wants changes, acquiesce pleasantly."

THE "FULL SERVICE" CONUNDRUM

One issue that comes up for freelance commercial writers is whether you can and are willing to provide marketing communications services in addition to copy. For instance, if you write brochures, will you also design the brochure, prepare film for the printer, supervise the printing, and deliver printed brochures to the client? Or do you, as some clients put it, "just write the copy"?

"You may at times find yourself entrusted with the 'whole ball of wax'—an assignment to handle the entire job, from initial research to having final camera-ready copy to go to the printer," says freelance writer Herman Holtz. "This happens quite often."

Some freelance commercial writers—those who don't have graphic capabilities or don't like to be involved in project management or production—often worry, "Will I be unable to get clients or lose jobs because I don't want to do [as Holtz puts it] the 'whole ball of wax'?"

Relax. If you want to do "just the writing," there's more business out there than you can handle. "We absolutely stick to writing copy," say the principals of B. K. Creative, a small copywriting firm specializing in direct-mail fund-raising copy. "Don't be a jack of all trades, master of none. In the long run, you'll be far better off."

If you like to see a project through from start to finish, there are more than enough clients who will pay you to do this, if that's your preference. As a rule of thumb, small businesses are most likely to want full service, while ad agencies and corporations are accustomed to hiring writers to do copy only and then having the material produced using their own staff or outside resources.

METHODOLOGY

An effective way to ensure client satisfaction with your methods of working is to let the client know those methods before he or she hires you. I do this by posting my working methods

for various tasks — copywriting, consulting, online marketing —
on the "Methodology" section of my Web site, www.bly.com.

In simple 1-2-3 fashion, a methodology document outlines
how you work with clients on a particular task, what you will
do for the client, and more important, what you will not do.
Clients will accept that you do not handle certain tasks or totally comply with their desires as long as you let them know
that in advance.

You can tell them these things verbally, but it's much more
effective to present your methodology and policies early in
the sales cycle. "When you tell a client 'this is my policy,' they
are more likely to accept it, precisely because it is a policy,"
says copywriter Joan Harris.

You should, of course, put your policies, terms, and conditions in your client agreement. But if the client sees something
in that agreement when you send a price quotation, she may
be taken aback and hesitate to sign your agreement.

That's why I like to get my working methods, which may
seem restrictive to some clients, out of the way early. So by the
time the client gets my agreement, there are no surprises, and
resistance is eliminated.

Here, for instance, is the Methodology page from my Web
site on the subject we just discussed: the fact that many clients
need graphic design and I don't provide it.

METHODOLOGY FOR GRAPHIC DESIGN, PRODUCTION,
AND PROJECT MANAGEMENT
Clients frequently ask whether we can bid on a direct-mail
package or e-mail marketing campaign "as an ad agency." They
may want us to do the design along with the copy, manage a
direct-mail project from start to finish, or otherwise provide a
single source for their direct mail and e-mail marketing needs.
Here's what we can — and cannot — do:

1. Basically, I'm a freelance copywriter—not a creative services agency, marketing communications firm, ad agency, list broker, or boutique.
2. My specialty is writing copy that sells. Period. I add little or no value performing any other function. Writing powerful copy is the primary value I deliver to my clients.
3. If you need graphic design as well as copy, I will refer you to one of several graphic artists I regularly recommend to my clients.
4. These designers are listed on the Vendors page of www .bly.com under the heading "Direct Mail Graphic Design." You can get a quote for the design from them directly (the most efficient route), but we don't mind doing this for you on your behalf.
5. I can give the designer considerable guidance—as much or as little as you and she would like. My copy comes with a copywriter's rough. It's drawn neatly in Microsoft Word, making the design easy to follow (copy elements are clearly keyed into the layout).
6. Whether you use your designer or ours, we would like to get (but do not insist upon) a PDF of the layout before the piece goes to press. I will review it at no charge to make sure the elements are laid out correctly and that everything works.
7. We also proofread the PDF for you thoroughly, again at no charge, and usually find typos that our clients miss. However, you are responsible for the final proofing.
8. If you need agency-style project management with an account executive, we have several freelance project managers we recommend. These are on the bly.com Vendors page under "Project Management."
9. If you need list recommendations, just go to one of my recommended list brokers on the bly.com Vendors page under

the heading "Mailing List Brokers." There is no need for me to get involved, but if you want me to talk with the broker on your behalf or review their list recommendations and give you my opinion, I can do so on a consulting basis.

10. My forte is writing copy for solo mailings. I can give advice on marketing strategy or campaign planning, but if you need a formal marketing plan, I will probably recommend you to one of the consultants listed on the bly.com Vendors page.

15

COMMON PROBLEMS AND HOW TO HANDLE THEM

Everyone who is a self-employed writer, consultant, or professional has problems with clients sooner or later. Any freelancer who says "I never have any problems" is either not telling the truth or has so little business that problems haven't come up. Why will you eventually have conflict with your clients?

1. They will not like something you write and this will offend you.
2. They will behave in a rude or offensive manner.
3. You will do something that is not to their liking, and they will complain about it or vent unhappiness in other ways.
4. You are both human beings, and human beings—even the nicest ones—sometimes have trouble getting along.
5. One or both of you will say or do something under pressure or in the heat of the moment that the other resents.
6. You will have a miscommunication that results in misunderstanding, and the client will blame you.
7. Either you or your client will change fees, payment terms, or other ways of doing business, and this will upset the other person.

8. Or one of any of a dozen other reasons why people argue, fight, or get angry.

There is nothing wrong with a little conflict now and then, so long as it blows over quickly, is resolved pleasantly by you, and doesn't prevent normal friendly business relations between you and your client.

If you are getting into blow-ups with clients all the time, perhaps you do not select your clients carefully enough, or else you are too short-tempered and need to be more in control.

In any case, most small problems do not become big ones if you know how to handle them correctly. Below are some of the most common freelance problems you will encounter in handling clients, along with some guidelines on how to resolve them.

PROBLEM NO. 1: YOU AND THE CLIENT HAVE FUNDAMENTAL DISAGREEMENTS ON HOW TO DO THE PROJECT AT HAND

This is a case where you want to be wild and creative, and you feel the client is unreasonably conservative in his approach to the assignment. Or where the client says your approach isn't "exciting" enough and you feel it is just right and works perfectly.

The secret to handling this problem is to prevent it from happening in the first place. This is done by carefully prescreening prospects and selecting only those clients whose creative philosophy, style, and business approach are similar to your own.

If a client has a certain ingrained style of working, he is not going to change it to accommodate a freelancer he hires to do one job. Rather, the company is looking for someone to execute the project along the basic lines they are comfortable with. They may want you to improve on what they've done in the past, but they don't want you to fundamentally, radically, alter it.

Only an ad agency or marketing consultant working with the agency on a long-term strategic basis has any hope of changing the client's basic way of thinking, and even then only with great difficulty. A freelancer (you) definitely isn't going to waltz in and revolutionize their business philosophy and style overnight.

For this reason, clients should choose writers—and writers should work with clients—who have a similar style, philosophy, and tone.

If you are uncertain as to whether you should work with clients because you are uncomfortable with their approach, then have them look at your samples and make them understand this is the type of writing they will be getting from you.

At the same time, look at their past work and make sure you are comfortable with it. If you don't like their style, or they don't like yours, pass on the project. They are not the right clients for you. You may indeed convince them to hire you. But you will be at odds with them from the moment you sign the contract.

It's much better to work for a client that likes and is looking for your style. This ensures compatibility and eliminates the risk of basic disagreements in execution and style.

Another technique to ensuring that you deliver what clients want is to ask them what they want. Do they want copy that's fanciful and creative, or professional and businesslike? Do they want a brochure that makes a sales pitch or is loaded with product facts and figures?

To be successful, you must give your clients copy that (a) pleases them; (b) achieves the result they desire; or (c) does both. Which of these two objectives is the priority depends on the client.

As a rule, direct marketers, entrepreneurs, retailers, business owners, and others who have bottom-line responsibility and who are able to measure the results of what you do for them, such as the response rate to a sales letter, want copy that they think is good. But they're also concerned with results, and will at least listen to any suggestions or advice you give on increasing the copy's performance.

PROBLEM NO. 2: YOU AND THE CLIENT HAVE FUNDAMENTAL DISAGREEMENTS ON YOUR WORKING ARRANGEMENT AND THE TERMS OF YOUR RELATIONSHIP

This is similar to problem No. 1, except here the conflict is not on creative philosophy, marketing tactics, or writing style, but on working arrangements.

For example, some clients love meetings, endless meetings. I find too many meetings to be unproductive, a waste of time. Therefore, a client who wants to get together and "brainstorm" three times a week is probably not a good client for me.

To make sure you don't have a conflict in working style, discuss your working preferences up front and at the same time try to learn any preferences the client may have. This can be done through questioning, such as, "Do you feel we need to meet, or can we handle the assignment by phone and e-mail?" Or, "Do you need progress reports, or would you prefer that I simply submit my copy when it is ready?"

This way you can gauge the client's expectations and preferences and see whether they fit your working style. This helps you make a decision about whether to accept or pass on the assignment.

PROBLEM NO. 3: THE CLIENT DOESN'T LIKE YOUR COPY

You need to distinguish between the client's asking for revisions, which is normal, and the client's fundamentally disliking your copy.

Most clients will ask for some revisions, although some do not. Revisions are normal, and as long as the revision process does not fundamentally destroy the flow, style, and power of the text you have written, my advice is: Just do it.

The problem arises when the client has no respect for the work you have done, doesn't like it, and rips it apart. This can happen verbally, when the client is rude and openly critical about your work, or on paper, where every other sentence or word of your copy is crossed out or circled.

How do you handle this? First, stay calm. Maybe the client has not hired a writer before, didn't know what to expect, and panicked when the copy was not 100 percent as he thinks he would have written it.

In this case, try to find out what the client liked, what he didn't like, what he wants changed, and why. After such a session, the client often calms down and discovers that the copy is much better than he thought and that only a few things are off the mark.

When faced with a major revision, politely but firmly force the client to be as specific as possible in his or her criticisms. Don't allow general comments to pass unclarified. Instead, insist that the client specify exactly what he doesn't like and what substitution or change is desired.

Explain that without this specific commentary, you are unable to proceed further with the revisions. You might even build such a statement into your sales literature and client contract.

In rare instances, the client may be an irrational person who is not interested in getting a good job but simply delights in torturing freelancers and other outside vendors. The best way to handle this client is politely but distantly.

Grit your teeth, put up with the client long enough to do a satisfactory revision, then send your bill and move on to the next client. Refuse to work for this client again despite any promises for an easier next assignment—it will never happen.

If any client treats you in a rude, abrasive, or undignified manner, do not allow it. Tell him that you will not tolerate it. If it continues one second longer, get up, walk away, and pursue collection until your bill is paid.

PROBLEM NO. 4: THE CLIENT IS LATE PAYING YOUR BILL

This does not mean that they don't intend to pay you, although that is a possibility. More likely, they either forgot or just are slow payers. Many Fortune 500 firms routinely pay invoices in 60 or 90 days, despite the fact that you wrote "net 10 days" or "net 30 days" on your bill. It's just a fact of life you'll have to live with.

But what happens when a reasonable time has passed and you still have not received payment? Then you begin your collection cycle. This is a series of letters and phone calls designed to remind the client that the bill is still unpaid and to get her to pay it.

The first contact is a letter. Never get angry or accuse the client of deliberately cheating you in this first letter. It serves as a reminder and makes the assumption that the client meant to pay you but simply forgot. This prods her to pay without making her feel guilty. You can use the model dunning letter series reprinted in appendix F.

Your goal is not to put the client in a compromising position or to prove that you are right and she is wrong, but simply to get the check she owes you.

Another way to get bills paid faster is either to give a small discount for prompt payment (e.g., "Deduct $X if paid within 10 days") or to charge the legal interest rate for overdue bills (e.g., "2½% service charge for bills 30 days or more past due").

PROBLEM NO. 5: THE CLIENT REFUSES TO PAY
THE BILL OR CAN'T PAY IT

If after the intensive collection effort, you still haven't been paid, it means that the client either can't or doesn't intend to pay your bill.

Now is the time to write a strong letter saying that if you do not receive payment within two weeks, you will have no choice but to take legal action to collect the bill. This means court.

Send this letter certified mail, return receipt requested, to prove that the client received it. If you don't hear back, wait the two weeks, then send a second letter stating the same thing.

If you still don't hear, hire a collection agency or attorney or take the client to court. The more paperwork you have—a signed contract, a purchase order, copies of any printed pieces the client produced using your copy—the better your chances of collection.

TIP: Always make a photocopy of the first check you receive from a client. This ensures that you have a record of their business bank account number, making it easier to collect any judgment you obtain against them. Getting an advance payment from any new client ensures that you always have such a check on file.

PROBLEM NO. 6: THE CLIENT PRESENTS YOU
WITH AN UNREASONABLE DEADLINE

First, what is a reasonable deadline? From your point of view, it is enough time to do the job properly without being rushed. This means doing the job at a normal pace without overtime or putting off other work to accommodate the client.

Clients often do not understand that they are not your only client or that you have other work. They will often give a deadline regardless of your schedule and act as if it's a given that you will accept it.

The key to solving this problem is client education. I begin early, addressing this point in my sales literature, explaining that (a) my normal turnaround time is two to three weeks; but (b) sometimes if I am busy the waiting period may be three or four weeks or longer; and (c) if I do take on their job, I promise to get it done by the deadline agreed upon.

However, I make it a point not to promise that I will always be able to do their projects, no matter what the deadline.

The definition of a "rush" job varies with the writer and the client. For me, two to three weeks is an acceptable deadline, although I will try to push for three weeks on difficult or complex assignments. I rarely promise anything in less than one or two weeks, and a turnaround within the same week the job is assigned is, for me, a rush.

Yet I know of other writers who consider one week or less a standard turnaround time. One writer even advertises a 24-hour turnaround. I guess she is just not terribly busy, and so quick turnaround is the advantage she sells and advertises.

Freelance video scriptwriter Steve Yankee gives his clients a card that says: "You can have it fast. You can have it good. You can have it cheap. Pick any two." Many clients, however, will try to get it fast, good, *and* cheap. Be flexible and accommodating, but don't overpromise. You don't want to set deadlines that you can't keep, charge so little that you have to work all the time and burn out, or promise what you can't deliver.

As for myself, I sell quality, expertise, and the ability to write copy that generates results. I do not emphasize low price or fast turnaround, although I will always try to accommodate the deadlines and budgets of current clients.

Okay. Let's say you get a phone call, and it's a client or prospect with an assignment. Only it's a rush assignment. How do you handle it?

• If you're not busy, then you might agree to handle the job, either at your normal fee or with an added charge for rush service. But make sure the client understands that you are bending over backward to accommodate him or her. Don't let on you are sitting around doing nothing. Clients want to hire writers who are busy and successful, and you must project such an image.

• If you are too busy to take on the project, and the call is from a prospect (someone who has not hired you yet) rather than a regular client, simply say, "It sounds interesting and I'd like to handle it. However, I am booked solid for the next eight weeks [or however long it is until you could do the job]. If you can wait until then, great. If not, I'll have to pass."

A more serious problem is getting the same call from a regular client when you are too busy. Obviously, you want to maintain the client's goodwill, and clients do not like it when you turn them down. Yet you should not take on more work than you can realistically handle.

In this case, the first step is to see if the deadline is real (that is, it exists because of an actual event, such as a sales meeting or trade show date), or if it is artificial (the date was picked arbitrarily or because the client wants the job done "as soon as possible").

To ascertain this, say to the client, "April twenty-second is a real rush for me and I'm not sure I'd be able to do the job you want in such a short time frame. Let me ask: What happens if you get the copy from me a week later?" The client thinks about it, realizes that it makes no difference, and so you get a one-week-longer deadline. Or the client wants it sooner, and you negotiate a compromise deadline date.

If the client can't or won't budge on the deadline, you have a difficult decision. If you fear the client will react negatively if you refuse, and if you can do the job even though it means working nights and weekends, you may decide for the sake of the relationship to go ahead and do it.

However, you can compensate for this by charging a higher fee, and also by pointing out to the client (without making too big a deal of it) that this is an exception to your policy and that you are doing him a favor. Let him know, in a polite way, that only for him would you agree to such a deadline, and that if anyone else called you would have said no.

PROBLEM NO. 7: YOUR PRICE IS TOO HIGH

Freelancers tell me they feel terrible when they quote a price to the client that is too high. Their instant reaction is to apologize and immediately offer the client a lower price, so they can proceed with the work.

What a mistake! For several reasons.

First, no other profession apologizes for charging a decent fee. When was the last time your doctor, dentist, or attorney acted ashamed or embarrassed or apologetic for the fee they charged? Never—because they are skilled professionals entitled to a professional fee. And you are, too.

Second, it's ridiculous to lower a price simply because the customer cannot afford it. Does the real estate agent lower the price on a $250,000 home to $180,000 simply because your budget is $180,000? Instead, they show you the $180,000 house you can afford and leave the $250,000 house to a buyer with more money.

And so it is with selling a professional service. Some will be able to afford you. Some won't. So what? Sell to clients who can afford you, and let the others buy a less expensive service until their funds reach the level where they can afford you.

Third, many writers tell me they charge lower fees because they feel sorry for the client or because the client is small.

Again, absurd. This isn't charity work we're talking about,

folks. It's business. That client who hires you is going to make a lot of money from your writing, and is in business to make money, not save the world. So please don't consider him or her a charity case.

You would be surprised to find out how wealthy most of these self-proclaimed "poor" companies really are. Don't be fooled.

Many years ago, I lowered the price on a brochure because the client said his business was struggling and if I helped him now, he'd reward me later on with lots of work. I agreed. When we parted in the parking lot, I drove off in my 1984 Chevette, and couldn't help but notice that his car was a shiny new black BMW. And because he was cheap with his business, the client did little promotion and had no further jobs of any significance to give me.

Fourth, and most important, if you immediately lower your $2,000 price quotation to $1,000, then the client has to believe that your original quotation was inflated and meaningless. What's the solution? It's to determine a fair price, quote it to the client, and then stop. Don't say anything more.

If you feel uncertain as to what to charge, there is nothing wrong with asking clients, "What is your budget?" If they don't have a budget, ask, "Do you have a dollar figure in mind as to what you would like to pay for this?" The answer lets you know whether their budget is in line with your fee structure or there's simply not enough money to hire you.

As soon as the client says, "The price is too high," or implies it with her silence, you may feel you have to justify the price or you may immediately begin to apologize and offer a lower price, or say something like, "Well, I'm flexible; I'll work within your budget."

The first person who talks after the price is presented loses the negotiation. So let the client do the talking. Don't back down. Remain the calm, cool professional. If the client does say the price is too high, you simply go over the quotation, explaining what the client is getting and what it costs.

If she still objects, you say, "I understand. I'm expensive, and my service is not for every client. If you hire me, you will get your money's worth in terms of quality and results—more than your money's worth. But it's your decision. If you decide to go ahead, just let me know." And then end the phone call.

You'll be shocked at how frequently the clients who "don't have the budget" or "can't afford you" come back a week later and meet your price. And those that don't? You can either negotiate a mutually acceptable price with them or pass on the job. It's up to you.

"Do not sell yourself short by giving your talent away," state the "Business Practice Recommendations" of the Self-Employed Writers and Artists Network (see appendix A). "Once you start to sell yourself cheaply, it's next to impossible to receive higher fees from the same clients in the future. An unrealistically low fee can be perceived as low quality; therefore, the prospect of getting better assignments becomes slim."

PROBLEM NO. 8: THE CLIENT WON'T SIGN YOUR CONTRACT

You should always have a contract, proposal, letter of agreement, purchase order, or other piece of paper that serves as a written record of your agreement with the client. And it should always be returned to you with the client's signature (and preferably an advance check) before you begin the job.

In a recent seminar, a freelance graphic artist complained to me, "The idea of a contract is all well and good, but most of my work is rush. By the time I write the letter, send it off, have the client sign it, and mail it back, the deadline for the job has passed."

This is a psychological weapon clients use. The argument is "Yes, I will sign your contract. But the job is a rush, and I don't expect you to hold me up on formalities. So begin without your contract and I'll get it to you — trust me."

One partial solution to this problem is simply not to take on rush jobs, as explained under Problem No. 6. Don't do jobs in two to three days, do them in two to three weeks, so there is plenty of time to get the paperwork before you begin.

Another solution is to have a standard agreement form you can e-mail as an attached PDF to the client immediately. This is less time-consuming than drawing up a new letter of agreement for each client. For a copy of my standard client contract, see appendix F.

One more good idea: Buy a fax machine. Having a fax machine virtually eliminates any excuses from the client. You e-mail the client a PDF of your agreement. They sign it and fax it back to you.

Nowadays my response to clients who say there isn't time to sign a contact is "As we agreed, I need the signed contract before we can begin. So give me your e-mail address. I will e-mail you a contract in a few minutes. Sign it and fax it back to me, and I'll have what I need to begin today." If an advance check is required, I tell the client to send the check overnight via Federal Express or Express Mail. With e-mail and fax, there is no reason on earth why the client can't receive, sign, and return to you the signed contract within minutes after his phone call.

PROBLEM NO. 9: PEOPLE ON THE CLIENT'S STAFF ARE UNCOOPERATIVE

As a writer, you cannot operate in a vacuum. Often you must work with the client and others in his organization to get the job done. So, what do you do when people on the client's staff are uncooperative?

First, don't lose your cool. Even though the person may not

be directly involved with the project, a complaint about you could create problems in the relationship.

You see, that person is a part of the company team, while you are just an outsider. If someone has to take a fall, a manager will find it easier to blame or dismiss an outside consultant rather than an employee.

So, treat everyone in the client organization with politeness and respect, even if they don't deserve it. You are not helpless if someone gives you a hard time, but displaying anger is not the solution. Have minimal contact with them: only as much as is needed to get the job done. The rest of the time, simply ignore them.

I've found that e-mail is a great tool for dealing with people I dislike speaking with in person or over the phone. I simply e-mail my communications and let them do the same. Dealing with them is easier if I don't have to hear their voice.

Finally, if someone is a total roadblock, you have no choice but to let your client know this. Don't do it emotionally, but simply inform the client that Joe or John or Mary is not being cooperative. Suggest alternatives, such as another person you can work with or another way to proceed. Often the client knows John or Mary is a troublemaker, appreciates your telling him so, and is all too happy to get John or Mary out of the picture.

PROBLEM NO. 10: THE CLIENT CANCELS THE JOB MIDWAY

Does your contract have a clause that outlines what happens if the client decides to cancel the project? If not, you might want to add one. A standard cancellation clause reads as follows:

> XYZ Company will have the right to terminate this agreement at any time upon notice to me. In such an event, XYZ will compensate me for the hours actually worked on the project

through the date and time of cancellation, plus any out-of-pocket expenses incurred by me up to that time.

This means that if the client cancels on Tuesday at nine A.M., you have the right to bill him for all labor and materials up to that instant. To be fair, you should in exchange turn over to the client all work completed to date.

Instead of basing the kill fee on the number of hours worked, you can base it on the level of progress you have made in the job as a percentage of the total project price. One possible kill-fee schedule is as follows:

- 10 percent of the fee if the client has given a go-ahead and then cancels before you have started work
- 25 percent if you have started working on the job but haven't submitted copy
- 50 percent if you have submitted an outline or copy platform but have not yet written a draft
- 75 percent if you have submitted a first draft but not done a revision
- 100 percent if you have already done a draft and one or more rewrites

PROBLEM NO. 11: THE PROJECT IS MORE WORK THAN YOU BARGAINED FOR

This happens a lot. In your eagerness to clinch the assignment, you underestimate the amount of work involved in order to quote the client a lower fee. Then, once you start work, you discover the project is much more involved than you anticipated, and you are not making much money on it.

What to do? Again, this is one of those problems best solved by preventing it from happening in the first place. So when you do estimates and quote fees, make sure you are being realistic.

If anything, make your quotation a little high to protect yourself from unexpected complications and snags.

Once the client has agreed to your fee and signed your contract, she understandably does not expect to pay more without good reason. Saying "I underestimated the job" is unprofessional and not likely to bring about an increase in fee. In fact, it probably diminishes your status in the eyes of the client.

Your only hope for a higher fee is when you can legitimately claim that the client has increased or changed the scope of the project after the estimate was made and the contract signed.

For example, you agreed to write a single sales letter for $2,000, and during the job the client decides she needs a second version aimed at a different market. You certainly are entitled to charge her an additional fee for creating the second version.

How much should that fee be? For doing versions of a sales letter or e-mail, the version is typically pretty much the same as the original, except with a different headline and lead. If I am charging $2,000 for the sales letter, each version is an additional $500.

A separate contract or "change order" amending your original agreement should then be sent to the client for signature and a signed copy returned to you before you proceed with this new work. As always, get it in writing!

PROBLEM NO. 12: THE CLIENT WANTS THE ENTIRE PACKAGE, INCLUDING DESIGN AND PRINTING, NOT JUST COPY

As a writer, you are selling writing services, and your agreements with clients should make this clear. Referring to what you deliver as "copy" in a letter of agreement or contract means that you deliver text in manuscript form, not desktop publishing pages or artists' layouts.

If the client is going to have the piece you are writing designed in-house or by a professional graphic artist but wants to get your ideas on layout, you can include instructions within your manuscript to guide the designer. Or you can offer to do a rough pencil sketch, which you should call a "copywriter's rough."

I draw my copywriter's roughs in Microsoft Word so I can include them in the Word file in which I submit my copy. Figure 15-1 shows a typical copywriter's rough.

Some writers take jobs to the next step, delivering laser proofs or computer files of pages that have been designed using a desktop publishing program. Writers who do this say they can increase the fees they charge by offering design along with writing services.

Maybe. My experience is that a good commercial writer can earn much more per hour than a desktop publisher, so the

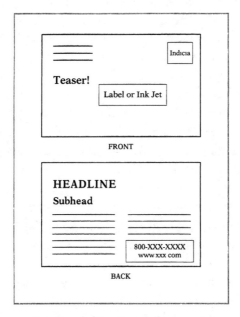

Fig. 15-1. Copywriter's Rough for a Postcard

hours you spend designing pages would be better spent writing. As a rule, the majority of clients are looking for regular manuscript and will not require you to do design. When the projects are manuals and newsletters, you may run into clients who want design along with copy.

For brochures, annual reports, and other documents that require more sophisticated design, you don't have to get involved in graphic design if you don't want to. Some clients will only hire you if they can get copy and graphics from a single source, but there are thousands who routinely buy "copy only" from writers, then turn that copy over to an in-house or outside graphic designer.

Large corporations and advertising agencies usually buy copy separately from design. Smaller firms are more likely to look for a one-stop service. There are numerous exceptions at both ends, of course.

When it comes to answering the question "Do you also handle graphics and printing?" you have two options.

Option 1 is to explain that you are a writer and what you deliver to the client is copy in manuscript form: hard copy and in computer format. If you choose this option, the client may ask you to recommend graphic designers, printers, and photographers to handle those portions of the project, and this is a request you should be able to comply with.

Seek out and form an informal referral network with other creative services firms that handle the portions of corporate and marketing communications you don't. I post a list of my recommended graphic artists on the "Vendors" page of my Web site, www.bly.com. You should be able to say to the client, "Here are two or three design firms I refer my clients to regularly and that can do this job for you."

If you are unable to give a referral to a designer when a client asks, then the client may hesitate to contract with you for the copy, worried that she won't be able to find someone to transform the copy into a finished design. So having a referral network of creative services in allied fields is extremely important for writers who offer a "copy only" service, as I do.

Option 2 is to offer the complete package, then subcontract graphic artists, photographers, illustrators, printers, and other vendors to deliver the complete package the client wants. If you want to do this, fine, but it's not necessary. If you prefer not to get involved with graphics, you certainly don't have to.

16

BUILDING YOUR FREELANCE WRITING BUSINESS

You may reach the point in your career where you are so busy you can't or don't want to take on more business.

The temptation is to stop marketing and selling your services. After all, marketing is costly and time-consuming. Why should you continue your sales efforts if you don't need to make more sales?

You should not put a halt to your marketing program even when you are extremely busy because it could hurt you in the future. "I was so busy that I stopped selling myself," said one woman at a luncheon meeting of freelancers in New York. "My current projects kept me busy for three months straight. But when I finally finished the work and looked up, I had nothing, not a single assignment or even a lead, because I had shut down my marketing program."

You can reduce your marketing activities when you are extremely busy, but don't stop them altogether. Remember, most writing assignments are over quickly. You need to cultivate contacts today so that you will have clients and hot prospects six months from now. As successful entrepreneur and bestselling author Harvey MacKay puts it, "Dig your well before you're thirsty."

GETTING INTO NEW MARKETS AND AREAS

Most of us start freelancing by writing things similar to what we did at our full-time jobs. A hospital publicist is most likely to begin freelancing by writing press releases and newsletters for local hospitals. A copywriter employed by a department store will probably begin freelancing by writing retail space ads and newspaper inserts.

The reason we start this way is that clients like to hire someone with experience in their areas. But at some point, we want to break away from our narrow specialty and move into other areas. How do we convince clients to hire us to do something in which we have little or no proven experience?

The best way is to work for ad agencies, public relations firms, TV producers, or other vendors that serve clients in several different areas. Initially, you will get hired because of your expertise in a specific field.

But once you demonstrate to an ad agency client that you can write, you may get asked to write copy for other accounts the agency handles. Almost every time I have gotten the opportunity to write in a new field, it has been for an ad agency or PR client who trusted me because I had proved myself doing the type of copy I was experienced in.

Of course, occasionally someone from an organization may call you directly and not care whether you have experience in that field. Perhaps you were referred by a client who praised your work. Or he or she read your article in an advertising magazine and decided you were the writer for the organization. Whatever the reason, you are being given an opportunity to do something different. Take it!

The positive side of doing something new is that it is fun, exciting, interesting, and challenging. Also, it gives you experience and writing samples you can use to sell yourself to get additional assignments in the new area.

The negative side is that it takes a lot more time to do something unfamiliar than to write the type of copy you've done a hundred times before. Therefore, your profit per hour is likely to be lower. This is the price you pay for breaking into a new area, and it's well worth it.

Because you have to eat and pay the rent, I suggest you balance your workload between your bread-and-butter assignments and forays into new fields. To ensure a good income, at least 80 percent of your assignments should be in your established area of expertise, with the remaining 20 percent in new areas. This achieves a good balance of income versus self-education.

INCREASING YOUR PROFITS

Although freelance writing offers a wonderfully free and unrestricted lifestyle that few other professions can match, the income potential of the freelancer is limited by the number of hours he or she can work.

You are one person. You can handle only so many assignments in a month or a year. You can charge only so much per assignment. This establishes a clear upper limit to your income, although for the top freelancers this can be in the hundreds of thousands of dollars per year.

How can a freelancer increase his or her income? There are six basic methods:

1. Write faster.
2. Increase fees.
3. Look for royalty arrangements.
4. Hire assistants.
5. Start a company.
6. Find additional profit centers.

Let's look at each of these in a bit more detail:

1. Write Faster

This is the surest way to greater profits. If it takes you two days to complete a $500 assignment, your profit is $250 per day. But if you could do it in half a day, your profit would be $500 for that half day, or $1,000 a day.

Speed develops with experience. The first time you are asked to write a sales letter for a client, it is all new to you, and you will spend many hours agonizing over the format, outline, and wording to get it just right.

But by the time you sit down to write your hundredth letter, you've already worked through most of the knotty problems of how to structure and write effective direct mail. As a result, you can do it faster because you know how to.

Just because you do your work fast, does it mean that you aren't doing as good a job as someone who spends weeks agonizing over the same assignment? Not at all. "It is axiomatic, in cognitive science, that there is no necessary correlation between profundity of thought and length of time spent on thought," writes William F. Buckley, Jr., in the *New York Times Book Review.*

Freelance writer Milt Pierce goes a step further. His belief is that copy written quickly is better because it comes more naturally. When a writer writes slowly, says Milt, it is because he is struggling to come up with ideas.

2. Raise Your Fees

Another way to make more money writing is to charge more per hour or per project. But raising fees is a tricky business. Here's what I've learned about it:

• Don't raise your fees by astronomic amounts. Restrict fee increases to no more than 10 to 20 percent at one time.

- Don't raise fees too often. Once a year is reasonable.
- When you raise fees, you will price yourself out of the range of certain clients and certain types of businesses. At the same time, you will begin to attract a higher-level clientele—companies that can and do pay top dollar for premium service from top professionals. These clients are usually better to work for than clients who haggle over every penny.
- Give current customers a reason for your price increase. Tell your clients you will continue to charge them your old prices for the rest of the year as a special favor to them. Then they pay your new prices starting on January 1 of the new year.
- Resist backing down from your new fees to your old when clients protest. Otherwise, prospects will think your new rates are meaningless and don't really apply to them. However, if a lot of people complain, perhaps your new fees are too high and should be adjusted to more realistic levels.
- Know where your prices put you in the market before you change them. It's reasonable for a low-priced writer to raise fees. But if you're already on the high side, and clients are straining to pay your bills, an additional 20 percent may price you out of the market.
- A fee raise doesn't have to apply across the board to every item on your fee schedule. For example, if you are gaining a reputation as a great annual report writer, you can raise your fee for an annual report, but leave other prices unchanged.

3. Look for Royalty Arrangements

When you write copy for which you are paid a royalty or mailing fee (see chapter 5), you free yourself from being an hourly laborer and gain a source of passive income.

For instance, if you negotiate a mailing fee of $20,000 for

every million direct-mail packages a client mails using your copy, you make $20,000 every time they print and mail another million of those letters—even though you are doing no additional work. With passive income, you make money without any additional labor on your part.

Don't count on royalty income when projecting your revenues for the year; consider it all as "gravy" or extra income. But sometimes royalty income can be substantial and in rare cases exceed your regular income from project fees. I recently read in a magazine that Merv Griffin made more than $7 million in royalties for writing the theme song for the TV show *Jeopardy*, and that the royalties from the song "Happy Birthday" total more than a million dollars a year.

4. Hire Assistants

If you are already a self-employed writer, you know that mundane tasks—online research, proofreading, addressing envelopes, going to the post office, filing, licking stamps, making photocopies—can eat up time that could be more profitably spent working on assignments.

One way to increase your productivity and profits is to hire an assistant. For years, Sig Rosenblum, one of the top freelancers specializing in direct mail, had a secretary employed Monday through Friday, 9 to 5, whom he kept busy all the time. Says Sig, "The only way you can make money is writing or thinking. When you do anything else, you are losing money. Get a secretary!"

Milt Pierce also used assistants for many years. He finds them valuable for doing library research, providing him with background material he needs to write his direct-mail packages, books, articles, and ads.

Other writers, however, do not find assistants helpful; they feel that in the time it takes to explain to an assistant what needs to be done and to check what was done, they can do it quicker themselves.

Another consideration is workload. Unlike Sig, many free-lancers, especially those just starting out, don't have nearly enough work to keep a full- or even part-time secretary busy. An alternative is to find people who can assist you, when needed, on a freelance basis.

Look in your local newspaper and Yellow Pages and ask other writers about proofreaders, word-processing services, re-searchers, editors, indexers, and other resources. You can call on them to help you when you're busy; when you're not, you do everything yourself.

5. Start Your Own Company

Carrying the idea of assistants one step further, you can go be-yond "freelancing" and start a company. For example, some freelancers start small companies providing editorial services. They get assignments from clients for a fee, then pay other freelancers to do the work at a lower rate. Other freelancers go on to build their own ad agencies or public relations firms.

However, running an ad agency or other company is not the same as being a self-employed individual. As a company presi-dent you are expected to do many other things in addition to writing. These include finding and hiring employees, manag-ing employees, much closer day-to-day contact with clients, travel, meetings, business planning, and "wining and dining" of clients.

Also, running a company involves a lot more administra-tion, management, and paperwork than a simple one-person freelance writing business. It may make you richer (then again, you could lose money, too), but it will certainly complicate your life.

"Employees can give you a measure of leverage and help you earn more in less time by multiplying yourself," explains Internet marketer Terry Dean in the book *The E-Code* (John Wiley & Sons). "The negative side is they also require a lot of hand-holding and watching over. If you have a lot of employees, you'll end up spending as much time watching over them as you do getting any real work done."

So making the decision to expand your operations comes down to this: Do I like the lifestyle of freelancing? Or do I want to take on the challenge of building my wealth through a company of my own? Only you can answer, depending on your personality.

"I don't like taking orders, and I don't like giving them," says Don Hauptman, a successful New York freelancer, explaining why he prefers to work alone, without employees or assistants.

One other point to keep in mind: As your company grows, you will spend more time selling and managing your business, less time writing. If you prefer to spend most of your time at the PC, as I do, then freelancing—not building an empire—may be more your style.

6. Find Additional Profit Centers

Another way to make more money is to get involved in other business ventures, or "profit centers," besides writing. A profit center is any activity that makes money for you. These profit centers don't have to be companies. They can simply be activities you do to earn additional income.

A good example of a writer who has made a fortune through profit centers is Andrew Linick, Ph.D. Known as the "copyologist," Dr. Linick is one of the most successful freelance mail-order writers of all time.

Using his knowledge of direct marketing, Dr. Linick has created a number of lucrative profit centers. He serves as marketing consultant to some of the top corporations in the country, advising them on how to create and run marketing programs. He has his own advertising agency, LNK Advertising. He writes, self-publishes, and sells his own books and reports through direct mail. He writes magazine articles on photography and self-defense (two of his many interests) and sells equipment and self-published books in both fields. Dr. Linick is also the director of the Copywriter's Council of America, an organization that matches clients with freelance direct-mail copywriters who have experience in their specific product lines.

Another writer who branched out into profit centers is novelist Lawrence Block, author of *Eight Million Ways to Die.* Block offered a $100 seminar for freelance writers, which he gave all over the country. He also repackaged the seminar as a $10 book, which he sells through full-page ads in *Writer's Digest.*

Think about starting another activity that might be a nice supplement to your full-time writing. If you use a particular software package in your work, for example, you might offer training to others who need to learn the system.

Or maybe you studied accounting before becoming a writer. Why not write and promote a home correspondence course on how to be a tax preparer? The possibilities for adding profit centers to your business are endless.

BURNOUT AND HOW TO AVOID IT

In some ways, freelance writing is easier than other jobs: no boss, no commute, interesting work, and you set your own hours.

At the same time, writing is very difficult. Every assignment means coming up with new ideas, new headlines, new words almost from scratch. Unlike a teacher, who might give the same basic set of lectures each year, the writer is always inventing something new. And that can be tiring.

Burnout is feeling tired and unenthusiastic about your work. Symptoms include lack of energy, insomnia, difficulty waking up in the morning, nervous stomach, poor digestion, feeling jittery, getting easily irritated, boredom, depression, even anger and resentment toward your work.

Many, many writers and other freelancers suffer from burnout or start to feel burned out at one time or another. The most dangerous period is five to seven years after starting as a freelancer. At this stage of their freelance careers, many writers feel that they

- have reached the peak of their income potential.
- are bored doing the same old thing and don't see any changes ahead.
- make decent money but want either greater wealth or the security of a 9-to-5 job.

Although burnout can strike any writer at any time, most writers who survive their fifth anniversary and remain enthusiastic tend to enjoy the business and stay in it for a long time.

If you feel you are beginning to experience burnout symptoms, there are several remedies:

1. *Go on vacation.* A week or two in the sun may be all that's needed to rejuvenate your spirit.
2. *Reduce your workload.* Cut back for a while. Take time to relax, sleep, work in the garden, read paperbacks, watch TV, and smell the roses.
3. *Do something different.* Start writing that novel you've always been talking about. Or go back to school and take courses for the M.B.A. you've always wanted.
4. *Socialize more.* Isolation can be a contributing factor to burnout. Join some writers' clubs or associations. Establish phone and pen-pal relationships with other writers. Have lunch with writer friends in your area.
5. *Add variety.* If all your clients are industrial manufacturers, take on a client in fund-raising, politics, or some other area that's different from what you usually work on. Remember the old adage "Variety is the spice of life."

6. *Add a profit center.* Maybe being a full-time writer is not for you. Perhaps you want to spend a part of each day in a non-writing business, such as giving seminars, consulting, mail order, or running some other business enterprise.

7. *Part-time job.* Some writers achieve good balance by working at a part-time writing job one or two days a week, then freelancing the rest of the time.

8. *Switch careers.* If you feel truly burned out with no hope of getting better, perhaps it's time for a career change. Maybe one of your clients has a staff writing position you can fill. Or maybe you want to work in something totally unrelated to writing. The change needn't be permanent. You can always go back to writing when you're ready. (Just don't mention this when interviewing for a staff job!)

CLIENT CONFLICTS

As good a writer as you are, and as nice as your clients may be, conflicts may arise. No business relationship runs smoothly 100 percent of the time. On occasion there is bound to be some friction between you and your clients.

Writing is a peculiar trade because writers often take criticism of their work as an attack on their integrity, ability, or worth as human beings, which they shouldn't. This is understandable because writing is a highly individual art.

Two printers handling a printing job will present the client with finished pieces that look pretty much the same. But two writers taking on the same assignment will produce two pieces of copy that vary tremendously in style, organization, and content. For two writers to produce two identical pieces of copy would be a one-in-a-billion event, on a par with the earth colliding with the sun.

You can eliminate most unpleasantness and conflict by

taking criticism on a business rather than a personal level. When a client says, "I think this section needs to be rewritten," he is not saying, "Your writing stinks!" He is just saying that the section needs to be rewritten. Your response should not be to rant and rave (I know you wouldn't, but you'd be surprised at how many writers do!), but to say, "Fine. Tell me what you want changed."

A small percentage of clients may be abusive, irrational, or have a way of working that is just not to your liking. There is no reason to continue working for such people. Just finish up the assignment to the best of your ability, send your invoice, and move on to bigger and better customers. "I have wholeheartedly rejected the customer-is-always-right mentality," writes Dale Feuer, contributing editor of *Training* magazine. "The fact is that being a customer doesn't exempt a person from having to exercise common courtesy in dealing with other adults; it doesn't give people license to behave like boors. By the same token, service is not synonymous with abject subjugation."

Occasionally, you will sense that a client is angry with you for no reason that you can figure. Your best bet is to bring the problem out into the open. Say: "Bill, you seem upset. Is there something I did to make you angry?"

Often you will find people take offense at things that seem trivial to you. A client may be upset because you sent your bill too quickly . . . or not quickly enough . . . or you weren't available to meet with her last Tuesday . . . or he doesn't understand why you won't attend his company's annual sales meeting in Weebigosh, Arkansas, without getting paid for your time.

The best you can do is to acknowledge the problem and try to solve it. If the client doesn't like getting invoices too quickly, make a note to delay sending his invoices for a few extra days. On the other hand, if the client is angry because he thinks you should attend his sales meeting for free, explain your billing procedures and why you feel you have to charge for attending.

Sometimes you can fix what's wrong. Other times, you can make the client see things your way. If neither works, politely apologize and try to get the client at least to see that you can "agree to disagree." You want to please the client, but you cannot do everything every client wants, the way they want, at the price they want to pay. So don't even try. You have to establish fair and reasonable ways of working and stick with them as best you can.

HANDLING CONFLICTS BETWEEN COMMERCIAL AND EDITORIAL WORK

A special kind of client conflict can occur when you write public relations materials for clients. "As a freelance corporate writer, I am paid by corporations to write articles for them for promotional purposes," one writer told me in a letter. "But in addition, I sometimes write as a journalist for the same magazines in which these ghosted promotional articles appear. Is this wrong? Sometimes the magazine wants to pay me a writer's fee for a ghosted article a corporate client has sponsored me to write and already paid me for. Is this ethical?"

My general answer to ethics questions is "If it makes you uncomfortable, it's probably unethical." Also, if the editor doesn't know what you are doing, but would disapprove if she did know, it's probably unethical.

Different people in public relations would answer this writer's questions in different ways. My personal views are these:

The issue of simultaneous payment for articles by sponsoring companies and trade magazines will come up infrequently, since most technical magazines do not pay for articles. When it does come up, it's certainly okay for a company to pay you to write the article, and if a magazine wishes to pay for that article, that's okay, too. However, since the company is sponsoring the article and paying for its creation, one could argue that any payment from the magazine should go to them, not you.

Here's how I handle it: My client is usually the public relations manager or marketing director of the company. Usually, he or she assigns an engineer or other employee as the expert to work with me, the writer, in preparing the article. The expert provides the technical information, I do the writing.

If the magazine offers payment, I recommend to the public relations manager that the payment (which is usually a small honorarium, not a significant fee) go to the employee, not me. This eliminates possible ethical violations, is economically fair to the client, rewards the employee, and creates goodwill all around.

I think most trade editors are aware that companies write these articles for promotional purposes, not for the sake of writing them or the honorarium. And they understand that a freelancer like you is getting paid by the company to put the article together. However, I wouldn't make a big deal of it either way. I explain to the editor that I am working with XYZ Company and we are proposing to give them an article on topic ABC. If they ask my role, I explain that I am "helping" the engineer or manager with the editing of the article. In twenty-six years of ghosting articles for engineers and managers, no editor has ever questioned this or been turned off by it.

CONTINUING YOUR EDUCATION

"Every really good creative person in advertising whom I have ever known has always had two noticeable characteristics," writes James Webb Young in his book, *A Technique for Producing Ideas*. "First, there was no subject under the sun in which he could not easily get interested. Second, he was an extensive browser in all sorts of fields of information."

The same can be said of all writers who deal primarily with information. Everything you read, hear, see, or observe becomes grist for the mill and may end up in your next ad, letter, booklet, or article.

Therefore, it pays to become a collector of information and a student of everything for life. British scientist John Eccles, quoted in *BusinessWeek,* puts it best: "We must keep discovering and discovering and discovering . . . and we must not claim to have the last word on anything." Donna Lyle, writing in *Catalog Success,* says, "In our Information Society, knowledge is the primary economic mover. No longer can you leave your school days behind you. Lifetime education is the new norm."

In addition to becoming more knowledgeable about writing, you want to learn more about business and how it works. You should also make an effort to learn more about the fields you write about.

Become an "information collector." Clip and save articles of interest. Collect booklets, pamphlets, reports, and brochures. Start a reference library and add to it whenever possible.

Become a student for life. Take courses and seminars; attend lectures. Read widely in books, magazines, business journals, and newspapers. Browse Web sites and join discussion forums on the Internet.

Become an observer. Pay attention to how people behave in business and social situations. Become interested in people. Ask them what they do, what they are interested in, what their life is like. You never know when a comment or fact will become a key point in a piece of copy you write. Never stop reading, listening, learning.

Seek out people who are successful and learn from them. Pick out the techniques that make them successful and adapt these techniques for your own use. Read books and articles by successful people you know and admire.

BE PERSISTENT . . . NEVER GIVE UP

When it comes to making money as a freelance commercial writer, you can do it. But not every day will be a success. Some days the business will be fun and easy, while other days you'll shake your head in despair. Some weeks you'll make a fortune, others a pittance. The short term is not important. What matters is how you handle things over the long haul, week after week, year after year.

As a freelancer, you will make many contacts that do not produce the response you would have wished for. People will be too busy to talk, too uninterested, too preoccupied. Your service will not be right for them. Or it will be right for them, but they do not wish to make a decision to use your services right now.

The tendency is to give up. Don't. The number-one reason for failure in selling freelance services is not sticking to it. Going out and selling yourself as a writer takes guts, hard work, and strong will to call prospects on the phone and go to meetings day after day, week after week, even in the face of seeming failure.

"Too often, ambitious people with dreams and talent fall short, even flat on their faces, because they give up too soon," writes motivational speaker Roscoe Barnes III in his book *Discover Your Talent and Find Fulfillment* (McKinley & Henson). "One of the keys to success is determination. A person needs determination to succeed in anything. Sometimes you have to grit your teeth, clench your fists, and refuse to give up."

Those who are persistent in sales eventually succeed. Those who give up fail to achieve their objective.

"Press on," said Calvin Coolidge. "Nothing in the world can take the place of persistence. Talent will not; nothing is more common than unsuccessful men with talent. Genius will not; un-rewarded genius is almost a proverb. Education will not; the world is full of educated derelicts. Persistence and determination alone are omnipotent."

Sales trainer Paul Karasik says sales is like a 15-round boxing match in which 90 percent of salespeople give up during round 14. "If they would only stay on their feet and keep slugging for one more round, they'd be standing at the final bell," notes Paul.

Winston Churchill put it this way: "Never give up."

Do not let rejection stop you. "Be it sport or business, you don't excel until you've been knocked around a little," says Chip Ganassi, a race-car driver and winning owner. When you get rejected, you learn how to do your sales calls better so the next person says "yes."

Certainly you want good results. If you are not getting them, don't give up. Instead, try something different. Or intensify your efforts. Or do both. When interviewed by *Target Marketing* magazine, catalog entrepreneur J. Peterman said, "If something fails and it destroys you, you should have been a nine-to-fiver. To be an entrepreneur, you can't be afraid of failure."

We all have dry spells where nothing seems to work out. Other times, you can't write fast enough to keep up with demand.

I find it is usually rain or shine, feast or famine, in freelancing. The dry spells and the busy periods usually balance themselves out. So don't give up if you start with a dry spell, even a long one. It will break, and success will come.

Persistence pays. Many of your competitors fail because they give up too early. The more effort you make, the greater the results.

Many would-be freelance commercial writers are like the job hunters who complain, "I responded to three help-wanted ads and didn't get any interviews." If you want to get interviews, send out 300 letters, not three. Likewise, if you want to generate business, send out 300 mailing pieces, not three or thirty. One freelancer told me, "The more work I do, the more successful I get."

Many people approach their sales tasks with fear and discomfort. What about you? If you have a lot riding on the success of your sales and marketing efforts, then it's only natural to be nervous.

Am I telling you not to be afraid? No. As motivational speaker and sales trainer Dr. Rob Gilbert says, "Courage is not the absence of fear. Courage is feeling the fear and doing it anyway." It doesn't matter how you feel about promoting and selling yourself. It only matters what you do.

As a rule, it's better to do something than nothing. Too many people do nothing. Or they do something, but not enough. Discussing her success in sales, Jane Trahey, a Chicago advertising executive, once told me, "I like to have a lot of balls up in the air at one time. This increases the odds that at least one will stick."

A tremendous mistake is to have too low a level of sales and marketing activity. If your response rate is one positive response for every 20 calls, and you make just five calls today, your chances of hearing "yes" today will be only one in four. However, if you make 40 calls, you are likely to produce two new leads or acquire two new customers. The greater your effort, the better your results.

Continual sales and marketing is the best way to ensure a steady flow of assignments at a relatively high fee level. If you stop marketing while you're busy, there's a good chance you'll have no orders coming in once the current peak period is over. You will get peaks and valleys in sales volume, rather than the steady, continuous high you want.

Even if you already have all the business you need for now and the foreseeable future, it's still a good idea to continue with your sales plan. Why? When you have more prospects than you can handle, you can pick and choose. You can do business with those who fit best in terms of need, personality, projects, and budget, and have the luxury of turning the rest away.

And by generating more demand for your product or service than the supply, you eliminate the need to negotiate and lower prices, as so many of your competitors do. When people are lined up to buy, checkbook in hand, you can set your price and stick with it. This increases not only your gross sales but also your profit margins.

17

BECOMING A MILLIONAIRE THROUGH WRITING, SAVING, AND INVESTING

Parting Advice on Your Career as a Freelance Writer

In this book, I set a round number for your financial goal: earning $100,000 a year or more in your freelance copywriting business.

When you earn at the six-figure level, as I am convinced you can, then accumulating a net worth of a million dollars, a number frequently touted in the financial media as the net worth you need to retire, becomes a realistic goal.

So in the first 16 chapters, I showed you methods that can help you increase your earnings to $100,000 a year or more.

In this final chapter, you'll see how you can parlay your six-figure income into a seven-figure nest egg—and become a self-made millionaire just through writing, saving, and investing.

MANAGING YOUR MONEY

Unless you are wealthy or have a large income from sources other than your writing, I recommend that you try to save your money and build a nest egg. "You can't get rich doing piece-work, no matter how high your hourly rate," a doctor in my town told me recently. "You have to invest to multiply the money you earn."

Although current tax laws have taken away some of the advantages of SEP, IRA, and other retirement plans designed for self-employed individuals, they are still among the best investments you can make.

Remember, as a self-employed individual, you won't be getting a nice pension from your company after twenty or thirty years of service—you have to create your own. Let your accountant or financial planner show you how much to invest in retirement funds and what type of plan is best.

In addition, a portion of your income should go into relatively safe investments: money markets, mutual funds, tax-free bonds, government notes, and whatever else your financial adviser recommends.

Your goal should be to build a nest egg of liquid investments, so if for any reason business were to slow down for a time, you could live comfortably off your savings. Having $50,000 or $150,000 or $250,000 in the bank can be a tremendous psychological boost for the freelancer. Instead of having to live entirely from hand to mouth, assignment to assignment, you can rest easier, knowing your investments can generate a portion of your income for you.

Never spend all your money as soon as you get it. Try to save 10 to 40 percent of fees paid to you by clients.

Remember, the checks you receive from clients represent income you still have to pay tax on. You need to have enough cash on hand to make estimated quarterly tax payments, plus any extra you owe on April 15. If you are in the top brackets, your tax bills will be approximately 38 percent of your gross income.

A home is a good investment for the freelancer, because a portion of your mortgage and other household expenses can be deducted as a business expense. This amount is directly proportional to the amount of space in your home you set aside as an office.

Try not to get too deeply in debt. Try to have a little extra cash in the bank rather than buying luxury items with money you don't have. It can be unpleasant and unsettling to have to depend on getting a check from a client to pay this month's bills.

My father once told me, "Money is not important, as long as you're happy." But I disagree. Copywriter Ted Nicholas, writing in his "Direct Marketing Success Letter," says, "The happiest possible life ideally rests on a balance between four elements: health, career, personal relationships, and money." I share Ted's view.

The most important piece of advice I can give to writers as far as investing and money is concerned is: Start early. In fact, start now. Don't wait.

YOUR KEY TO FINANCIAL INDEPENDENCE: START SAVING NOW!

No matter what your vocation, investing and saving should be everyone's "second career." The longer you wait to begin your second career as an investor and saver, the more difficult it will be to achieve your financial goals and retire in relative comfort and wealth.

Why is getting an early start so important? Compound interest. Investments earn annual returns ranging from 1 to 25 percent and sometimes much more. Naturally, the longer you hold an investment and it earns a return, the more its value increases.

But thanks to compound interest, the increase in value is not merely linear, it's almost exponential. Therefore, when you start early, your investments will grow in value much more spectacularly than someone who gets a late start. In his book *Money Doesn't Grow on Trees* (Cumberland House), investment counselor Mark Dutton says, "Compound interest is the eighth wonder of the world."

For instance, Merrill Lynch says that a person who puts $2,000 a year in an IRA starting at age eighteen will retire with more than double the savings of a person who starts only ten years later, at age twenty-eight.

Wayne Kolb, my accountant, had an even more dramatic example in his "Tax Planning" newsletter: Let's say an eighteen-year-old invests $2,000 annually in an IRA through age twenty-five, with an annual return average of 10 percent, and then stops. By age sixty-five, his IRA will be worth more than $1 million! Not a bad return for a $16,000 investment.

By comparison, if a person waits until age twenty-five to start an IRA, as I did, he or she will need to invest $2,000 a year until retirement to have $1 million. Two thousand dollars a year for forty years, from age twenty-five to sixty-five, is $80,000—meaning the person who started his IRA seven years later, at age 25 instead of 18, had to put in five times the investment of the person who started earlier.

But whatever your age when you read this, if you haven't started investing in earnest, the best advice I can give is do so now. Not in a week, but now. An example from Prudential Securities dramatizes this point: If you open an IRA at age 50, and contribute $2,000 a year earning 8 percent compounded monthly, at age 65 your IRA will be worth $54,300.

Had you opened the same IRA when you were 25, and put in the same amount of money annually earning the same rate of return, at age 65 your IRA would be worth more than half a million dollars—almost ten times as much.

Be a saver. Invest. Americans are notoriously behind the rest of the world when it comes to accruing wealth. The average American family saves less than 1 percent of their earnings each year, compared with nearly 10 percent in the U.K. and almost 13 percent in Sweden.

Before you spend your paycheck, invest at least 10 percent of it. My habit is to invest in increments of $10,000. Once

I have an extra $10,000 in my bank account, beyond the balance I need to maintain to pay bills and living expenses, I invest it, whether in a mutual fund, bond, or stock. I advise you to do the same.

In addition to investing more, spend less. Lower your expenses. Do not throw money away. Combine abundance with thrift. When my net worth reached a million dollars in my late thirties, I was driving an eleven-year-old Chevrolet Chevette, for which I had paid $6,500 in 1984.

Likewise, long after I became a self-made millionaire, we still lived in a modest three-bedroom colonial in a middle-class town. Could we have afforded a grander house in a snootier town? Yes, and eventually my wife forced me to make such a move!

But I'd rather have money in the bank than a huge mortgage payment to make every month. Our old house wasn't showy, but it was comfortable, and we didn't need more.

There's an old saying: "Money isn't everything in business; it isn't the sole factor defining success; but it is how people keep score." Throughout your life, you will often ask yourself, "Am I successful?" The search for a meaningful answer can be difficult and frustrating. Many of us spend our lives in search of that answer.

At least the money portion can be measured. Don't sacrifice your life for money. Don't put it so far ahead of the other elements of your life—family, friends, health, career, accomplishment, personal fulfillment—that these other elements go largely unfulfilled.

But do make the accumulation of wealth a priority in your life. When you have enough money that you can describe yourself as "comfortable," that's indeed how you feel: more secure, more content, less worried, proud of what you have accomplished, and more comfortable with who, what, and where you are in life. This I can attest to from personal experience.

Calculating the amount of money you need to retire is easy, according to Michael Masterson, cofounder of the American Writers and Artists Institute. Here's how: Take whatever you earn per year now and multiply it by ten. Say you earn $100,000 a year now, and you want to have the same income in retirement.

Ten times $100,000 is a million dollars, and that's the retirement nest egg you need. Reason: If you invest that at 10 percent, you will have an investment income of $100,000.

How do you accumulate that nest egg? Masterson says there are three things you have to do:

1. Increase your income.
2. Develop equity, either through real estate investments or businesses you own.
3. Reduce your spending so that your income exceeds your expenditures.

A WORD FROM WOODY

David Wood, a successful freelance copywriter known to his friends and clients by his nickname Woody, says, "The first book I read after going out on my own in January 1990 was Bob Bly's *Secrets of a Freelance Writer*. And what it taught me would have taken years to learn on my own, not to mention the tens of thousands of dollars my mistakes would have cost me.

"When I turned fifty in February 2000, I celebrated the auspicious occasion by sharing with readers of my *Foster's Sunday Citizen* newspaper column a number of random observations on life I'd gained during my first half-century."

Here is an abbreviated version of that column. You can decide for yourself how much wisdom David has acquired (in my opinion, it's considerable):

- One does not have to be especially bright in order to be successful. Some people are lucky, some use intimidation, others just outwork the competition. The surest path I've found to success is to surround yourself with smart people, listen to what they have to say, then make decisions based on your own judgment.
- Dogs are the world's greatest creation. No other person or creature will ever give you such steadfast loyalty and unconditional love and demand so little in return.
- If you tell someone you're going to do something then, for cripe's sake, do it!
- Political correctness is simply a cover for being a dishonest phony. Say what you really think and be willing to accept the consequences. People will respect you for it, even if they don't always love you.
- Everyone should live alone for at least five years, preferably before they reach forty. You learn an enormous amount about yourself, develop confidence, and improve your chances of successfully living with others.
- Most people who dream of success aren't willing to put forth the effort it requires.
- Lying isn't worth the effort. If you always tell the truth you only have to remember one story.
- The best way to deal with a bully is to outbully him.
- People who smoke have no self-respect.
- In general women are nicer—and smarter—than men. They just haven't yet figured out how to capitalize on it and seize the power from us.
- If you've achieved success, you owe it to others to share the lessons you've learned.
- People who don't read a lot are boring.
- Always print out a copy of anything important that's stored on your computer. Don't ever trust the little beige box.

- Most people are intimidated or just plain too lazy to complain and fight back when they are wronged, especially by large organizations. The big guys know that — it's why they're so arrogant.
- Don't expect to feel good unless you eat and drink sensibly and exercise regularly.
- The smartest people don't have all the answers — they just know where to find them.
- There's no friend like an old friend.
- Always trust your instincts. Nine times out of ten they're right.
- When it comes to the big things in life, like where you live and who you love; don't ever settle.
- And, most important, never take yourself too seriously.

PUTTING YOUR CAREER IN PERSPECTIVE

To sum up my thoughts about being a freelance commercial writer, based on twenty-three years in the field:

- Do your best.
- Keep your promises.
- Meet all deadlines.
- Set priorities, doing first things first.
- Help your clients.
- Take care of yourself.
- Focus on what the customer wants and give it to him or her.
- Keep your files organized.
- If it feels wrong or makes you uncomfortable, walk away.
- Save and invest your money.
- Spend as much time as you can with your children while they are young and still want you.
- Be dedicated to your craft.

- Be a lifelong student—of copywriting, business, and the topics on which you write.
- Be humble, not arrogant.
- Learn to say no. Don't overbook or overcommit.
- Expect and learn to live with highs and lows.
- Keep cool, calm, and collected. Don't allow anger to interfere with your thinking and actions.
- Bill on time and make sure you get paid.
- Treat others fairly.
- Confirm things in writing.
- Make sure others treat you fairly.
- Do work you enjoy.
- Give your clients more than their money's worth on every assignment.
- Handle a variety of assignments while developing yourself as a specialist in one or more fields.
- Charge fair, reasonable fees.
- Don't undercharge.
- Be willing to walk away.
- Keep in touch with your clients and prospects.

Be happy while you're living, for you're a long time dead.

—Old Scottish proverb quoted by David Ogilvy,
Confessions of an Advertising Man

SOURCES AND RESOURCES

FREELANCE PLACEMENT AGENCIES
These companies match freelance commercial writers with potential clients who may need their services. Fee arrangements vary.

Copywriter's Council of America
7 Putter Lane
Middle Island, NY 11953
(631) 924-8555

Creative Freelancers
99 Park Avenue, Suite 210A
New York, NY 10016
(888) 398-9540
www.freelancers.com

Direct Marketers On Call
45 Christopher Street
New York, NY 10014
(212) 691-1942
www.dmoc-inc.com

Paladin Staffing Solutions
South Dearborn Street, #305
Chicago, IL 60603
(888) 725-2346
www.paladinstaff.com

Staffwriters Plus
2150 Joshua's Path, #102
Hauppauge, NY 11787
(631) 582-8828

ASSOCIATIONS, CLUBS, ORGANIZATIONS

American Medical Writers
Association
160 Fifth Avenue, Suite 625
New York, NY 10010
(212) 645-2368

American Writer's Institute
245 NE 4th Avenue, #102
Delray Beach, FL 33483
(561) 278-5789
www.awaionline.com

Direct Marketing Association, Inc.
1120 Avenue of the Americas
New York, NY 10036-6700
(212) 768-7277

Direct Marketing Club of
New York
224 Seventh Street
Garden City, NY 11530
(516) 746-6700

Education Writers Association
2122 P Street NW, #201
Washington, DC 20037
(202) 452-9830
www.ewa.org

Florida Freelance Writers
Association
CNW Publishing, Editing &
Promotion, Inc.
P.O. Box A
North Stratford, NH 03590
(603) 922-8338

International Association of
Business Communicators (IABC)
One Hallidie Plaza, Suite 600
San Francisco, CA 94102
(415) 544-4700
www.iabc.com

National Association of Science
Writers
P.O. Box 890
Hedgesville, WV 25427
(304) 754-5077
http://nasw.org

National Mail Order Association
2807 Polk Street NE
Minneapolis, MN 55418-2954
(612) 788-1673
www.nmoa.org

National Writer's Union
113 University Place, 6th floor
New York, NY 10003
(212) 254-0279
www.nwu.org

Outdoor Writers Association
of America, Inc.
121 Hickory Street, #1
Missoula, MT 59801
(800) 692-2477

Self-Employed Writers and
Artists Network (SWAN)
P.O. Box 175
Towaco, NJ 07082

Society of American Travel
Writers
1500 Sunday Drive, #102
Raleigh, NC 27607
(919) 861-5586

Society for Technical
Communication
901 North Stuart Street,
Suite 904
Arlington, VA 22203
(703) 522-4114
www.stc.org

MAILING LISTS

Creative Access
3701 North Ravenswood Avenue,
#207
Chicago, IL 60613
(312) 440-1140

Edith Roman Associates
One Blue Hill Plaza, 16th floor
Pearl River, NY 10956
(800) 223-2194
www.edithroman.com

SOFTWARE

Act
1505 Pavilion Place
Norcross, GA 30093
(770) 724-4000
www.act.com

Telemagic
(800) 835-MAGIC
www.telemagic.com

Word for Windows
(800) 426-9400
www.microsoft.com

PowerPoint
(800) 426-9400
www.microsoft.com/office

Scriptor Professional Script
Formatting Software
138 North Brand Boulevard, #201
Glendale, CA 91203
(818) 843-6557
www.screenplay.com

BOOKS, PERIODICALS, AND E-ZINES

BOOKS

Bly, Robert. *The Copywriter's Handbook: A Step-by-Step Guide to Writing Copy That Sells, Third Edition.* New York: Henry Holt, 2006. How to write effective copy.

Bowerman, Peter. *The Well-Fed Writer.* Atlanta: Fanove Publishing, 2000. Marketing and self-promotion for freelance commercial writers.

Boyd, Amanda. *Writer's Digest Handbook of Making Money Freelance Writing.* Cincinnati, Ohio: Writer's Digest Books, 1997. Collection of useful articles on the commercial aspects of freelance writing.

Cates, Bill. *Unlimited Referrals.* Wheaton, Md.: Thunder Hill Press, 1996. How to get lots of referral leads.

Collins, Mary Claire. *How to Make Money Writing Corporate Communications.* New York: Perigee, 1995. How to freelance for large corporations.

Davis, Paul D. *How to Make $50,000 or More a Year as a Freelance Business Writer.* Rocklin, Calif.: Prima Publishing, 1992. Good advice on starting and running a freelance commercial writing business.

Floyd, Elaine. *Make Money Writing Newsletters.* St. Louis, Mo.: Newsletter Resources, 1994. How to make money writing and producing promotional newsletters for corporations, small businesses, and nonprofits.

Flynn, Nancy. *The $100,000 Writer: How to Make a Six-Figure Income as a Freelance Business Writer.* Holbrook, Mass.: Adams Media,

2000. Shows how to earn $100,000 a year as an editorial services consultant.

Foote, Cameron. *The Creative Side of Business.* New York: William Morrow, 1996. Comprehensive and informative guide to the business of freelancing for corporations and ad agencies.

Holtz, Herman. *How to Start and Run a Writing and Editing Business.* New York: John Wiley & Sons, 1992. How to make money doing freelance editing and writing for corporations, nonprofits, individuals, and the government.

Kopelman, Alexander. *National Writer's Union Guide to Freelance Rates & Standard Practice.* New York: National Writer's Union, 1995. Somewhat dated guideline to rates.

Shaw, Eva. *Ghostwriting: How to Get into the Business.* New York: Paragon House, 1991. How to ghostwrite books for executives, companies, celebrities, and other clients.

Slaunwhite, Steve. *How to Start and Run a Successful Copywriting Business.* North Vancouver, B.C.: Self-Counsel Press, 2001. Excellent guide to getting started as a freelance copywriter.

Sorenson, George. *Writing for the Corporate Market: How to Make Big Money Freelancing for Business.* Denver, Colo.: Mid-List Press, 1990. A successful writer who works in the business market tells how you can follow in his footsteps.

PERIODICALS

Advertising Age
740 North Rush Street
Chicago, IL 60611
(312) 649-5200

Adweek
49 East 21st Street
New York, NY 10010
(212) 529-5500

BtoB
740 North Rush Street
Chicago, IL 60611
(312) 649-5260

Commerce Business Daily
Government Printing Office
Washington, DC 20401
(202) 512-0132

Creative Business
275 Newbury Street
Boston, MA 02116
(617) 424-1368

Direct Marketing
Hoke Communications
224 Seventh Street
Garden City, NY 11530
(516) 746-6700

DM News
19 West 21st Street
New York, NY 10010
(212) 741-2095

Freelance Success
801 Northeast 70th Street
Miami, FL 33138
(305) 757-8857

Freelance Writer's Report
45 Main Street
P.O. Box A
North Stratford, NH 03590
(603) 922-8338

New Writer's Magazine
Sarasota Bay Publishing
P.O. Box 5976
Sarasota, FL 34277-5976
(813) 953-7903

Public Relations Journal
33 Irving Place
New York, NY 10003
(212) 998-2230

Sales and Marketing Management
633 Third Avenue
New York, NY 10017
(212) 986-4800

Target Marketing
North American Publishing Co.
401 North Broad Street
Philadelphia, PA 19108
(215) 238-5300

The Writer
Kalmbach Publishing Co.
21027 Crossroads Circle
P.O. Box 1612
Waukesha, WI 53187
(800) 533-6644

Writer's Digest
1507 Dana Avenue
Cincinnati, OH 45207
(513) 531-2690

Writer's Journal
27 Empire Drive
St. Paul, MN 55103
(612) 486-7818

E-ZINES

"Bencivenga's Bullets"
www.bencivengabullets.com
Master copywriter Gary
Bencivenga's can't-miss
e-newsletter based on his
decades of tested results.

"The Copywriter's Roundtable"
www.jackforde.com
John Forde's superb e-newsletter
on copywriting.

"The Direct Response Letter"
www.bly.com
My monthly e-newsletter on
copywriting and direct marketing.

"Early to Rise"
www.earlytorise.com
Daily e-newsletter on business
success, wealth, and health by
marketing guru Michael
Masterson.

"Excess Voice"
www.nickusborne.com/excess_
voice.htm
Nick Usborne's e-newsletter on
online copywriting. Informative
and great fun.

"Marketing Minute"
www.yudkin.com/markmin.htm
Weekly marketing tip from
consultant Marcia Yudkin.

"Paul Hartunian's Million-Dollar
Publicity Strategies"
www.prprofits.com
Great marketing e-newsletter
focusing on publicity.

"The Success Margin"
www.tednicholas.com
Ted Nicholas's must-read
marketing e-zine.

"The Well-Fed Writer"
www.wellfedwriter.com
Peter Bowerman's
e-zine on succeeding
as a freelance commercial writer.

WEB SITES

www.awaionline.com
Home study courses and
conferences on copywriting.

www.monthlycopywriting-
genius.com
Monthly Copywriting Genius
Regular reviews of winning
promotions and interviews
with the copywriters who
wrote them.

www.smallbusinessadvocate.com
The Small Business Advocate
Radio show and Web site
dedicated to small business.

www.theadvertisingshow.com
"The Advertising Show" (radio
show on advertising).

www.agora-inc.com/reports/
700SCBMO/W700D643/
Mailbox Millionaire
Home-study course on
how to start and run a
profitable direct-response
business.

DIRECTORIES

Bacon's Publicity Checklist
332 South Michigan Avenue
Chicago, IL 60604
(800) 621-0561
Media lists for mailing press
releases.

Directory of Major Mailers
North American Publishing Co.
401 North Broad Street
Philadelphia, PA 19108
(215) 238-5300
Good prospecting directory for
direct-mail writers.

Encyclopedia of Associations
Gale Research
Book Tower
Detroit, MI 48226
(313) 961-2242
Good prospecting directory for
writers who want to do work for
associations.

*Interactive Multimedia
Sourcebook*
R. R. Bowker
121 Chanlon Road
New Providence, NJ 07974
(908) 464-6800
Good prospecting directory
for writers who want to do
CD-ROMs, Web sites,
and other interactive
multimedia projects.

NJ Source
Calsun, Inc.
P.O. Box 327
Ramsey, NJ 07446
(201) 236-9099
Lists New Jersey ad agencies,
printers, and other suppliers.

*O'Dwyer's Directory of Corporate
Communications*
J. R. O'Dwyer & Co., Inc.
271 Madison Avenue
New York, NY 10016
(212) 679-2471
Prospecting directory that lists
communications directors at
large corporations and
associations.

*O'Dwyer's Directory of Public
Relations Firms*
J. R. O'Dwyer & Co., Inc.
271 Madison Avenue
New York, NY 10016
(212) 679-2471
Prospecting directory of public
relations firms.

Philadelphia Creative Directory
153 James Mill Road
Elverson, PA 19520
(610) 286-7990
Lists Philadelphia-area ad
agencies, printers, and other
suppliers.

Standard Directory of Advertisers
R. R. Bowker
121 Chanlon Road
New Providence, NJ 07974
(908) 464-6800
Excellent prospecting directory
of major national advertisers.

Standard Directory of Advertising Agencies
R. R. Bowker
121 Chanlon Road
New Providence, NJ 07974
(908) 464-6800
The best prospecting directory
for advertising agencies.

Standard Rate and Data Service
1700 Higgins Road
Des Plaines, IL 60018-5605
(800) 851-7737
www.srds.com

Comprehensive directory of
publications that accept
advertising.

Thomas Register
Thomas Publishing Company
One Penn Plaza
New York, NY 10119
(212) 290-7200; (212) 695-0500
www.thomasnet.com
Lists thousands of businesses
that advertise and would be good
potential clients for you.

Writer's Market
F&W Publishing
1507 Dana Avenue
Cincinnati, OH 45207
(800) 289-0963
Lists magazines you can write
for and their editorial
requirements.

BOB BLY'S INFORMATION KIT

"WELCOME" LETTER

Thanks for your interest in my copywriting services. . . .

Now, maybe you asked for this information kit out of curiosity. Some folks do . . . especially those who have never hired a freelance copywriter before.

But more likely you need a good business-to-business copywriter — someone who combines writing skill and sales ability with technical know-how and product knowledge.

Whatever your reason for calling or writing, you want to know more about a writer before you hire him. If we were sitting face-to-face, chatting in your office, you'd ask me questions. Let me try to answer a few of those questions right here.

"What are your qualifications as a copywriter?"

As a freelancer, I've written copy for more than 100 agencies and advertisers. And I'm the author of 60 books, including *The Copywriter's Handbook* (Henry Holt), *The Perfect Sales Piece* (John Wiley), and *The Complete Idiot's Guide to Direct Marketing* (Alpha).

I've given seminars on copywriting and direct marketing for numerous corporations and associations. I have also taught copywriting at New York University.

Before becoming a freelancer, I was advertising manager for Koch

Engineering (an industrial manufacturer) and a staff writer for Westinghouse. The attached material will give you the full story.

"Do you have a technical background?"

I have a bachelor's degree in engineering from the University of Rochester. And 95 percent of the work I do is in industrial, high-tech, business-to-business, and direct response.

I've written copy about computers, chemicals, pulp and paper, mining, construction, electronics, engineering, pollution control, medical equipment, industrial equipment, marine products, software, banking, financial services, health care, publishing, seminars, training, telecommunications, consulting, corporate, and many other areas.

In the computer field, for example, I'm the author of five computer books, including *A Dictionary of Computer Words*, published by Dell/Banbury.

Most important to you, I'm a business-to-business, direct-response copy specialist.

Writing business-to-business copy isn't something I do to pass the time between TV commercials. Rather, it's my bread and butter. So I put all my skill, knack, and know-how into every piece of business-to-business copy I write.

And, after writing hundreds of ads, articles, brochures, and sales letters for people like you, I've learned how to sell to corporate executives, entrepreneurs, managers, purchasing agents, technicians, engineers, professionals, and other business and technical buyers.

"Do you have experience in my field?"

If you sell to business, industry, professionals, or through direct response, chances are I already have experience dealing with your type of product or service or with something very similar.

Take a look at my writing samples enclosed with this letter. Do they seem "right up your alley"? If not, give me a call, and I'll send additional samples that are closer to your area of interest.

"What kinds of assignments do you handle?"

I cover the full spectrum. About 80 percent of my business is writing direct-mail and e-mail marketing for business, industrial, and high-tech clients. The rest involves creating a wide assortment of marketing communications materials, including ads, feature articles, slide presentations, film and videotape scripts, press releases, newsletters, catalogs, case histories, annual reports, product guides, manuals, and Web sites.

My specialty is my ability to write clear, credible, persuasive copy about a wide range of business products and services, from the simple to the highly technical.

I am able quickly to grasp complex marketing problems and understand sophisticated technologies. Clients appreciate the fact that I can sit down with engineers, scientists, systems professionals, and other specialists, ask intelligent questions, and speak their language.

What's more, my copy gets results. One ad, written for a manufacturer of pollution control equipment, was the number-one inquiry producer in four consecutive issues of *Chemical Engineering* magazine.

Another piece of copy, a direct-mail campaign I wrote for a telephone company, won the Direct Marketing Association's Gold Echo Award . . . and generated a 50 percent response rate (and $5.7 million in revenue) for the client.

I can't predict how many responses my ad, mailer, or literature package will pull for you. But I can—and do—guarantee your satisfaction with the copy you receive from me.

"Why does your letterhead say 'copywriter/consultant'?"

In addition to writing copy, I also work with many of my clients as a consultant, helping them plan marketing campaigns that generate maximum response.

They're pleased and happy to get on-target advice that works—at an affordable fee—and they like the fact that I don't charge a monthly retainer.

"Your fee schedule lists a price for a 'copy critique.' What's that?"

A Copy Critique provides an objective review of an ad, sales letter, brochure, or direct-mail package. You can have me critique either an existing piece or a draft of copy in progress. It's up to you.

When you order a Copy Critique, you get a written report that analyzes your copy in detail. I tell you what's good about it and what works, what doesn't work, what should be changed . . . and how. My critique covers copy, design, strategy, and the offer. It also includes specific directions for revisions and rewriting, although I do not write or rewrite copy for you under this arrangement.

A Copy Critique is ideal for clients who want a second opinion on a piece of copy, or who need new ideas to inject life into an existing package that's no longer working. It also enables you to sample my services at far lower cost than you'd pay to have me write your copy from scratch.

"Speaking of money, how much does it cost to hire you for a project?"

For any copywriting assignment—a direct-mail package, a sales letter, an ad, a brochure, a feature article, an audiovisual script—just let me know what you have in mind and I'll quote you a price. The enclosed Schedule of Estimated Fees gives typical prices for a variety of different projects.

"Who are your clients and what do they say about your copy and counsel?"

"Working with Bob Bly was easy," reports Robert Jurick, CEO of Fala Direct Marketing. "Bob Bly is more than a copywriter; he becomes part of the client and writes with understanding and sense. His copy resulted in several projects from some of our big accounts."

Andrew Frothingham, former ad manager of Ascom/Timeplex, comments: "When I was the ad manager at Timeplex, I used Bob Bly a lot, because he has the best understanding of any writer I found of the issues in the world of high technology."

"I would like to express my thanks for your assistance in helping us develop a marketing program via the mass media," writes Stan Stevens, president, Personal Health Profile. "I was impressed with your professionalism, knowledge of the field, willingness to extend yourself, and your eagerness to help us succeed. It was a real pleasure working with you."

"How long will it take you to write my copy?"

Ideally I like to have two to three weeks to work on your copy. That gives me the time to polish, edit, and revise until I'm happy with every word.

However, I realize you can't always wait that long. So if the job is a rush, just tell me the date by which you must receive the copy. If I take on the job, I guarantee that you will have the copy on your desk by this date—or sooner.

No matter what the deadline is, the copy I submit to you will be right. You can depend on it.

"What happens if we want you to revise the copy?"

Just tell me what you want improved and what the changes are, and I'll make them—fast. There is no charge for rewriting. Revisions are included in the flat fee we've agreed to for the assignment, provided they are assigned within 30 days of your receipt of the copy and are not based on a change in the assignment after copy has been submitted.

Most clients are pleased and enthusiastic about my copy when they receive it. But if you are not 100 percent satisfied, I will revise the copy according to your specific guidelines—and at my expense.

"How do I order from you?"

Putting me to work for you is easy. First, just tell me what you're selling and whom you're selling it to. Send me your brochure, catalog, or any other literature that will give me the background information I need to write your copy. But don't worry about organizing anything. I'll do that. If I have any questions, I'll pick up the phone and ask.

If you'd like to get together to go over the job in person, we can do that, too. I'd be delighted to meet with you, wherever and whenever you wish.

When you give me the go-ahead, I'll write the assignment for you. You will receive your copy on or before the deadline date. And remember, it is guaranteed to please you.

Dozens of firms—including Medical Economics, Agora Publishing, Prentice Hall, G. E. Solid State, IBM, Allied Signal Aerospace, and Edith Roman Associates—have found my copy ideal for promoting business, industrial, and high-tech products and services and direct-response offers.

So . . . why not try my service for your next sales letter, direct-mail package, feature article, press release, ad, or brochure? I promise you'll be delighted with the results.

Regards,
Bob Bly

P.S. If you have an immediate need call me right now at (201) 385-1220 or fax me the details on my dedicated fax line: (201) 385-1138. There is no charge for me to discuss your job with you and give you a cost estimate. And no obligation to buy.

BIOGRAPHY

BUSINESS-TO-BUSINESS, HIGH-TECH, DIRECT-RESPONSE COPY

BOB BLY is an independent copywriter and consultant with more than 15 years' experience in business-to-business, high-tech, industrial, and direct marketing. A winner of the Direct Marketing Association's Gold Echo award and an IMMY from the Information Industry Association, Bob has written copy for such clients as ITT Fluid Technology, Medical Economics, M&T Chemicals, Wallace & Tiernan, PSE&G, Brooklyn Union Gas, Samsung, Sony, Ascom/Timeplex, G.E. Solid State, Plato Software, IBM, AT&T, Agora Publishing, McGraw-Hill, Louis Rukeyser's Wall Street, CoreStates Financial Corporation, Swiss Bank, Value Rent-a-Car, Hyperion Software, Alloy Technology, EBI Medical Systems, Citrix Systems, Allied Signal, The BOC Group, John Wiley & Sons, DataFocus, and Graver Chemicals.

Bob is the author of over 60 books, including *The Advertising Manager's Handbook* (Prentice Hall), *Business-to-Business Direct Marketing* (NTC Business Books), and *The Copywriter's Handbook* (Henry Holt). Other titles include *Targeted Public Relations* and *Selling Your Services*, both from Henry Holt, and *Keeping Clients Satisfied*, from Prentice Hall. His articles have appeared in *Business Marketing, Direct, Computer Decisions, New Jersey Monthly, Writer's Digest, Amtrak Express, Science Books & Films*, and *Direct Marketing*.

Bob has presented marketing, sales, writing, and customer service seminars for numerous groups, including the Publicity Club of New York, Women in Communications, Direct Marketing Association, Independent Laboratory Distributors Association, American Institute of Chemical Engineers, American Chemical Society, Business Marketing Association, International Tile Exposition, Direct Marketing Creative Guild, Women's Direct Response Group, Direct Media Coop, and American Marketing Association. He also taught business-to-business copywriting and technical writing at New York University.

Bob writes sales letters, direct-mail packages, e-mail marketing campaigns, ads, brochures, articles, press releases, newsletters, and other marketing materials clients need to sell their products and services to businesses. He also consults with clients on marketing strategy, mail-order selling, and lead-generation programs.

Bob Bly holds a B.S. in chemical engineering from the University of Rochester. He is a member of the American Institute of Chemical Engineers, the Business Marketing Association, and the Newsletter and Electronic Publishers Association.

For a FREE information kit, or a free, no-obligation cost estimate for your next project, contact:

Bob Bly
22 E. Quackenbush Avenue
Dumont, NJ 07628
Phone (201) 385-1220
Fax (201) 385-1138
E-mail rwbly@bly.com
Web site: www.bly.com

TESTIMONIALS

WHAT THEY SAY ABOUT BOB BLY'S COPY AND COUNSEL

"Bob, this is great! It always amazes me how quickly the important concepts are captured and highlighted. Thanks."

— Adrienne Pierce, The BOC Group

"I thought you would enjoy seeing the fruits of your labor on the recent diaphragm valve literature. This is a good example of taking product literature and making it more market oriented. We worked diligently to produce a high quality brochure—and I think we succeeded. Thanks very much."

— John Porpora, ITT Fluid Technology Corporation

"When I was ad manager at Timeplex, I used Bob Bly a lot, because he has the best understanding of any writer I found of the issues in the world of high technology."

—Andrew Frothingham, Ascom/Timeplex

[additional testimonials go here]

CLIENT LIST

BOB BLY: CLIENTS/EXPERIENCE (A PARTIAL LIST)

ABC (network television)

Abcor (ultrafilters)

Academic Information Services (book publisher)

Agora Publishing (newsletter publisher)

Boardroom (newsletter publisher)

BOC Gases (industrial gases)

[additional clients and descriptions of their businesses go here]

BOB BLY'S FEE SCHEDULE

SCHEDULE OF ESTIMATED FEES

Print ad	$950–$3,000+
Sales letter	$2,000–$8,500+
Direct-mail package, lead generation	$2,500–$6,500
Direct-mail package, mail order	$6,500–$9,500+
Renewal series	$1,000–$1,500/letter
Blanket renewal insert	$2,000–$2,500
Magalog	$9,500–$15,000
Self-mailer	$2,500–$4,500
Postcard or double postcard	$1,500–$2,000
Brochure	$750–$1,000/page
Data sheet	$1,500
Catalog	$750/page
Newsletter	$750/page
Feature story	$1.50/word
White paper	$4,000–$5,000
Press release (1–2 pages)	$750
Audiovisual or multimedia script	$200–$250/minute

Web site home page	$1,500–$2,500
Web site, other pages	$750–$1,000/page
e-mail, short copy	$1,250–$2,500
e-mail, long copy	$2,500–$4,500
e-zine ad	$500
Landing page, long copy	$7,500
Telemarketing script	$1,500–$2,500
Radio commercial (six-spot package)	$2,000–$3,000
Copy critique	$750–$1,500

TERMS

Purchase order or letter of authorization required for all jobs. Copywriting fees for initial projects are payable 50% in advance, balance upon delivery. Copy critique fees are payable in full, in advance.

All revisions must be assigned within 30 days of receipt of copy. Rewrites are made free of charge unless the revision is based on a change in the assignment made after copy is submitted.

Listed fees are guidelines only. Call today for a prompt price quotation on your specific assignment.

NOTE: This fee schedule current as of May 2005 and valid for 90 days from date of receipt. Be sure to call for current fee schedule when ordering copy or consulting service.

MODEL DOCUMENTS

**SELF-PROMOTION LETTERS TO
GENERATE SALES LEADS**

Here is the sales letter I used to launch my freelance copywriting business in 1982. I mailed it to creative directors at 500 advertising agencies that handled industrial accounts, pulling the list from the *Standard Directory of Advertising Agencies* (see appendix B). I received 35 replies—a 7 percent response.

HOW AN ENGINEER AND FORMER AD MANAGER CAN
HELP YOU WRITE BETTER ADS AND BROCHURES

For many people, industrial advertising is a difficult chore. It's detailed work, and highly technical. To write the copy, you need someone with the technical know-how of an engineer and the communications skills of a copywriter.

That's where I can help.

As a freelance industrial and high-tech copywriter who is also a graduate engineer, I know how to write clear, technically sound, hard-selling copy.

You'll like my writing samples, ads, brochures, catalogs, direct mail, PR, and A/V. And you'll like having a writer on call who works only when you need him.

Here are my qualifications:

I have an engineering background (B.S., chemical engineering, University of Rochester). I started out writing brochures and A/V scripts for the Westinghouse Defense Center. After I left Westinghouse, I became advertising manager for Koch Engineering, a manufacturer of process equipment.

In my freelance work, I've handled projects in a wide variety of industries, including computers, software, chemicals, industrial equipment, electronics, publishing, banking, health care, and telecommunications.

My articles on business communications have appeared in *Business Marketing, Computer Decisions, Amtrak Express, Chemical Engineering,* and *Audiovisual Directions.* And I'm the author of *The Copywriter's Handbook* (Henry Holt), *A Dictionary of Computer Words* (Dell/Banbury), and nine other books.

Now, I'd like to help you create ads, brochures, and other promotions. Call me when your creative team is overloaded, or when the project is highly technical.

I'd be delighted to send you a complete information kit on my copywriting services. The package includes a client list, fee schedule, biographical information, and samples of my work.

Just complete and mail the enclosed reply card and the kit is yours, at no cost or obligation to you, of course.

Sincerely,
Bob Bly

P.S. Mail the reply card today and I'll also send you a free copy of the much reprinted article, "10 Tips for Writing More Effective Industrial Copy."

I eventually developed another letter, printed below, that did even better, and this is the one I now use. I mail this letter in a business envelope with a reply card to potential clients. From some mailing lists, response has been as high as 10 percent:

Dear Marketing Professional:

"It's hard to find a copywriter who can handle business-to-business and high-tech accounts," a prospect told me over the phone today, "especially for brochures, direct mail, and other long-copy assignments."

Do you have that same problem?

If so, please complete and mail the enclosed reply card, and I'll send you a free information kit describing a service that can help.

As a freelance copywriter specializing in business-to-business marketing, I've written hundreds of successful ads, sales letters, direct-mail packages, brochures, data sheets, annual reports, feature articles, press releases, newsletters, and audiovisual scripts for clients all over the country.

But my information kit will give you the full story.

You'll receive a comprehensive "welcome" letter that tells all about my copywriting service—whom I work for, what I can do for you, how we can work together.

You'll also get my client list (I've written copy for more than 100 corporations and agencies) . . . client testimonials . . . biographical background . . . samples of work I've done in your field . . . a fee schedule listing what I charge for ads, brochures, and other assignments . . . helpful article reprints on copywriting and advertising . . . even an order form you can use to put me to work for you.

Whether you have an immediate project or a future need or are just curious, I urge you to send for this information kit. It's free . . . there's no obligation . . . and you'll like having a proven copywriting resource on file—someone you can call on whenever you need him.

From experience, I've learned that the best time to evaluate a copywriter and take a look at his work is before you need him, not when a project deadline comes crashing around the corner. You want to feel comfortable about a writer and his capabilities in advance so when a project does come up, you know whom to call.

Why not mail back the reply card TODAY, while it is still handy? I'll rush your free information kit as soon as I hear from you.

Regards,
Bob Bly

P.S. Need an immediate quote on a copywriting project? Call me at (201) 385-1220. There is no charge for a cost estimate. And no obligation to buy.

Reply Card for Self-Promotion Letter

Bob:
[ ] Please send more information on your copywriting services.
[ ] Give me a call. I have an immediate project in mind.
[ ] Not interested right now. Try us again in _____
                                                         (month/year)
Name _____ Title _____

Company _____ Phone _____
Address _____
City _____ State _____ Zip _____
My business is· _____
Type of copy I need:
[ ] Ads   [ ] Direct mail   [ ] Brochure
[ ] A/V script   [ ] PR   [ ] Other: _____

SELF-PROMOTION LETTER TARGETED TO A SPECIFIC
INDUSTRY

Here is a version of the above sales letter aimed specifically at potential clients in the software industry. It generated a response of 5 to 10
percent using various lists.

Dear Software Marketer:

"It's tough to find a copywriter who can produce result-getting
copy for software, computers, and related high-tech products
and services," a prospect told me over the phone the other day.

Do you have that same problem? If so, please complete and
mail the enclosed reply card, and I'll send you a free information kit describing a service that can help.

As a freelance copywriter specializing in direct marketing, I've
planned and written successful lead-generating and mail-order
copy for over a hundred software and high-tech companies.

These include Computron, Hyperion Software, IBM, On-Line
Software, DataFocus, Cartesia Software, Mortice Kern
Systems, Yourdon, Syncsort, Micro Logic, Citrix Systems,
Plato Software, McGraw-Hill, Ascom/Timeplex, U.S. Robotics,
Sony, Atech, Advanced Systems Concepts, Wolfram Research,
Symantec, Digital Linguistix, G.E. Solid State, AT&T,
CorSoft, AlliedSignal, HB Pascal & Co., Letraset, and Chubb
Institute.

Does my copy work?

- Convergent Solutions was getting a 1 to 2 percent response
  to mailings for its C3S/ADS application development tool.
  A simple wording change to the beginning of their sales letter increased response to 5 percent—more than double the
  control.
- Another mailing campaign, promoting disaster recovery
  services, pulled a whopping 56 percent response . . . and
  generated an immediate $5.7 million in sales for U.S. West.
  (The mailing won a Gold Echo award from the Direct
  Marketing Association.)

- On a space ad for Chubb Institute, a computer training company, we doubled the number of inquiries produced over all previous ads, simply by changing the presentation of the offer.

To see some of these successful ads and mailings . . . and others more related to your product . . . just complete and mail the enclosed reply card today.

You'll receive a complete information kit, including copywriting samples, client list, testimonials, fee schedule, and more. For fastest delivery, call (201) 385-1220.

Sincerely,
Bob Bly

P.S. Respond now and I'll also send you a free tip sheet, "20 Secrets of Selling Software in Print." This reprint is packed with proven techniques for increasing the selling power of your software ads, direct mail, and brochures.

COPY DISCLAIMER

I have the following text as a file on my computer and I insert it at the top of the first page of every manuscript when submitting copy to clients. Its purpose: to let them know the copy should be reviewed in a timely manner.

A Note to Reviewers

Please keep in mind that this is a preliminary draft. As you read, you may find extraneous information you want to delete, or think of missing information you want to add. You may want to change the organization of the piece, or make wording changes to heads and body copy. Please do so without hesitation, marking your comments directly on this manuscript. That will give us the best draft possible. At this point, you can make as many changes as you want, without cost or delay of any kind. NOTE: If we do not hear back from you within 30 days, we will assume there are no changes and that you approve the copy as is.

SAMPLE PRESS RELEASE

You can generate stories about yourself in the business and trade press by sending press releases to editors at the publications your prospects read. Here's a sample of an effective press release that got results for the writer:

FOR IMMEDIATE RELEASE

Richard Armstrong
250 W. 57th St., Suite 1527
New York, NY 10019
CONTACT: Richard Armstrong
(202) 333-0646

NEW BOOKLET TAKES THE GUESSWORK OUT OF HIRING FREELANCERS
Six Questions to Ask before You Hire a Freelance Copywriter

You're struggling to meet a tight deadline when suddenly a new job lands on your desk that has to be done before the first one.

Your staff copywriter just handed you a piece of copy that's so tired you can almost hear it yawn.

Your boss calls with an urgent project. But just before he hangs up, he says, "This time, I want to see something new, not the same old junk."

Sound familiar?

If so, you may be thinking about hiring a freelance copywriter. But before you do, there's a new booklet that might help.

Richard Armstrong, a New York-based freelancer, has published a free booklet to help advertising agencies, direct-mail companies, and public relations firms separate the good from the bad when it comes to hiring freelance writers.

Entitled "Six Questions to Ask before You Hire a Freelance Copywriter," the eight-page pamphlet is free to anyone who writes Mr. Armstrong at 250 West 57th Street, Suite 1527, Dept. DM, New York, NY 10019 or calls (202) 333-0646.

"For many companies, hiring a freelance copywriter is the only way to get first-class creative talent," the booklet begins.

"But watch out! As you look for a qualified freelancer, you're likely to meet everyone from moonlighting agency copywriters to unemployed surfers.

"Worst of all," continues the pamphlet, "you may find a novelist or a magazine writer who thinks that because he has published 'real writing,' working on your little brochure will be a cinch."

By knowing what questions to ask, however, clients can make sure they hire the right freelancer at the right price.

"What with the recent 'mega-mergers' on Madison Avenue," said Mr. Armstrong recently, "we're going to be seeing a lot more people on the street calling themselves freelance copywriters. Some of them are bound to be very good. But others might just be using freelancing as a way to tide themselves over between jobs. I hope my booklet will give clients some useful guidelines to finding the right freelancer for the job."

SAMPLE ARTICLE QUERY LETTER

You can promote yourself by publishing how-to and informational articles related to commercial writing in trade and business magazines read by your potential clients. To propose an article to an editor, use a query letter. The sample query below got me an assignment to write an article on letter writing for *Amtrak Express* magazine; they even paid me $400!

Mr. James A. Frank, Editor
Amtrak Express
34 East 51st St.
New York, NY 10022

Dear Mr. Frank:

Is this letter a waste of paper?
Yes — if it fails to get the desired result.
In business, most letters and memos are written to generate a specific response, close a sale, set up a meeting, get a job interview, make a contact. Many of these letters fail to do their job.

Part of the problem is that business executives and support staff don't know how to write persuasively. The solution is a formula first discovered by advertising copywriters, a formula called AIDA. AIDA stands for Attention, Interest, Desire, Action.

First, the letter gets attention . . . with a hard-hitting lead paragraph that goes straight to the point, or offers an element of intrigue.

Then, the letter hooks the reader's interest. The hook is often a clear statement of the reader's problems, his needs, his concerns. If you are writing to a customer who received damaged goods, state the problem. And then promise a solution.

Next, create desire. You are offering something: a service, a product, an agreement, a contract, a compromise, a consultation. Tell the reader the benefit he'll receive from your offering. Create a desire for your product.

Finally, call for action. Ask for the order, the signature, the check, the assignment.

I'd like to write a 1,500-word article on "How to Write Letters That Get Results." The piece will illustrate the AIDA formula with a variety of actual letters and memos from insurance companies, banks, manufacturers, and other organizations.

This letter, too, was written to get a specific result: an article assignment from the editor of *Amtrak Express*.

Did it succeed?

Regards,
Bob Bly

P.S. By way of introduction, I'm an advertising consultant and the author of five books, including *Technical Writing: Structure, Standards, and Style* (McGraw-Hill).

SAMPLE PITCH LETTER TO GET SPEAKING ENGAGEMENTS

Another excellent way to market yourself is by giving talks and speeches to groups of advertising and marketing professionals. Here's a model query letter you can use to generate such engagements:

Ms. Jane Smiley
Program Director
Women in Engineering
Big City, U.S.A.

Dear Ms. Smiley:

Did you know that, according to a recent survey in *Engineering Today*, the ability to write clearly and concisely can mean $100,000 extra in earnings over the lifetime of an engineer's career?

ᕀ For this reason, I think your members might enjoy a presentation I have given to several business organizations around town, "10 Ways to Improve Your Technical Writing."

As the director of Plain Language, Inc., a company that specializes in technical documentation, I have worked with hundreds of engineers to help them improve their writing. My presentation highlights the 10 most common writing mistakes engineers make, and gives strategies for self-improvement.

Does this sound like the type of presentation that might fit well into your winter program schedule? I'd be delighted to speak before your group. Please phone or write so we can set a date.

Regards,
Blake Garibaldi, Director
Plain Language, Inc.

FORM FOR KEEPING TRACK OF SALES LEADS

Date _____ Source of inquiry _____ Response via _____
Name _____ Title _____
Company _____ Phone _____
Address _____ Room/floor _____
City _____ State _____ Zip _____
Type of business: _____
Type of accounts (if an ad agency): _____
Type of projects: _____
For: [ ] immediate project   [ ] future reference
[ ] project to be started in: _____
                                        (month/year)
STATUS:
[ ] Sent package on (date): _____
[ ] Enclosed these samples: _____
[ ] Next step is to: _____
[ ] Probability of assignment: _____
[ ] COMMENTS: _____

CONTACT RECORD:
Date: _____ Summary: _____

CLIENT QUESTIONNAIRE

To gather information you need to write your copy, you have to ask clients questions. Some copywriters send questionnaires to the client in advance of doing the writing. The client answers by mail, fax, e-mail, a phone call, or in a meeting.

COPYWRITER'S QUESTIONNAIRE

1. What are all the product benefits?
2. What are all the features of the product?
3. How is the product different from and, hopefully, better than the competition?
4. What does the buyer expect when he or she plunks down a few dollars for the product? And do we deliver?

5. What methods, approaches, and sales techniques is the competition using?

6. How does the audience for my product differ from the general public?

7. How much can my buyer reasonably expect to pay?

8. Does my average buyer have a credit card or a checking account?

9. Will my product be purchased for business or personal use?

10. Can I expect to get multiple sales from my buyer?

11. What is the logical back-end product to sell someone after he has purchased my product? ["Back end" refers to other products in your product line you can offer to someone who has bought the primary product featured in your ad.]

12. Will I need to show my product in color?

13. What's the "universe," i.e., the total number of potential customers?

14. Who will buy my product: teenagers or octogenarians . . . men or women . . . executives or blue-collar workers?

15. Is there a market for overseas sales?

16. Should I offer time payments?

17. Will my product be a good gift item?

18. Should my copy be long or short?

19. What should the tone of my copy be?

20. Should I test the price?

21. Should I test copy approaches?

22. Is there a seasonal market for my product and am I taking advantage of it?

23. Are testimonials available from satisfied customers?

24. Do I need photographs or illustrations?

25. Which appeals have worked in the past for this product?

26. What objections might arise from a prospective customer? How can I overcome these objections?

27. Should I use a premium?

28. Should I offer a money-back guarantee?

29. Is this item also sold by retail? Are there price advantages I can stress for buying direct from the ad?

30. Should I consider a celebrity testimonial?

31. Can I tie in my copy to some news event?

32. Can I tie my copy to some holiday or seasonal event?
33. Does my product sell better in a particular region or climate?
34. Should I consider using a sweepstakes?
35. Can my product be sold through a two-step advertising campaign? [In a "two-step campaign," ads generate inquiries rather than direct sales.]
36. What must I do to give the reader a sense of urgency so he or she will buy my product now?
37. Can I use scientific evidence in my sales approach?
38. Have I allowed enough time to write, design, produce my ad, and place my insertion order?
39. Can I get my customer to order by telephone?
40. What unsuccessful approaches have been used to promote this product?
41. Can I get powerful "before" and "after" pictures?
42. Assuming the ad is successful, is the client prepared to fill all the orders?

SOURCE: Milt Pierce. Reprinted with permission.

SAMPLE PROMOS

SAMPLE ADS

You can run ads promoting your freelance commercial writing services in local business magazines, association newsletters, advertising trade publications, and other media. Classified or small (one- or two-inch) classified display ads work best. Here are some of the more successful ads I have run over the years:

I WRITE ADS!

Over 75 corporations and ad agencies count on my crisp, accurate, hard-sell copy for ads, brochures, direct mail, PR, and A/V scripts. High-tech, industrial, and business-to-business advertising my specialty. Call or write for free information kit: Bob Bly, 22 E. Quackenbush Avenue, Dumont, NJ 07628, phone (201) 385-1220.

CALL THE HIGH-TECH COPY PRO

I specialize in industrial and high-tech copy: computers, electronics, chemicals, software, telecommunications, heavy equipment, banking, health care, corporate, and many other products and services. To receive full details by mail, call today. Bob Bly (201) 385-1220.

IMPROVE YOUR DM RESULTS!

SEND FOR FREE REPORT . . .

I specialize in writing lead-getting sales letters, DM packages, and ads for high-tech and business-to-business clients and agencies. For FREE report, "23 Tips for Creating Business-to-Business Mailings That Work," phone or write: Bob Bly, 22 E. Quackenbush Avenue, Dumont, NJ 07628, (201) 385-1220. Also ask for a free information kit on my copywriting services.

Full-Page Ad for Bob Bly's Copywriting Services in *DM News*

This ad ran in *DM News* where it generated 75 replies. See page 353.

Fractional Ad for Russ Phelps's Copywriting Services in *DM News*

Russ reports this ad was very successful, prompting calls from potential clients who told him, "I was going to hire another copywriter, but then I read your ad and figured I'd better talk to you first." See page 354.

SAMPLE SELF-PROMOTION BROCHURE FOR A FREELANCE COPYWRITER

My Commitment To You

Powerful and Persuasive Sales Writing

Whether you're selling products or services, in the B2B or B2C market, it is critical you get your message out powerfully and persuasively. You must make an impression. When I write for you, you will. Your sales message will go to your prospects in a clear, well-written professional manner. Count on it.

Committed To Serving You

I give you the service you need and deserve. Your goals are my goals. Your success is my success. I don't write to see my name in a by-line; I write to help you. That's what I'm all about. I write, you profit.

Reliability

I know what it means to have others rely on me. I know what it means to live up to expectations. So, when you work with me, I'll meet your deadlines. I'll take care of what you need and I'll do it all knowing you're counting on me to deliver. I will.

Call James McGovern
561-628-2211

Jim's Background

I'm James McGovern – Jim. I'm an independent freelance copywriter with extensive experience in the aviation industry including a B.S. degree from the US Air Force Academy and service as an Air Force pilot. My experience also includes the financial services industry and civilian aviation.

My background and training make me an ideal writer for both technical and non-technical sales and marketing material. I'm available to write web site text, sales and marketing letters, direct mail packages, brochures and other sales related material for both the business to business market and business to consumer market.

Contact Information

You Can Reach Me At:

561-628-2211

or

Impressioncopywriting@adelphia.net

Writing Samples Available Upon Request

Impression Copywriting
James McGovern
Aviation Copywriter
561-628-2211

"I bring you a unique combination of aviation expertise and skillful use of salesmanship in print."

Photo Courtesy of US Air Force

Specializing In Aviation Marketing And Sales Communication

SAMPLE CONTRACTS, FEE SCHEDULES, AND COLLECTION LETTERS

CONTRACT FOR COPYWRITING SERVICES

This is the standard agreement I use with my clients. But I am not an attorney, and any contracts you use should be reviewed by your lawyer.

Copywriting for [Project]

Dear [Name]:
Thank you for hiring Bob Bly to write [project] for [company]. Here are the terms we discussed. Would you please read this through to make sure these are terms you agree to and send a REPLY e-mail that all is fine? (Please include this e-mail in your reply.)

FEE
The fee for the [project], which includes [describe elements if applicable], is $xxxx.

NOTE ABOUT FEES
We require a deposit of half the project fee up front and we invoice the balance upon completion of the project. We accept credit cards via phone or checks made payable to "Center for Technical Communication."

DEADLINE
You will have first draft copy by [Day/Date] by 3:00 p.m. (Eastern time). We do not miss deadlines, so if you have not received your copy on the date it is due, please call us immediately so we can resend it.

PLEASE NOTE: Once we agree on deadlines, they are contingent on getting your go-ahead and deposit by [DATE]. Bob's schedule does fill up quickly and we regret that we can't hold dates without payment.

REVISIONS
Up to two revisions are included at no extra charge unless they are based on a change in the assignment made after the copy is submitted.

All revisions must be assigned within 30 days of your receipt of the first draft of copy. After that, additional rewrite may be made at a fee to be negotiated separately from this agreement.

We make our best attempt to be available to make revisions. Bob can turn around minor revisions in 2–3 business days and major revisions may take longer.

CAVEATS
If you cancel or put the project on hold once Bob has begun work, a kill fee may be applied. Let me know if you'd like a copy of our kill fee schedule.

This fee is for copywriting, which we define as creating text for promotional material from content provided by the client. Research to create original content if needed would be an additional fee to be quoted separately.

Background material sent to Bob Bly in preparation for copywriting assignments is not returned to the sender unless specific arrangements have been made with Fern Dickey in writing prior to the project.

Although you are not required to do so, Bob recommends that you send him a PDF of the [piece] before [printing/sending], so he can review it, make sure the elements are positioned effectively, and make sure all revisions work effectively.

Also, although Bob makes every effort to make your copy comply with the law, he is not an attorney. Therefore, it is your responsibility to submit all copy for legal review. You are also responsible for final proofreading of all the copy.

RESULTS

There are many factors in your marketing—product, market, price, list, demand, consumer preferences, major events—that Bob cannot control. Therefore, while he can and does guarantee your satisfaction with his copy before you test it, he does not promise and cannot guarantee specific results.

Thank you, [Name].

Regards,

SAMPLE LETTER OF AGREEMENT

If you find a contract too formal and intimidating, you can confirm assignments in writing with a simple letter of agreement, such as the one reprinted below. Consult your lawyer before using this letter.

Date

Mr. Joe Jones
President
Big Corporation
Anytown, U.S.A.

Dear Mr. Jones:

Thanks for choosing Bob Smith & Associates to handle your job #3333. Job 3333 is a series of three capability brochures. I will write these brochures for you and provide such marketing and editorial consulting services as may be required to implement the project.

My base fee for the services I described above is $10,000. That fee estimate is based on 100 hours of working time at my hourly rate of $100, and includes time for copywriting, editing, tele-conferencing, meeting, consulting, travel, and research.

Copy revisions are included in my base fee, provided that at such time as the total time devoted by me shall exceed 100 hours, I shall bill you for additional working time at the rate of $100 per hour.

Out-of-pocket expenses, such as toll telephone calls, photocopies and computer printouts, fax charges, messengers, and local and out of town travel, incurred in connection with the project, will be billed to you in an itemized fashion.

Payment of the base fee will be made as follows: One-third of the above-mentioned base fee is due upon my commencement of work; one-third upon delivery of first draft copy; and one-third is due upon completion. Payment for expenses will be made within ten days following receipt of invoice.

Sincerely,
Bob Smith

ACCEPTED AND AGREED
By _____ Date _____

CONFIDENTIALITY AGREEMENT
Some clients may ask you to sign a confidentiality agreement saying you won't share the client's proprietary information with other people. If the client wants you to make such a promise but doesn't have their own confidentiality agreement, you can use a confidentiality memo as shown below.

TO: Sue Simon, ABC Systems
FROM: Bob Bly, phone (201) 385-1220
DATE: 12-11-05
RE: Nondisclosure agreement

1. "Confidential information" means any information given to me by ABC Systems.

2. I agree not to use, disseminate, or share any confidential information with my employees, vendors, clients, or anyone else.

3. I will use reasonable care to protect your confidential information, treating it as securely as if it were my own.

4. I won't publish, copy, or disclose any of your confidential information to any third party and will use my best efforts to prevent inadvertent disclosure of such information to any third party.

5. The copy I do for you shall be considered "work for hire." ABC Systems will own all rights to everything I produce for you, including the copyright. I will execute any additional documents needed to verify your ownership of these rights.

Sincerely,
Bob Bly

LETTER REQUESTING REFERRALS

One of the best sources of sales leads is referrals from existing clients. If your clients aren't giving you as many referrals as you want, here's a letter you can use to ask for more:

Ms. Joan Zipkin
Acme Retail Outlets
Anytown, U.S.A.

Dear Joan:

I'm glad you liked the spring catalog I recently completed for you.

Like you, I'm always on the lookout for new business. So I have a favor to ask.

Could you jot down, on the back of this letter, the names, addresses, and phone numbers of a few of your colleagues who might benefit from knowing more about my services? (Naturally, I don't want the name of anyone whose product line competes with your own.)

Then, just mail the letter back to me in the enclosed reply envelope.

I may want to mention your name when contacting these people. Let me know if there's any problem with that.

And thanks for the favor!

Regards,
Sam Tate

LETTER FOR SOLICITING TESTIMONIALS FROM CLIENTS

After completing a job successfully, you can use this letter to solicit a testimonial from the client. A sheet of paper filled with testimonials is a very powerful addition to a promotional package and convinces prospects you are good at what you do (see my promotional package in appendix C). I always send a self-addressed, stamped envelope and two copies of the letter. This way the recipient doesn't have to make a copy of the letter or address and stamp her own envelope.

Mr. Andrew Specher, President
Hazardous Waste Management, Inc.
Anywhere, U.S.A.

Dear Andrew:

I have a favor to ask of you.

I'm in the process of putting together a list of testimonials, a collection of comments about my services from satisfied clients like yourself.

Would you take a few minutes to give me your opinion of my writing services?

No need to dictate a letter—just jot your comments on the back of this letter, sign below, and return it to me in the enclosed envelope. (The second copy is for your files.)

I look forward to learning what you like about my service . . . but I also welcome any suggestions or criticisms, too.

Many thanks, Andrew.

Regards,
Bob Bly

YOU HAVE MY PERMISSION TO QUOTE FROM MY
COMMENTS, AND USE THESE QUOTATIONS IN ADS,
BROCHURES, MAIL, AND OTHER PROMOTIONS USED TO
MARKET YOUR FREELANCE WRITING SERVICES.

Signature _____ Date _____

LETTER FOR GETTING PERMISSION TO USE
EXISTING TESTIMONIAL

Some clients will send you letters of testimonial unsolicited. Before
you use them in your promotions, get their permission in writing, using this form letter:

Mr. Mike Hernandez
Advertising Manager
Technilogic, Inc.
Anytown, U.S.A.

Dear Mike:

I never did get around to thanking you for your letter of
8/15/04 (copy attached). So . . . thanks!

I'd like to quote from this letter in the ads, brochures, direct-
mail packages, and other promotions I use to market my
writing services — with your permission, of course.

If this is okay with you, would you please sign the bottom of
this letter and send it back to me in the enclosed envelope. (The
second copy is for your files.)

Many thanks, Mike.

Regards,
Bob Bly

YOU HAVE MY PERMISSION TO QUOTE FROM THE
ATTACHED LETTER IN ADS, BROCHURES, MAIL, AND
OTHER PROMOTIONS USED TO MARKET YOUR
FREELANCE WRITING SERVICES.

Signature _____ Date _____

SAMPLE INVOICE

Here is a typical invoice to send a client upon completion of a job:

Invoice for Services Rendered   July 15, 2005

From: David Willis
15 Sunnyville Drive
Anyplace, U.S.A.
(201) 123-4567

Social Security #123-45-6789

To: XYZ Corporation
Anytown, U.S.A.
ATT: June Chapman, Advertising Manager

For: Copy for MAXI-MIX equipment brochure

Reference: Purchase order #1745

Amount: $2,200

Terms: Net 30 days

THANK YOU.

SAMPLE COLLECTION LETTERS

LETTER NO. 1

Dear Jim:

Just a reminder . . .

. . . that payment for the brochure I wrote for you (see copy of invoice attached) is now past due.

Would you please send me a check today? A self-addressed stamped reply envelope is enclosed for your convenience.

Regards,
Bob Bly

LETTER NO. 2

Dear Jim:

I haven't gotten payment for this invoice yet. Did you receive my original bill and follow-up letter?

If there is any problem, please let me know. Otherwise, please send me a check for the amount due within the next few days.

Thanks,
Bob Bly

LETTER NO. 3

Dear Jim:

This is the third notice I've sent about the enclosed invoice, which is now many weeks past due.

Was there a problem with this job I don't know about? When may I expect payment?

Sincerely,
Bob Bly

LETTER NO. 4

Dear Jim:

What do you think I should do?

Despite three previous notices about this invoice, it remains unpaid.

I haven't heard from you, and you haven't responded to my letters.

Please remit payment within 10 days of receipt of this letter. I dislike sending you these annoying notices, nor do I like turning accounts over to my attorney for collection. But you are leaving me little choice.

Sincerely,
Bob Bly

P.S. Please be aware that the copyright on the copy I wrote for you for this assignment does not transfer to your company until my invoice has been paid in full.

THANK-YOU LETTER TO CURRENT CLIENTS

Copywriter Robert Lerose sends this letter each year to his active clients. You can develop a similar letter of appreciation to let your clients know you value your relationship with them.

Dear Roger:

As copywriter, I make my living with words, so I choose them carefully.

With the year drawing to a close, I like to reflect on the preceding twelve months. When I look back, there's one special word that bears repeating.

Thanks.

Thank you . . .

. . . for entrusting your assignment to me.

. . . for placing your faith in my abilities and judgment.

. . . for being judicious with your revisions.

. . . for teaching me valuable lessons you acquired through your own experience.

. . . for compensating me without complaint.

. . . for writing or speaking about my services with elegance and generosity.

. . . for your devoted patronage that permits me to practice the craft I love in the style I like.

. . . for being a partner, not a taskmaster.

May you find health and prosperity throughout the seasons!

Warmest regards,
Robert Lerose

TYPICAL FEES FOR COMMERCIAL FREELANCE WRITING PROJECTS

SCHEDULE OF ESTIMATED FEES

Print ad	$950 – $3,000+
Sales letter	$2,500 – $8,500+
Direct-mail package, lead generation	$4,500 – $6,500
Direct-mail package, mail order	$6,500 – $9,500+
Renewal series	$1,000 – $1,500/letter
Blanket renewal insert	$2,000 – $2,500
Magalog	$12,500 – $15,000
Self-mailer	$2,500 – $4,500
Postcard or double postcard	$1,500 – $2,500
Brochure	$750 – $1,000/page
Data sheet	$1,500 – $2,000
Case study	$2,000 – $2,500
Catalog	$750/page
Newsletter	$750/page
Feature story	$2,500 – $3,500
White paper	$4,000 – $5,000
Press release (1 – 2 pages)	$750 – $1,000
Audiovisual or multimedia script	$200 – $250/minute
Telemarketing script	$2,000 – $2,500
Radio commercial (six-spot package)	$2,000 – $3,000
Copy critique	$750 – $1,500

TERMS:

Purchase order or letter of authorization required for all jobs. Copywriting fees for initial projects are payable 50% in advance, balance upon delivery. Copy critique fees are payable in full, in advance.

All revisions must be assigned within 30 days of receipt of copy. Rewrites are made free of charge unless the revision is based on a change in the assignment made after copy is submitted.

Listed fees are guidelines only. Call today for a prompt price quotation on your specific assignment.

NOTE: This fee schedule current as of December 2005 and valid for 90 days from date of receipt. Be sure to call for current fee schedule when ordering copy or consulting service.

ONLINE COPYWRITING FEE SCHEDULE

Long-copy landing page (microsite) — $7,500
A long-copy dedicated Web site designed to sell a consumer product — such as a newsletter, e-book, or conference — directly. The online equivalent of a 6- to 8-page sales letter.

Medium-copy landing page — $5,500
The online equivalent of a 2- to 4-page letter. Used for b-to-b offers and products that require less description (e.g., software).

Short-copy landing page — $2,000 - $2,500
A simple landing page for a product or offer. Often used for white papers, software demos, and other inquiry fulfillment. The online equivalent of a trade ad: headline, a few paragraphs of descriptive product copy, and order portion.

Landing page versions — 25% - 50% of above fees
Creating a different front-end for an A/B split test. Price is based on the assumption that Bob Bly is writing the version at the same time he is writing the original landing page.

Hard-copy version of landing page — 50% + 2 cents
Bob's fee to turn the landing page he wrote for you into a direct-mail package is 50% of the original copywriting fee plus a mailing fee of 2 cents per piece after a test of 50,000 pieces.

Transaction page—$950
Similar to a short-copy landing page but with even less descriptive product copy; a page designed primarily as an online reply form where the visitor can either order the product or (if lead generation) request a free white paper or other information.

Long-copy e-mail—$2,500-$3,500
An e-mail designed to sell a product directly by driving the recipient to a landing page. The online equivalent of a 2- to 4-page sales letter.

Teaser e-mail—$1,500-$2,500
A short e-mail designed to drive readers to a microsite or long-copy landing page where they can order the product. The online equivalent of a 1/2- to 1-page sales letter.

Lead-generation e-mail—$1,500-$2,000
Similar to the teaser e-mail but the purpose is to drive the readers to a landing page or transaction page where they can request a free white paper or other information.

Online e-mail conversion series—$1,000-$1,500 per effort
A series of follow-up e-mail messages, sent via auto responder, designed to convert an inquiry into a sale.

Online ad—$500
A 100-word classified ad to run in an e-zine and drive readers to a microsite or landing page.

E-mail capture pop-under page—$750-$1,500
A window that appears when visitors attempt to exit your Web page without ordering; offers free content in exchange for the visitor's e-mail address.

"Mail order" package #1—$9,500 (value: $13,500)
Everything you need to sell a newsletter or other consumer product online; includes a long-copy landing page, three teaser e-mails, and three online ads. This option is recommended for marketers with access to large e-lists.

"Mail order" package #2—$9,500 (value: $13,500)
Everything you need to sell a newsletter or other consumer product online; includes a long-copy landing page, pop-under page to capture

e-mail addresses, and three conversion e-mails to convert inquiries to sales. This option is recommended for marketers who drive traffic to their site primarily through search engines.

Web site package #1 — $5,500–$6,500

A small business or single product line Web site consisting of a home page and up to 5 additional pages.

Ongoing site copy maintenance — 3% of gross sales or $5,000 a month

For a royalty of 3% of gross sales, we remain on call to make minor tweaks and updates, and provide new test versions, at no additional fee. Copywriting of major new tests and versions is quoted separately.

Home page, simple ("ad style") — $1,500–$2,000

Simple home page with a headline and up to 300 words of text describing the company or site.

Home page, complex ("tabloid style") — $2,000–$3,000

Complex home page with multiple headlines and copy sections. Often used in membership and subscription Web sites. Also used in sites highlighting news or content in multiple product lines or subject areas.

Banner ad — $500–$1,000

Banner ad designed to generate click-throughs to a microsite or landing page.

INDEX

ABOUT THE AUTHOR

ROBERT W. BLY is a freelance copywriter specializing in business-to-business, high-tech, and direct marketing.

Mr. Bly has more than twenty-five years of experience writing ads, brochures, direct-mail packages, sales letters, publicity materials, e-mail campaigns, white papers, booklets, special reports, newsletters, landing pages, and Web sites for more than 100 clients including Grumman, AlliedSignal, AT&T, IBM, Lucent Technologies, Medical Economics, McGraw-Hill, Phillips Publishing, Forbes, KCI, Agora Publishing, Ken Roberts Company, and EBI Medical Systems.

He has won a number of industry awards including a Gold Echo from the Direct Marketing Association, an IMMY from the Information Industry Association, two Southstar Awards, an American Corporate Identity Award of Excellence, and the Standard of Excellence award from the Web Marketing Association.

Mr. Bly is the author of more than sixty books including: *The Complete Idiot's Guide to Direct Marketing* (Alpha Books) and *Internet Direct Mail: The Complete Guide to Successful E-mail Marketing Campaigns* (NTC Business Books).

His articles have appeared in such publications as *Cosmopolitan, Chemical Engineering, Computer Decisions, Business Marketing, New Jersey Monthly, The Parent Paper, Writer's Digest, City Paper, Early to Rise, Successful Meetings, Sharing Ideas, DM News, Amtrak Express,* and *Direct Marketing.*

Robert W. Bly has taught copywriting at New York University and has presented sales and marketing seminars to numerous corporations, associations, and groups including: the American Marketing Association, Direct Marketing Creative Guild, Women's Direct Response Group, American Chemical Society, Publicity Club of New York, and the International Tile Exposition. He has been a guest on dozens of radio and TV shows including CNBC and CBS's *Hard Copy,* and has been featured in periodicals ranging from *Nation's Business* to the *Los Angeles Times*.

Mr. Bly is a member of the Business Marketing Association, Newsletter and Electronic Publishers Association, and the American Institute of Chemical Engineers. His e-zine, "Direct Response Letter," goes to more than 60,000 subscribers monthly.

For more information, contact:

Robert W. Bly
Copywriter
22 E. Quackenbush Avenue
Dumont, NJ 07628
Phone: 201-385-1220
Fax: 201-385-2238
E-mail: rwbly@bly.com
Web site: www.bly.com

CPSIA information can be obtained at www.ICGtesting.com
Printed in the USA
LVOW13s2036240713

344425LV00001B/1/P